NASA MISSION AS-506

APOLLO 11

1969 (including Saturn V, CM-107, SM-107, LM-5)

To the 400,000

"We would like to give special thanks to all those Americans who built the spacecraft; who did the construction, design, the tests, and put their hearts and all their abilities into those craft. To those people tonight, we give a special thank you, and to all the other people that are listening and watching tonight, God bless you. Good night from Apollo 11."

Neil Armstrong,
Dedication transmitted on the 23rd July 1969, on the way home from the Moon.

A catalogue record for this book is available from the British Library

ISBN 978 1 84425 683 9

Library of Congress control no. 2009923195

Published by Haynes Publishing,
Sparkford, Yeovil, Somerset BA22 7JJ, UK
Tel: 01963 442030 Fax: 01963 440001
Int. tel: +44 1963 442030 Int. fax: +44 1963 440001
E-mail: sales@haynes.co.uk
Website: www.haynes.co.uk

Haynes North America Inc.
861 Lawrence Drive, Newbury Park,
California 91320, USA

Printed and bound in the UK

Conversion factors

Note: *All distance and velocity figures quoted in the text of this book are given in Imperial units, as would have been the case at the time of the Apollo missions.*

Distance

feet	0.3048	metres
metres	3.281	feet
kilometres	0.6214	statute miles
statute miles	1.609	kilometres
nautical miles	1.852	kilometres
kilometres	0.54	nautical miles
nautical miles	1.1508	statute miles
statute miles	0.86898	nautical miles

Velocity

feet/sec	0.3048	metres/sec
metres/sec	3.281	feet/sec
metres/sec	2.237	statute mph
statute mph	0.447	meters/sec
feet/sec	0.6818	statute mph
statute mph	1.4667	feet/sec
feet/sec	0.5925	nautical mph
nautical mph	1.6878	feet/sec
statute mph	1.609	kph
kph	0.6214	statute mph
nautical mph	1.852	kph
kph	0.54	nautical mph
statute miles/sec	1.609	km/sec
km/sec	0.6214	statute miles/sec

Volume (capacity)

US gallons	3.785	litres
litres	0.2642	US gallons
US gallons	0.833	Imperial gallons
Imperial gallons	1.201	US gallons
cubic feet	0.02832	cubic metres

Mass

pounds	0.4536	kilograms
kilograms	2.205	pounds

Pressure

pounds/sq inch	70.31	grams/sq cm
grams/sq cm	0.0142	pounds/sq inch

Propellant weights

RP-1 (kerosene)	Approx 6.7 pounds per gallon
Liquid oxygen	Approx 9.5 pounds per gallon
Liquid hydrogen	Approx 0.56 pounds per gallon

NASA MISSION AS-506

APOLLO 11

1969 (including Saturn V, CM-107, SM-107, LM-5)

Owners' Workshop Manual

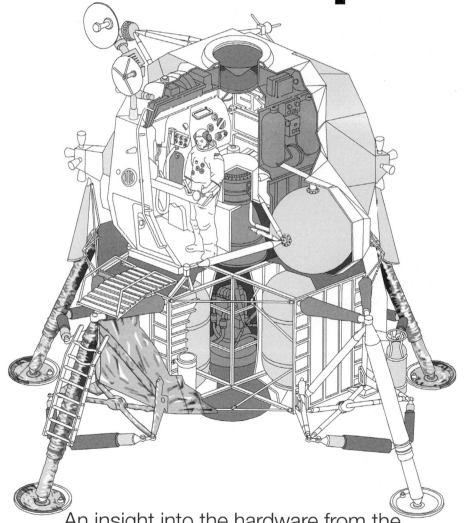

An insight into the hardware from the
first manned mission to land on the Moon

Christopher Riley and Phil Dolling

Contents

6	Introduction

The dream of space travel 9
World War Two rocket research 10
The Cold War 10
The space age begins 11
A space race 12
The dawn of Apollo 14
The first man in space and the
    new President 15
How would we fly to the Moon? 18
Apollo and the race to the line 24
The end of the decade 25
Apollo 11 prime crew 27
Apollo 11 backup crew 29
Apollo 11 Flight Directors 31

32	The Saturn rocket

The icon of Apollo 33
In the beginning 34
Saturn 1 39
Saturn 1B 40
Saturn V 43
Apollo 4 56

58	The Command and Service Modules

A new kind of spacecraft 60
Two spacecraft in one 61
Command Module 62
Service Module 77
Electrical Power 82
Life-support systems 83
Changes after the fire 84
Temperature regulation 85
Food 86
Toilet stops 87
Personal hygiene 90
To the Moon 91

94	The guidance, navigation and control system

The lynchpin of Apollo 93
A new integrated guidance
    system 97
Inertial Measurement Unit 98
The sextant 101
The computer 103
Apollo 11 – landings and alarms 110

112	The Lunar Module

In the beginning 114
Back to the drawing board 116
Weight watching 116
The descent stage 118
The ascent stage 121
The crew compartment 122
Overweight 126
Apollo 4 127
Apollo 5 – The LM's first flight 127
Flying the LM 127
Apollo 8 128
Apollo 9 – The LM's first manned
    flight 129
Apollo 10 – The LM's first flight
    to the Moon 130
How to land on the Moon 131
Apollo 11 – The LM's first
    landing 137
Preparing for lift-off 140

142	The space suits

A wearable spacecraft 144
Water-cooled garment 149
The pressurised inner suit 150
Outer protective suit (ITMG) 150
Helmet and visor assembly 151
Gloves and boots 151
Life-support backpacks 152
Waste management 155
Food and drink 155
First test flight for the Apollo suit 155
One small step 155
Where are they now? 157

158	Communicating from the Moon

For all Mankind 160
Talking across space 161
Conversations from the Moon 163
Mission Control 166
The Apollo beeps 168
TV from the Moon 168
Filming Apollo 169

172	Beyond Apollo 11 – the J-class missions

The Moon shot master plan 174
Apollo 12–14 176
Apollo 15–17 178
Apollo 18–20 (The cancelled
    missions) 180
The next Apollo 181
Misconceptions and
    conspiracy theories. 182
Why Did We Stop Going
    to the Moon? 183
Postscript 183
The legacy of Apollo 184

Epilogue 185

186	Appendices

Apollo acronyms and
    abbreviations 186
Table 1 – Missions 187
Field Guide to the Apollo
    hardware. 190
Table 2 – The fates of the
    Saturn V stages from the 15
    planned Apollo flights. 190
The spacecraft 192
Race to the Moon - timeline 194

Acknowledgements 196

LEFT Neil Armstrong, Michael Collins and Buzz Aldrin peer from the hatch of the Apollo 11 Command Module in June 1969, while conducting checks prior to their historic lunar landing mission. *(NASA)*

'Apollo was a grand attempt to reach beyond the world
of mundane life and to transcend the ordinary limits
of human existence through accomplishment of the
miraculous. Above all it was a story of engineers who
tried to reach the heavens.'

J. Bainbridge
Spaceflight Revolution

Introduction

Project Apollo was more than just a Cold War race to the Moon. In just eight years 400,000 people across America had come together to accomplish the seemingly impossible task of landing a man on the Moon and returning him safely to the Earth.

Achieving technical miracles and overcoming bureaucratic battles, daunting setbacks and tragedies, Apollo's engineers and scientists worked out how to transport human beings and their home comforts across a quarter of a million miles of hostile space to live and work on the surface of an unexplored alien world. It was the first time in the 4.6-billion-year history of our Solar System that life had left one world to visit another. Perhaps, given the apparent rarity of technological civilisations in the Milky Way, Apollo was also even something of galactic significance.

That we did all this at a time before the age of micro-computers, mobile phones and the internet, when slide rules were still in every engineer's top pocket, is even more exceptional. As Gene Cernan, the last man to leave his footprints on the Moon, said of Apollo, "The President had plucked a decade out of the 21st century and inserted it into the 1960s and 70s."

The inspiring astronomer and planetary scientist Carl Sagan summed up this boldness in his essay *The Gift of Apollo*. "They would use rockets not yet designed and alloys not yet conceived, navigation and docking systems not yet devised, in order to send a man to an unknown world – a world not yet explored, not even in a preliminary way, not even by robots – and we would bring him safely back, and we would do it before the decade was over. This confident pronouncement was made before any American had even achieved Earth orbit."

The fact that this was all achieved without loss of life in space had made it all look too easy. It seemed to most of us that President Kennedy had declared that we would go to the Moon, and a few years later we just went. It was as if humans were always destined to walk on the Moon, just another exploration box to tick. But the truth was that nothing about Apollo was guaranteed.

The collision of scientific know-how with ideological rivalry and the economic prowess to permit a president to make such a proclamation was unlikely, to say the least. But without the intellectual talents of the generation he challenged and their dogged determination to see it through at all costs Apollo might still never have succeeded.

LEFT Searchlight beams penetrate the darkness surrounding Apollo 8 on Pad 39A at the Kennedy Space Center on 20th December 1968. *(NASA)*

LEFT The ever-present goal of project Apollo – always there in the sky to remind those working on the project of what they were attempting. (NASA)

From the improbably gigantic Saturn V rocket to the individual stitching on a pressure glove the seven million engineered parts invented to fly a single mission all had to work perfectly. A single technical glitch could kill a crew and the entire programme was only ever one disaster away from possible cancellation. The reality of just how close to unreachable a lunar landing was in the mid-twentieth century is to be found in some of the stories recounted in this book.

Apollo was an achievement of profound historical, cultural and technological significance which should be remembered and celebrated as long as the human race survives.

LEFT The American flag heralds the flight of Apollo 11, the first human spaceflight to attempt a lunar landing. (NASA)

BELOW Geologist-Astronaut Harrison Schmitt, Apollo 17 Lunar Module Pilot, is photographed next to the American flag during extravehicular activity (EVA) on NASA's final lunar landing mission. The highest part of the flag appears to point toward our planet Earth in the distant background. (NASA)

The dream of space travel

In 1903, the same year as the Wright Brothers' first powered flight in a heavier-than-air machine, the Russian visionary Konstantin Tsiolkovsky published his first thesis on rocket propulsion, *The Exploration of Cosmic Space by Means of Reaction Devices*. The book described a super-cooled liquid hydrogen and oxygen powered rocket engine to propel his theoretical spacecraft.

It took American engineer Robert Goddard to turn Tsiolkovsky's concepts into reality. Goddard had first written about liquid propellants back in 1909 and by 1921 he was experimenting with them. On 16th March 1926 he launched his first liquid-fuelled rocket from his Aunt Effie's farm. The liquid oxygen and petrol powered rocket named 'Nell' only flew for 2.5 seconds – but it was a turning point in rocket-powered flight and a key step towards space travel. Before his death in 1945 Goddard's liquid-propelled rockets were reaching heights of over 8,300 feet and speeds of over 300mph. Others around the world inspired by Tsiolkovsky and Goddard were also experimenting with liquid-fuel rockets. Among them was the East Prussian aristocrat Wernher von Braun.

World War Two rocket research

Von Braun had taken Goddard's plans from various sources and used them to build his 1930s 'Aggregate' series rockets, later used by Adolf Hitler to carry the second of his 'vengeance weapons' (*Vergeltungswaffen*), the V2, to London. The first V2 to be used in anger lifted off from a park on the outskirts of The Hague on 7th September 1944, striking the suburb of Chiswick, in west London, and killing thirteen people. Propelled by alcohol and liquid oxygen

the rocket had climbed rapidly to a height of 23 miles and then arched down towards West London, travelling over 100 miles in six minutes. Von Braun described it later as his darkest day, reportedly commenting that "the rocket had worked perfectly except for landing on the wrong planet".

As Nazi power crumbled at the end of the war, von Braun strategically manoeuvred to surrender to the Americans on 2nd May 1945, near the town of Oberammergau in the Bavarian Alps. Two days before the area was handed over to the Soviets, the Americans evacuated von Braun and his team back to the United States. However, in the carve-up of Germany which followed, some of von Braun's engineers and their V2 rockets ended up in the Soviet Union. This played a part in the development of the Cold War and sowed the seeds of the Space Race and ultimately Apollo.

The Cold War

The first rocket-related salvo in the Cold War had effectively been fired in 1947, when it was announced that US Air Force pilot Chuck Yeager had broken the sound barrier in his rocket-powered Bell X-1 aeroplane. Across the United States and the Soviet Union each nation

BELOW Chuck Yeager poses beside the Bell X-1 'Glamorous Glennis' (named after his wife) in which he became the first man to break the sound barrier. *(TopFoto)*

RIGHT A V2 Bumper-WAC launch from the White Sands Missile Testing Range in New Mexico, during the 1940s. *(Mark Williamson)*

raced to outdo the other, sending their rockets to ever higher altitudes and faster speeds.

By the mid-1950s von Braun's Redstone rockets, which had evolved out of his V2 designs, were reaching 682 miles out into space; but they could not travel fast enough to reach orbital velocity. The race to achieve Earth orbit was formally launched in 1955 as part of the International Geophysical Year (IGY) – a global collaboration to study the physics of the Earth. On 29th July the United States announced that one of the goals of the IGY would be to place an artificial satellite into Earth orbit. Four days later, on 2nd August, the Soviet Union also declared its desire to launch an artificial satellite. The Soviet chief designer, Sergei Korolev, had first proposed using a rocket for launching a satellite in 1953, and felt his nation had a chance of beating the Americans to such a goal.

The space age begins

By March 1957 the Soviets had a rocket which was far more powerful than anything the Americans had built. It was called the R7 and Korolev was determined it would succeed. On 4th October 1957, after six unsuccessful attempts to orbit a satellite, and disobeying Premier Nikita Khrushchev's orders to cancel the project, Korolev's perfected R7 rocket rose from its pad at the Baikonur Cosmodrome carrying Sputnik 1 into orbit. Five minutes and 14 seconds after lift-off a highly polished 58-cm sphere emerged from its nose cone and the

four rod-shaped antennae begin to transmit their iconic 'bleep–bleep–bleep' broadcast announcing that the space age had arrived.

The world's first artificial satellite – Sputnik 1 – remained in orbit for 92 days, burning up in the atmosphere on 4th January 1958. An elated Premier Khrushchev, suddenly realising the technological, military and ideological advantages of success in space, began to steer funding from conventional arms towards this rocket technology. Korolev was asked to draw up plans for a spacecraft to carry the first humans into space atop a rocket.

A space race

The Soviet success was celebrated by many people around the world – who saw this technological marvel of their time as a great triumph of inspiring ingenuity. But for some there was a more sinister side to this sudden arrival of the space age. Over-flying another nation, even from space, brought with it the chance to spy and to drop bombs.

President Eisenhower came under strong public pressure to match the Soviet success in space and guard against this new threat from above. And so, with a small test satellite attached to the top of its third stage, the US Navy's Vanguard TV-3 rocket was rushed to the launch pad at Cape Canaveral in Florida just two months behind Sputnik 1. On 6th December 1957 the countdown clock reached zero and America held its breath as the Vanguard lifted off. One second later, and having risen only 4 feet, the rocket fell back onto the pad and exploded violently, hurling its payload clear of the inferno. The satellite, still transmitting, was found later in a nearby Florida swamp.

'Flopnik', as the press dubbed it, only served to humiliate Eisenhower further. The President turned to the US Army to save the nation's reputation and his own pride. Working day and night for the next 60 days, von Braun fast-tracked his new and ambitious four-stage Juno 1 rocket to completion, in what he optimistically called 'Project Orbiter'. Juno 1's first stage used a single Rocketdyne A-7 engine with the higher stages put together hurriedly using clusters of scaled-down Sergeant missiles.

To von Braun's relief the project lived up to

The Birth of NASA and the Mercury Seven

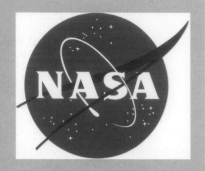

It had been America's tri-partheid approach to rocket powered flight through the three branches of its military which had cost the United States the first round of the space race. Unifying US rocket research and development into a single programme was essential if they were to regain the lead. And so in early 1958 a Space Act was drawn up in Washington and the National Advisory Committee for Aeronautics (NACA), which had already secretly begun researching the exploration of Earth orbit, was transformed into the National Aeronautics and Space Administration, (NASA).

On the 1st October 1958 NASA officially opened for business, with an annual budget of $340 million. Project Mercury – to place the first man in space began within a week and NASA took delivery of its first human rated Mercury capsule on the 1st April 1960. After a long fight the Army's Ballistic Missile Agency was finally transferred to NASA on July 1st that year, bringing with it von Braun's heavy lift rocket technology. The names of NASA's first astronauts 'the Mercury Seven' were announced to the world just ten weeks later on the 17th December 1958 – the fifty-fifth anniversary of the Wright Brothers' flight.

BELOW Informal photograph of the Mercury Seven, NASA's first selection of astronauts, in front of a Mercury Capsule and a larger Apollo capsule mock-up to the left. From left to right they are; Gordon Cooper, Wally Schirra (hidden), Alan Shepard, Gus Grissom, John Glenn, Deke Slayton and Scott Carpenter. *(NASA)*

its name, placing the US Explorer 1 satellite into orbit on 1st February 1958. Von Braun was hailed as the man of the moment and Eisenhower awarded his Army Ballistic Missile Agency (ABMA) a contract to build an even bigger booster – perhaps powerful enough to regain the lead. It would ultimately grow into a rocket which would be called the Saturn.

The dawn of Apollo

By the late 1950s detailed lunar mapping programmes had been undertaken by the US Air Force as a precursor to plans for its Lunex Project – a military outpost on the ultimate high ground – the Moon! Lunex aimed to have 21 airmen stationed in an underground lunar base by 1968. The US Army was also interested in colonising the Moon. In 1959 von Braun published the 'Project Horizon' feasibility study which laid out plans for establishing an Army lunar outpost to give the United States a scientific and military advantage over other nations. Horizon would harness von Braun's heavy-payload Juno rockets to land twelve soldiers on the Moon by December 1966. The purpose of both these military Moon programmes was to demonstrate conclusively that America could win any technological competition with the Soviets. It was felt strongly that no achievement short of a lunar landing would have the required historical significance to prove this.

But, whilst the United States military drew up elaborate plans for Moon bases, it was the Soviet Union which was first again with its own lunar exploration programme. In January 1959 an unmanned Soviet satellite called Luna 1 flew within 3,000 miles of the Moon.

NASA was quick to respond and, encouraged by the famous planetary scientist Harold Urey, it began to look into lunar exploration. Urey believed that, without an atmosphere or any of the geological activity which recycled the rocks on Earth, the Moon's crust could still hold clues to the history of the solar system. Driven by this, and the clear Soviet interest in the Moon, NASA quickly came up with a detailed programme of unmanned lunar probe missions which would culminate in

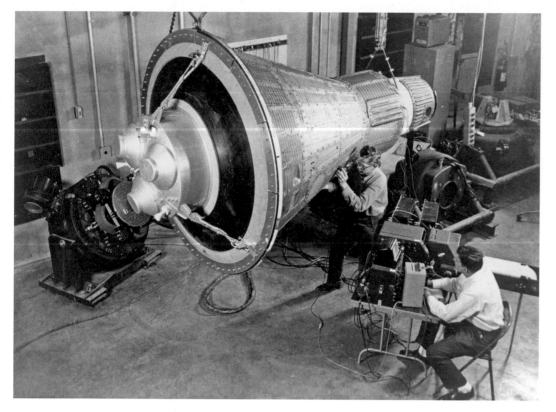

a manned landing on the Moon in 1970. The 10-year plan would cost between $12 and $15 billion dollars for the first five years and the agency recommended that work should start immediately on a new three-man spacecraft capable of a lunar flight.

Searching for a name for a project of such ambition, a senior NASA manager called Abe Silverstein turned to Greek mythology for inspiration. Silverstein felt that the image of Apollo – the son of Zeus – riding across the face of the Sun was suitably grand. And so, at the end of July 1960, NASA announced its intent to create a new advanced manned spaceflight programme called Apollo.

The first man in space and the new President

Before embarking on a flight to the Moon NASA had to prove that it could put a man into space and bring him back alive. Early attempts to launch life into space had not gone very well. In the late 1940s the US Army had flown two monkeys inside the nose cones of captured German V2 rockets. They did not

survive the flight. It was not until the 20th September 1951 that a monkey and eleven mice reached an altitude of over 50 miles inside an Aerobee sounding rocket before being parachuted safely back to the ground.

The first animal from Earth to go into orbit was a stray mongrel dog from the Moscow streets called Laika. It was November 1957,

RIGHT The famous 'hand shake' welcome. Chimpanzee Ham is greeted by the recovery ship Commander after his flight on the Mercury Redstone rocket. (NASA)

FAR RIGHT President John F. Kennedy and Nikita Khrushchev pictured together for the first time, in Vienna on 3rd June 1961. (TopFoto)

only a month after the Soviet Union's first orbital flight of Sputnik 1, but the new pressurised compartment Laika was housed in seemed to protect her long enough to establish that the rigours of launch and the weightlessness of orbit were not fatal.

Animal tests on the Americans' new man-rated Mercury space capsules began in January 1961 when a chimpanzee called Ham survived a sub-orbital Mercury flight on a Redstone rocket. The Soviets were also making sub-orbital animal flights with their new Vostok capsule at this time. The race to produce a tested orbital space capsule was neck and neck.

During this crucial time, on 20th January 1961, President John F. Kennedy took office. No one, not even NASA, knew what direction he would want to choose for the manned spaceflight programme. The new administration had been critical of Eisenhower's space policy and Kennedy's first move was to quickly appoint a new NASA chief. He picked James E. Webb – a former secretary of state under Truman and a director of the McDonnell Aircraft Company. Webb quickly became an enthusiastic supporter of NASA's plans for lunar exploration, but before he could sell the idea to Kennedy events on the other side of the world changed everything.

On 12th April 1961, just 12 weeks after Kennedy had come to power, the Soviets launched Yuri Gagarin into Earth orbit – making him the first spaceman in history. As if that was not enough to dent the reputation of the new US administration, five days later the CIA-backed Bay of Pigs invasion of Cuba was wiped out by Castro's forces. Kennedy badly needed something to restore public confidence and directed his pro-space Vice President, Lyndon B. Johnson, to find a space exploration goal at which America could beat the Soviet Union.

Johnson's conclusion was swift and categorical. America should adopt NASA's lunar landing programme as its official national goal. Kennedy was at first reluctant. Anxious about the risks and the costs of such an endeavour, he asked his advisors to find an alternative technological field to compete in. Johnson disagreed, insisting that it had to be space and declared "… to be first in space is to be first period, to be second in space is to be second in everything". A programme of lunar exploration was far enough out of reach for both superpowers to stand a chance of success, eliminating the booster gap and restoring something of a level playing field once more.

US national pride was briefly restored on 5th May 1961 when NASA successfully flew

ABOVE A close-up of astronaut Alan Shepard in his space suit seated inside the Mercury capsule. He is undergoing a flight simulation test with the capsule mated to the Redstone booster. *(NASA)*

its first astronaut, Alan Shepard, on a sub-orbital Mercury flight. Three weeks later Kennedy made a speech to Congress, entitled 'Urgent National Needs', in which he called for support to land a man on the Moon and return him safely to the Earth before the decade was out.

BELOW Astronaut John Glenn and technicians inspect artwork that will be painted on the outside of his Mercury spacecraft. John Glenn nicknamed his capsule 'Friendship 7'. *(NASA)*

Gagarin

On 12th April 1961, twenty-seven-year old Russian pilot Yuri Alexeyevich Gagarin stepped out of the cosmonaut preparation building at the launch site near Tyura-Tam (later named Baikonur) and climbed into a bus to be driven towards Korolev's SL-3 rocket, steaming on pad LC1 in the dawn light. With help from ground staff

ABOVE Yuri Gagarin on board the Vostok spacecraft in April 1961. *(TopFoto)*

he boarded his Vostok 1 spacecraft, mounted on top, and at 10:07 local time lifted off the Earth and into history.

Within a few minutes he had become the fastest man ever and as the final stage of the rocket hurled him to almost five miles a second and an altitude of over a million feet he also became the world's first space man.

Still unsure quite how a human being might react to the ride, medical staff had insisted that the spacecraft was controlled from the ground and Gagarin's controls were reportedly locked to prevent him from taking manual control. Reaching a maximum altitude of 196 miles he declared "The Earth is blue. How wonderful. How amazing." About one hour into the flight mission control fired the retrorockets over Angola to bring Gagarin down safely about 5,000 miles further north. The spacecraft's separate equipment module failed to detach at first, as it was designed to do, and the capsule initially began to tumble wildly as it re-entered the atmosphere, before proper separation.

Unable to land gently enough to ensure his survival, Gagarin was trained to eject from the capsule whilst still almost 23,000 feet high. Both he and the capsule landed separately by parachute 16 miles south west of Engels in the Saratov region of northern Russia. Gagarin had flown around the whole planet in just under 90 minutes and was back on Earth before lunch! Less than sixty years since the Wright brothers' first powered flight, Gagarin's orbit was an extraordinary leap in technology which captured the attention and imagination of the world like nothing else. Sending a man into space had proved to be the perfect way to demonstrate ideological supremacy.

How would we fly to the Moon?

With project Apollo now backed by Congress, it was important to agree on how a trip to the Moon should be made. Since the 1950s, the principal concept for a flight to the Moon involved a streamlined rocket blasting vertically off the Earth, flying straight there and then landing vertically tail first on a column of rocket thrust. After lunar exploration was completed it would then perform a similar vertical launch from the Moon and a landing on Earth. Popular in both science fiction and with military feasibility studies like the Air Force Lunex project, this 'direct ascent' as it was dubbed, also seemed an obvious solution for Apollo.

But direct ascent was not as straightforward as it first appeared. It would need a very powerful rocket to do the job, possibly as tall as the Empire State Building! Secondly no one really knew how the astronauts, sitting near the top, could land this flying skyscraper on the lunar surface tail-first. Such 'details' did not deter those in NASA's Space Task Group who had backed it. They already had a rocket design on the drawing board called 'Nova' which packed up to 30 million pounds of thrust, over four times more than the final Saturn V.

Wernher von Braun had been championing an alternative concept called Earth Orbit Rendezvous (EOR) since his US Army days in the late 1950s. His method would eliminate the need for one giant rocket, requiring instead a number of smaller Juno V (later Saturn V) booster rockets which would launch into orbit the collective hardware, for subsequent assembly before heading for the Moon. Now, as head of NASA's Marshall Space Flight Center, von Braun had been continuing to develop his EOR method – billing it as the only realistic way of reaching the Moon by the end of the 1960s.

Whilst EOR solved the giant-rocket problem, the difficulty of landing a huge Earth return rocket on the surface of the Moon remained and, with multiple Saturn rocket launches needed for each Moon shot, EOR could prove more expensive and would require daunting construction work in Earth orbit to assemble the final Moon vehicle.

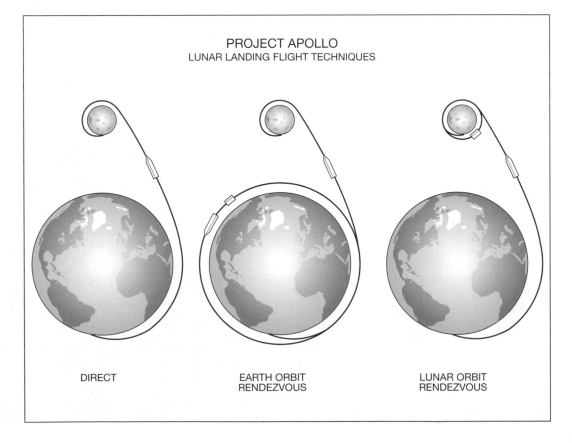

RIGHT Three of the methods on the table in 1961 to land a man on the Moon and return him safely to the Earth.
(Matthew Marke)

PROJECT APOLLO
LUNAR LANDING FLIGHT TECHNIQUES

DIRECT

EARTH ORBIT RENDEZVOUS

LUNAR ORBIT RENDEZVOUS

A third equally outlandish method for visiting the Moon, which had also been discussed since the late 1950s, was called Lunar Orbit Rendezvous (LOR). The idea, as the name suggests, involved a rendezvous in lunar rather than Earth orbit. A separate landing craft would then undock from a mother ship in lunar orbit to ferry two crewmen down to the Moon's surface. After their exploration this lander would ferry the crew back to the mother ship in lunar orbit before being discarded to leave a much smaller and lighter craft to be propelled back to Earth.

This low-weight energy-saving solution requiring only one launch vehicle. But in mid-1961 the rendezvous of two spacecraft had yet to be achieved in Earth orbit, let alone around the Moon. And with only 15 minutes of sub-orbital manned spaceflight experience it felt just too risky for NASA's managers to take seriously.

It took a lone voice from a team working on Moon shot trajectories at NASA's Langley Spaceflight Centre to get LOR considered alongside EOR and direct ascent. Against NASA protocol a young engineer on the team called John Houbolt vociferously lobbied NASA's Associate Administrator Robert Seamans until the agency started to see it as a realistic alternative whose benefits outweighed its drawbacks.

Finally, in June 1962, over a year after Kennedy's challenge had been announced, LOR was selected as NASA's method of going to the Moon. Whilst it would need techniques of rendezvous to be worked out, these were considered easier to achieve than the sheer number of Saturn V rockets needed for EOR or the impossibly large Nova rocket needed for direct ascent.

The origins of Lunar Orbit Rendezvous

It was a self taught Russian mechanic named Yuri V. Kondratyuk who is credited with coming up with the concept of Lunar Orbit Rendezvous in 1916. Realising that the entire spacecraft need not land, Kondratyuk described correctly how a small landing craft could leave the mother ship in lunar orbit, descend to the surface and then rejoin the larger craft. He expanded on this theory further in his self published 1929 book *The Conquest of Interplanetary Space*. Sadly Kondratyuk died in 1942, a generation away from seeing his foresight vindicated with Apollo.

At least two space scientists, Herman Oberth and an Englishman named Harry E. Ross kept Kondratyuk's ideas alive in the intervening years. Then in 1958 an American called Thomas Dolan of the Vought Astronautics Division doing some speculative work on lunar landing concepts also resurrected it as a highly efficient energy saving Moon shot concept. Whilst Dolan's company failed to win over NASA a young engineer called John Houbolt, working out of NASA's Langley Space Flight Center, championed LOR in late 1960 – lobbying NASA's top brass to adopt it as the only realistic way of getting to the Moon by the end of the decade.

BELOW John C. Houbolt at the blackboard, showing the space rendezvous concept for lunar landings. Houbolt was the person most responsible for pushing Lunar Orbital Rendezvous (LOR). *(NASA)*

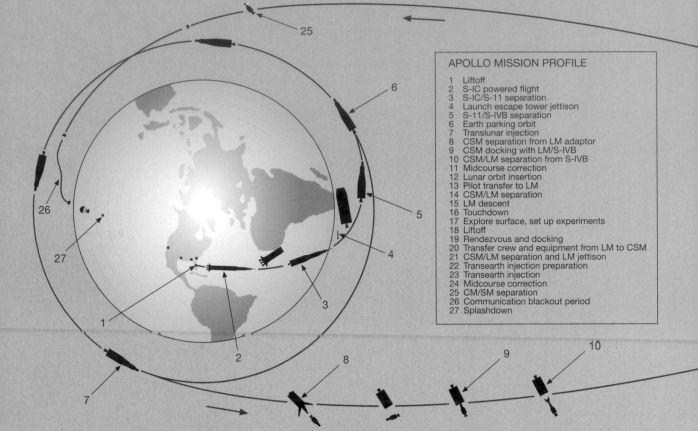

(Matthew Marke)

APOLLO MISSION PROFILE

1. Liftoff
2. S-IC powered flight
3. S-IC/S-11 separation
4. Launch escape tower jettison
5. S-11/S-IVB separation
6. Earth parking orbit
7. Translunar injection
8. CSM separation from LM adaptor
9. CSM docking with LM/S-IVB
10. CSM/LM separation from S-IVB
11. Midcourse correction
12. Lunar orbit insertion
13. Pilot transfer to LM
14. CSM/LM separation
15. LM descent
16. Touchdown
17. Explore surface, set up experiments
18. Liftoff
19. Rendezvous and docking
20. Transfer crew and equipment from LM to CSM
21. CSM/LM separation and LM jettison
22. Transearth injection preparation
23. Transearth injection
24. Midcourse correction
25. CM/SM separation
26. Communication blackout period
27. Splashdown

Lunar Orbit Rendezvous (LOR)

An Apollo Mission profile using the Lunar Orbit Rendezvous technique involved effectively transporting four separate spacecraft to the Moon; a Command and Service Module (the CSM), and Lunar Module (LM) consisting of a descent and an ascent stage. Stacked together at the top of the rocket, a single three stage Saturn V could place all of them into Earth orbit, (steps 1–6). Following a spacecraft 'health' check whilst still in a parking orbit, the final stage of the Saturn (the S-IVB) would then be reignited in an operation called Trans-Lunar-Injection, or TLI, (stage 7). Now on a course to intersect the Moon in three days' time the CSM would detach (stage 8) and turn 180 degrees to face the LM, still sitting inside the S-IVB. By slowing down very slightly to allow the SIV-B to catch up, the nose of the

Command Module (CM) could be docked with the top hatch of the LM (stage 9). Then, by accelerating gently away from the S-IVB, the LM could be extracted (stage 10).

Together the CSM, docked to the LM, would continue towards the Moon making any mid-course corrections which Mission Control deemed necessary (stage 11). The mission was now flying on a path called a 'free return trajectory' which would, if nothing more was done, harness the Moon's gravity to sling them back towards Earth. Attaining lunar orbit was only possible by making a burn called Lunar Orbit Insertion, or LOI, (stage 12) using the CSM's main engine to fire in the direction of travel, slowing down the spacecraft enough to be captured by the Moon's gravity.

The following day, the Commander (CDR) and the Lunar Module Pilot (LMP) would transfer to the LM, leaving the

(Matthew Marke)

Earth

240,000 miles

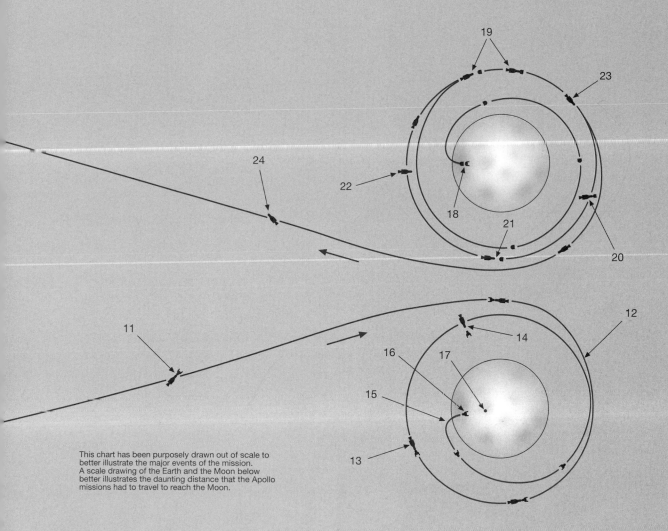

This chart has been purposely drawn out of scale to
better illustrate the major events of the mission.
A scale drawing of the Earth and the Moon below
better illustrates the daunting distance that the Apollo
missions had to travel to reach the Moon.

Command Module Pilot (CMP) in the CSM (stage 13). The
LM and CSM would then separate (stage 14) and using its
descent engine the LM would brake to slow down, putting
it on a trajectory which would intersect the Moon's surface.
Using the descent engine's variable thrust the pilots could
make a controlled – even pinpoint landing (stage 16). After
suiting up to depressurise the LM the two astronauts would
open the side hatch and climb down the ladder to explore
the Moon's surface (stage 17). After returning to the LM they
would ignite the ascent engine to blast them back up into
Lunar Orbit (18) leaving the descent stage on the surface.
The LM's ascent stage would then rendezvous and dock
with the CM and the astronauts would transfer themselves
and their equipment and rock samples back into the
CSM (stage 20).

With the LM's role over it would be jettisoned (stage
21) leaving the CSM to bring them home (stage 22) in a
procedure called Trans Earth Injection, or TEI, (stage 23)
to accelerate away from the Moon's gravity and head
back towards the Earth. As on the way out mid-course
corrections could always be carried out to fine tune the
spacecraft's trajectory (stage 24) and the point at which it
would hit the Earth's atmosphere. An hour before
re-entry the Service Module would be jettisoned from the
Command Module (stage 25) just leaving the very apex
of the original rocket stack to return to Earth. The heat
generated by re-entry would cause a brief period of
radio blackout (stage 26) before the main chutes were
deployed to carry the spacecraft to splashdown
(stage 27).

Moon

With LOR formerly adopted at the end of 1962 work could finally begin on commissioning a new lightweight Lunar landing vehicle, perfecting a Command Module to support it and deciding on a rocket to launch the whole stack. Whilst this engineering development work on Apollo got underway NASA's extended Mercury programme – named Gemini, set out to give the astronauts practice at space walks and rendezvous and docking of two craft in orbit – the new key to landing on the Moon.

The first manned Gemini flight blasted off from Cape Canaveral in March 1965. Over the next 20 months nine more manned missions would rehearse for Apollo in Earth orbit. Built by McDonnell (later McDonnell Douglas), the new Gemini spacecraft also tested life support systems and fuel cell technology. It was the first American manned spacecraft to carry an onboard guidance computer and crews also pioneered the use of in flight radar and artificial horizons. By the last Gemini flight (Gemini XII) in November 1966, NASA's astronauts had spent a total of almost 30 days in space. For the first time since Sputnik 1 kick started the space age nine years before, America had the edge in space, and perhaps even enough experience to fulfil President Kennedy's dream of reaching the moon before the decade was out.

But these were achievements which Kennedy never lived to see. Just a week after touring the Saturn V launch complex at

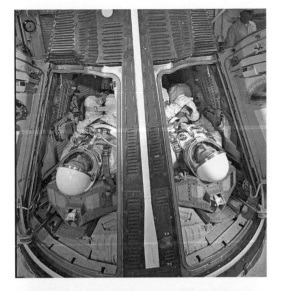

OPPOSITE Lift-off of Gemini-Titan 11 (GT-11) from Complex 19. The Gemini 11 mission included a rendezvous with an Agena target vehicle. *(NASA)*

LEFT Astronauts James McDivitt and Ed White inside the Gemini spacecraft for a simulated launch at Cape Canaveral, Florida on 13th May 1965. *(NASA)*

LEFT NASA successfully completed its first rendezvous mission with two Gemini spacecraft – Gemini VII and Gemini VI – in December 1965. *(NASA)*

BELOW Astronauts Edward H. White II (left) and James A. McDivitt inside the Gemini IV spacecraft wait for lift-off. *(NASA)*

BELOW On June 3rd, 1965, Edward H. White II became the first American to climb out of his his spacecraft and let go! White floated and maneuvered himself around the Gemini spacecraft for 23 minutes. *(NASA)*

Cape Canaveral with von Braun in November 1963, he was assassinated whilst on a trip to Dallas, Texas. Around the world many people remember where they were when they heard of his murder. The same would be said of one other day in history just six years away when an Apollo astronaut would become the first man to walk on the Moon.

Apollo and the race to the line

Towards the end of 1966, with the new Apollo Command Module behind schedule it was decided to bump the first Apollo flight to February the following year. The mission, commanded by Gus Grissom with crew mates Ed White and Roger Chaffee, was designed to test launch operations, ground tracking and the overall performance of the new spacecraft and Saturn rocket launcher. But during a routine practice countdown on the 27th January 1967 a spark from some exposed wires in the base of the Command Module set fire to the interior of the spacecraft. Quickly catching alight in the oxygen rich atmosphere the resulting inferno killed the crew within minutes and halted the entire Apollo programme.

By April of that year, an accident with the new Soviet Soyuz spacecraft, during its first flight, killing cosmonaut Vladimir Komarov, had also grounded the Russian Moon programme. No one would fly into space again until the following year. By then both super powers were readying themselves for missions which would go straight to the Moon. On the 18th September a new Soviet spacecraft called Zond was launched on a circumlunar flight carrying a cargo of turtles and other animals. The mission went well until the end, when it suffered a severe 10–15 G re-entry on its way home, discouraging its designers from flying a similar mission with a cosmonaut onboard.

Apollo 7 saw NASA's return to flight a few weeks later on the 11th October when Wally Schirra commanded a mission to test out the new improved Apollo Command Module in Earth orbit. The Soviets had the same idea, and just days after Apollo 7 splashed down in the Pacific Soyuz 3 was blasting into space to practise docking and rendezvous manoeuvres with the unmanned Soyuz 2 craft. Cosmonaut Georgi Beregovoi became the first Russian to return to space since Komarov's death.

By November the Soviets had perfected the Zond's return and another circumlunar mission carrying animals was dispatched. This time its parachutes let it down – deploying too early and failing to slow the capsule enough before it crash landed fatally on Earth. Despite these set backs six cosmonauts arrived at Baikonaur on the 23rd November to begin preparations for a manned Zond mission round the Moon. NASA knew that the Zond's rockets were not powerful enough to brake the craft in Lunar orbit, but Zond was still capable of flying a trajectory which would swing it round the Moon on a free return trajectory back to Earth; and potentially allowing the USSR to claim the historically significant first manned flight into deep space.

The Apollo Lunar (landing) Module was still not ready for spaceflight. But earlier in the year it had been decided to send Apollo 8 to the moon without it. The mission would be NASA's only chance of beating the Russians to a manned deep-space flight and could still teach the astronauts some useful lessons for the up coming landing missions. Commander Frank Borman, with crew mates Jim Lovell and Bill

Anders blasted off from Cape Kennedy at 12:51 UT on the 21st December 1968 and two hours and fifty minutes later became the first humans to leave Earth orbit and head for the Moon.

Testing out the onboard navigation system and making a visual reconnoitre of a potential landing site for Apollo 11 as they orbited the Moon ten times, the crew returned triumphantly six days later, splashing down before dawn in the Pacific Ocean on the 27th December 1968.

The successful flight of Apollo 8 came as a fatal blow to the Soviet Moon programme which was quickly re-purposed to concentrate on developing a space station for Earth orbit. But the race was far from over for NASA. With the clock still ticking on Kennedy's deadline, just twelve months away, and no spaceflight experience yet with their Lunar lander or the Apollo space suit there was much to be done on the two remaining flights before Apollo 11 could make the first attempt at a landing.

The end of the decade

Jim McDivitt, Dave Scott and Rusty Schweickart would sort out some of the remaining unknowns on their Apollo 9 flight in Earth orbit during March of 1969. In one of the most ambitious space missions ever carried out they put the LM through its maiden flight, testing navigation, rendezvous and docking systems, test firing the descent and ascent engines and pioneering techniques which would one day help to bring the crew of Apollo 13 safely home using the LM as a lifeboat. After overcoming a bout of space sickness, Rusty Schweickart had also climbed out of the LM hatch, to test the new Apollo space suit. He'd spent almost 40 minutes on the porch, putting the back pack's life support systems through its paces and marvelling at the view of Earth passing 150 miles beneath him.

Just two months later, Apollo 10 took the next LM to fly in space all the way to the Moon on NASA's one chance to test the Lunar Orbit Rendezvous technique in situ before the flight of Apollo 11. Gemini veterans Tom Stafford, John Young and Gene Cernan were selected to carry out this crucial flight. They had been training together for two years and were the

ABOVE A telescopic ground tracking camera at KSC follows the flight path of Apollo 8. *(NASA)*

BELOW Apollo 9's maiden flight of the Lunar Module in Earth orbit. *(NASA)*

ABOVE This oblique view, featuring International Astronomical Union (IAU) Crater 302 on the Moon surface, was photographed by the Apollo 10 astronauts in May of 1969. *(NASA)*

BELOW Earth viewed from the Moon, standing to the rear side of the LM. *(NASA)*

most experienced crew ever to fly together on an Apollo mission; a fact which reflected the challenges that lay ahead of them. The lunar environment was still poorly understood and the problems of precisely flying two manned spacecraft around the Moon to a successful rendezvous were daunting. Riding out a series of, at times hair raising, problems the crew made it to just 51,000ft above the lunar surface, paving the way for Apollo 11. As the Apollo 10 crew headed for home on May 23rd 1969, the next fully stacked Saturn V was already moving towards pad 39A for its historic landing mission.

On the 16th July 1969 the Apollo 11 crew Neil Armstrong, Michael Collins and Edwin 'Buzz' Aldrin rode into space on only the sixth Saturn V ever to fly. The three of them had worked together for the past year, first serving as the backup crew for Apollo 8. Together they had an impressive wealth of Gemini spaceflight experience and carried the combined knowledge of the six men who'd already flown to the Moon; not to mention the hundreds of hours of Apollo simulator time they'd accumulated during training.

In lunar orbit, on the 20th July 1969 Armstrong and Aldrin undocked their Lunar Module – 'Eagle' from Mike Collins in the Command Module 'Columbia', and began their historic descent to the surface. Computer alarms and fuel warnings plagued the next twelve minutes of their flight but with just 20 seconds of propellant remaining the two pilots dropped their Eagle gently onto the Moon.

This momentous moment, and the walk which followed, brought people around the world together in mutual admiration for what America had achieved. In less than eight short years, project Apollo had accomplished what many had thought impossible.

A triumph of this magnitude transcended nationhood. Sending men to another world had proved to be a unique demonstration of what our species was capable of. Collective pride in the ingenuity of Apollo briefly united the human race in a way that no politician, preacher or prophet had ever quite managed to do. But 400,000 engineers with a promise to keep to a President had achieved just that. On the plaque fixed to the legs of the Eagle they'd written the words "We came in peace, for all Mankind."

Apollo 11 prime crew

Neil Armstrong, Commander – Apollo 11

Neil Alden Armstrong was born on his grandparent's farm in Auglaize County, Ohio on the 5th August 1930. He was introduced to his first aircraft at the age of six when he got his first flight in a Ford Tri-Motor 'Tin Goose'. He had his pilot's licence by the age of 16. Fascinated by flight, he built a small wind tunnel in the basement of his home to experiment with the model planes he was designing and building. After leaving Blume High School in 1947, Armstrong won a US Navy scholarship to study aeronautical engineering at Purdue University. Two years later he had to suspend his studies, when he was called up to active service. He trained for his jet wings at the Pensacola Naval Air Station in Florida and joined his first squadron as their youngest pilot at the age of 20. Armstrong flew 78 combat missions during the Korean War.

Following his tour of duty in Korea he returned to Purdue and completed his Bachelor's degree in 1955. Outside the military, as a civilian once more, he joined NASA's Lewis Research Centre in 1955 and later transferred to NASA's High Speed Flight Station at Edwards Air Force Base, in California, where he flew as an X-15 project pilot making 7 flights – the highest to 207,500 feet and over 4,000 miles per hour. Other flight test work included piloting the X-1 rocket airplane, the F-100, F-101, F-102, F-104A Starfighter, F5D, B-47 and para-gliders. As a pilot of the B-29 'drop' aircraft he participated in the launches of over 100 rocket airplane flights. At the time of Apollo 11 he had logged over 4,000 hours of flying time.

Armstrong was selected as an astronaut by NASA in September of 1962 and served as a backup commander of the Gemini V mission. As Command Pilot for Gemini VIII he performed the first ever successful docking of two vehicles in space. The mission was terminated early due to a malfunctioning OAMS thruster, but the crew had demonstrated exceptional piloting skill in overcoming the problem and bringing the spacecraft back safely. He went on to serve as backup command pilot for Gemini XI and backup commander for Apollo 8. As

Commander of Apollo 11 he became the first human to set foot on the Moon on the 21st July 1969.

Armstrong acted as an accident investigator after Apollo 13, personally opposing the report's recommendations to redesign the service module's oxygen tanks which had caused the problem.

Following Apollo 11 Armstrong announced that he did not plan to fly in space again. He left NASA in August of 1971 and took up a teaching post at the University of Cincinnati, in the Department of Aerospace Engineering which he held for eight years. During the 1980s he accepted an invitation to appear in an advert for Chrysler and began to act as a spokesman for the company. He went on to serve on the board of directors for a number of other American companies. In 1986 he acted as vice-chairman of the commission appointed to investigate the Challenger Shuttle accident. His authorized biography *First Man* was published in 2005, putting right many of the rumours and myths which had emerged over the decades about the first man to walk on the Moon.

Neil Armstrong. *(NASA)*

had logged over 4,000 hours of flying time – including more than 3,200 hours in jet aircraft.

After applying for NASA's second call for astronauts in 1962 and failing to get selected, Collins re-applied the following year and entered astronaut service in October 1963. He served as backup pilot for Gemini 7 and prime pilot along with John Young for the 3-day Gemini X flight. Together they rendezvoused and docked with two separate Agena target vehicles in different orbits, and Collins made a challenging space walk to retrieve a micro-meteorite detection experiment from one of the target Agenas.

Collins was originally selected to fly on board Apollo 8 as CMP – but surgery to his back prevented him from taking up the place on this mission and he swapped places with Jim Lovell – to become the CMP for Apollo 11 instead. Collins acted as CapCom for Apollo 8 – issuing the historic command "You are Go for TLI" which signalled the moment when the first humans in history would leave Earth orbit for deep space.

Following his Apollo 11 assignment Collins settled in Washington as Assistant Secretary for Public Affairs. But the political life was not for him and a year later he left this position to become director of the National Air and Space Museum; a position he held until 1978. During this period he also attended the Harvard Business School and in 1980 he became Vice President of LTV Aerospace – a company based in Arlington Virginia. He resigned in 1985 to start his own business.

Collins is an outstanding writer and the author of four books including his autobiography published in 1974 – *Carrying the Fire: An Astronaut's Journey*. Of his experience alone in orbit whilst his crew mates explored the Moon below, Collins wrote that "the solitude of 45 minutes alone behind the Moon with a billion stars and 'God knows what else' was as exhilarating as walking on the surface."

Michael Collins. *(NASA)*

Michael Collins, Command Module Pilot, Apollo 11

Michael Collins was born in Rome, Italy on the 31st October 1930, where his father Major General James Lawton Collins was stationed at the time. During his years growing up the family lived all over the United States and even spent time in Puerto Rico, where he had his first flight in a plane called a Grumman Widgeon. He attended St Albans School in Washington D.C. and then chose to follow his father and uncle into the armed services – attending the United States Military Academy at West Point, New York. From here he picked the Air Force – striking out away from the US Army where his family were so well connected.

He served as an experimental flight test officer at the Air Force Test Center at Edward's Air Force Base, in California, where he worked on the performance, stability and control of jet fighters. Like Armstrong, before Apollo 11 he

Buzz Aldrin, Lunar Module Pilot, Apollo 11

Buzz Aldrin, (originally named Edwin Eugene Aldrin) was born on the 20th January 1930 in Montclair, New Jersey. He attended Montclair High School, New Jersey and went on to study at the United States Military Academy at West Point, New York for a Bachelor of Science degree, graduating in 1951. The following year he received his Air Force wings from Bryan, Texas and went on to serve with the 51st Fighter Interceptor Wing – flying 66 combat missions during the Korean War in F-86 Sabre fighter jets.

He went on to fly F-100 Super Sabre jets as a flight commander with the 36th Tactical Fighter Wing at Bitburg, Germany before taking leave to study for a doctorate in guidance for manned orbital rendezvous at MIT. On graduating he returned to the Air Force and was assigned to the Gemini Target Office of the Air Force Space Systems Division in Los Angeles.

In October 1963 Aldrin was selected as one of NASA's third group of astronauts and served as backup to the Gemini IX mission and a prime pilot for Gemini XII – for which he pioneered neutral buoyancy underwater training. Aldrin served as Lunar Module Pilot for Apollo 11 – the first manned mission to land on the Moon on the 20th July 1969.

In March 1972 Aldrin retired from NASA and returned to Edwards Air Force Base in a managerial role, which he struggled to feel satisfied by after the excitement of space flight. In many ways the hardest part of his assignment to the first mission to land on the Moon was returning to Earth – a sentiment reflected in his 1989 biography *Men From Earth*. In the book Aldrin admitted that he would rather have been on the 2nd or 3rd landing where he could have put his scientific talents to greater use and the emphasis would have been more on exploration. Alcoholism and a tendency for depression, which he'd inherited from his parents, plagued the 1970s and early 1980s. But in 1985 he returned to orbital mechanics – inventing the Aldrin cycler – a spacecraft trajectory which encounters Earth and Mars on a regular basis. Aldrin suggested it could be harnessed for carrying exploration equipment and people to the red planet, using little or no propellant; something which humanity might one day turn to in the centuries to come. In recent years Aldrin has proved to be a tireless promoter of human space exploration and the most industrious spokesman for mankind's first flight to the surface of another world.

Buzz Aldrin. *(NASA)*

Apollo 11 backup crew

Jim Lovell – Commander

James Arthur Lovell was born in Cleveland Ohio on the 25th March 1928. He attended the University of Wisconsin-Madison and the United States Naval Academy, and after graduating in 1952 he joined the US Navy – serving in the Korean War. He spent four years as a test pilot at the Naval Air Test Center in Patuxent River, Maryland and applied for the first intake of NASA Mercury astronauts in 1958. Lovell made it through to the short list and was rejected in the end for a trivial medical test result. He was selected in the second group in 1962 and went on to serve as a backup pilot on Gemini 4 and to fly into space on Gemini 6A in December 1965. He was the backup commander for Gemini 9A and in November 1966 made his

Jim Lovell. *(NASA)*

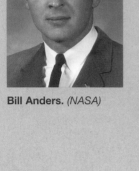

Bill Anders. *(NASA)*

second spaceflight as commander of Gemini 12; giving him the title of most experienced space traveller in history. During the Apollo programme he served as back-up for Apollo 9 (with Neil Armstrong and Buzz Aldrin) but switched places with Michael Collins to prime crew when the Apollo 8 and 9 missions were swapped around. Lovell flew the first manned Moon shot mission – Apollo 8 – in December 1968. As backup Commander for Apollo 11 he was scheduled to fly as prime commander for Apollo 14. This mission was swapped with Apollo 13 when it was felt Alan Shepard needed more time to train. Lovell flew to the Moon a second time in April 1970 on the ill fated Apollo 13 mission (see Chapters 2 and 7).

Bill Anders

William Anders was born in Hong Kong on the 17th October 1933. He attended St. Martin's Academy and Grossmont High School in La Mesa, California. He went on to study at the United States Naval Academy for a Bachelor of Science degree in 1955 and at the Air Force Institute of Technology in Ohio, for a Master of Science degree in nuclear engineering in 1962. The following year he was selected by NASA in the third group of astronauts, specialising in space flight radiation dosimetry and spacecraft environmental controls. He was the backup pilot for Gemini XI and Lunar Module Pilot for Apollo 8 – his first and only flight into space. Following his assignment as backup crew for Apollo 11 he accepted a job with the National Aeronautics and Space Council – which he needed to take up in August of 1969. In case Apollo 11 slipped by a month or more – a second backup Command Module Pilot – Ken Mattingly also began training for this role (see right). During the 1970s Anders devoted his time to nuclear power research, regulation and safety. In 1976, following a term as Chairman of the new Nuclear Regulatory Commission, Anders was appointed Ambassador to Norway. Looking for new challenges, the following year Anders turned to business and after a course at Harvard Business School he pursued management positions in a number of large American Companies. He still serves on NASA's Advisory Council and has established the William A. Anders Foundation – a philanthropic

Ken Mattingly. *(NASA)*

Fred Halse. *(NASA)*

organisation devoted to supporting educational and environmental issues.

Ken Mattingly

Thomas Kenneth Mattingly was born on the 17th March 1936 in Chicago, Illinois. He attended school in Hialeah, Florida and Miami Edison High School. He went on to receive a Bachelor of Science degree in Aeronautical Engineering from Auburn University in 1958 and joined the US Navy the same year. He received his wings in 1960, flying A-1H Skyraiders and A-3B Skywarriors off aircraft carriers for the next five years. Mattingly was a student at the Air Force Aerospace Research Pilot School when NASA selected him as an astronaut in April 1966. His first assignment was as Command Module Pilot on the Apollo 13, but eight days before launch he was exposed to German measles and it was thought best if he didn't fly. Jack Swigert took his place and as a result Mattingly was able to play a key part in getting the crew back safely following the accident 200,000 miles from home. Mattingly went on to fly as CMP on Apollo 16 – making remote sensing observations of the Moon from orbit 60 miles up during the three days that John Young and Charlie Duke were exploring the surface. After Apollo, Mattingly went on to serve in Astronaut Management on the Space Shuttle development programme. He commanded two shuttle flights – the first – a final test flight mission on Columbia (STS-4) in June 1982 and the second on a military mission in Discovery (STS-51C) in January 1985. Mattingly left NASA in 1989 and went on to work for several large American aerospace engineering companies; including Grumman and Lockheed Martin.

Fred Haise

Fred Wallace Haise was born on the 14th November 1933 in Biloxi, Mississippi. He attended the Biloxi High School and Perkinston Junior College before joining the Navy to train as a pilot. Following a spell as a Marine Corps fighter pilot he entered the University of Oklahoma graduating in 1959 with honours as an aeronautical engineer. He joined the Lewis Research Center the same year, moving to NASA's Dryden Flight Research Center at Edwards Air Force Base in 1963. He became an astronaut during NASA's third intake in 1966 and was the first of that group to be assigned to Apollo duties. He served as a backup LMP for Apollo 8 and 11 before flying to the Moon as prime LMP on Apollo 13. Despite his close brush with death, on this mission, Haise stayed with the Apollo programme – serving as backup on Apollo 16 and was scheduled to Command the Apollo 19 mission before its cancellation. Beyond Apollo Haise stayed on with NASA to help with the development of the Space Shuttle – flying five development drop test 'Approach and Landing' flights in the Shuttle Enterprise prototype vehicle. He retired from NASA in 1979 to become a manager at Grumman Aerospace, which he stayed with until 1996.

Apollo 11 Flight Directors

Cliff Charlesworth – launch and EVA

Cliff Charlesworth was born on the 29th November 1931 in Redwing, Minnesota. He grew up in Jackson, Mississippi – graduating from Mississippi College in 1958 with a degree in physics. He joined the Navy as a civilian scientist and also worked briefly on the Army's Pershing Missile programme before joining NASA in 1962. Charlesworth was a flight director on Gemini XI and Gemini XII in 1966 and Apollo 8 in 1968, before his assignment as Flight Director for launch and the first Moon walk on Apollo 11. After Apollo Charlesworth acted as manager of NASA's Earth observation missions and as deputy manager of the shuttle payload integration and development programme. Charlesworth died of a heart attack in January 1991, aged just 59.

Gene Kranz – lunar landing

Eugene Francis Kranz was born on the 17th August 1933 in Toledo, Ohio. He attended the Central Catholic High School and went on to graduate from Saint Louis University in 1954. Kranz joined the US Air Force Reserve, completing his pilot training in 1955. He was

sent to South Korea to fly F-86 Sabre aircraft for patrol operations of the demilitarised zone. After finishing this tour of duty he left the Air Force to work for the McDonnell Aircraft Corporation before joining NASA's Space Task Group at the Langley Research Center in Virginia. Working under NASA's original Flight Director Chris Kraft, Kranz cut his spaceflight teeth on the Mercury and Gemini programmes, before serving on Apollo. Although he directed the historic first landing on the Moon, covering descent and landing of the Eagle on Apollo 11, he is best known for his role commanding the white team at Mission Control during Apollo 13. Kranz's final shift as a NASA Flight Director was for the launch of Challenger from the Taurus Littrow valley on Apollo 17 – mankind's final departure from the Moon.

Glynn Lunney, lunar ascent

Glynn S. Lunney was born on the 27th November 1936 and grew up in Old Forge, Pennsylvania. He studied engineering at college and went on to study for a Bachelor of science degree in Aerospace Engineering at the Universities of Scranton and Detroit, studying part time whilst working for a National Advisory Committee for Aeronautics (NACA) programme run by the Lewis Research Center in Ohio. NACA was turned unto NASA just one month after Lunney graduated and he got transferred quickly to the Langley Research Center in Virginia – becoming a member of the Space Task Group. He was just 21 years old – the youngest on a team tasked with the creation of NASA's manned space programme. Like Kranz he worked through Project Mercury and Gemini – defining the procedures for space flight as they went along. During Apollo's development phase he took charge of the launch escape system boiler plate test flights at White Sands. He served as lead Flight Director for Apollo 7 – the programme's first manned flight since the Apollo 1 fire. Lunney also played a key role in returning the Apollo 13 crew to Earth – coming on shift an hour after the explosion and leading the tiger teams appointed to solve the seemingly insurmountable problems which the accident posed. Ken Mattingly called it the most magnificent display of personal leadership that he'd ever seen.

Cliff Charlesworth. *(NASA)*

Gene Kranz (left) and Glynn Lunney. *(NASA)*

Chapter 1

The Saturn rocket

It is 9th November 1967 and a team of world-class rocket engineers are about to do something no one has ever attempted before. Not only have they designed and built the largest, most complex rocket they can conceive, with three powerful stages stacked one above the other, but more significantly they are about to test fly all three stages in one almighty 'mother of all maiden flights'. As if that is not enough the stack will also carry the first live Apollo spacecraft into space.

As the heaviest object ever to fly lifts off at 7.00 that morning, the five first-stage F1 engines create a man-made earthquake which registers on seismometers as far away as New York City. The shockwave which follows prompts one spectator to question whether the Saturn V had risen or if Florida has in fact sunk! Beneath the behemoth, heat from the engines is turning parts of the concrete pad to glass and melting the metal guard rails. Cameras mounted strategically to record the lift-off are blown off the pad and into the swamp beyond.

Two and a half minutes into the launch, as the first stage begins to run out of propellant, the NASA announcer starts the countdown to the ignition of the second stage. Everyone who has worked on the second stage around the country is praying with their eyes closed and their fingers in their ears. "Three, two, one … first stage cut off … Second stage ignition" declares the commentary. "We have second stage ignition!" he repeats, his voice tinged with surprise and joy.

The Saturn V is born. It will be the first of 13 unforgettable flights and not a single one will be lost.

The icon of Apollo

The engineering bravado needed to take on Kennedy's challenge was epitomised by the Saturn V rocket, and the stories of the men who created the greatest booster rocket ever to fly are tales of boldness beyond belief. The iconic Saturn rocket embodied the audacity of project Apollo. It was the most public declaration of the engineering miracles required to carry mankind to another world.

Built to outrun the gravitational pull of the entire planet Earth, when stacked together the whole rocket would tower 363 feet high.

LEFT The giant Saturn V Apollo Moon rocket stands flood-lit on the pad, ready to fly. *(NASA)*

RIGHT This photograph shows an early moment of the first test flight of the Saturn V vehicle for the Apollo 4 mission, photographed by a ground tracking camera, on the morning of November 9th, 1967. *(NASA)*

BELOW A composite image of the moment of lift off for all 13 Saturn V flights of the Apollo and Skylab era. *(NASA)*

Even on paper, it seemed like an unbelievable idea. Daring to embark on its construction demanded huge faith from the engineering team who had conceived it. Perhaps it was only because NASA had originally planned an even larger rocket called Nova that building and flying the relatively 'less ambitious' Saturn V rocket seemed worth attempting.

People watching a launch described the guttural quake, that rolled towards them like thunder, as an intense physical experience. One journalist wrote of a Saturn V lifting off that "in the bedlam of launch there were momentarily no critics of the space programme". Riding it was something else. All 26 men who rode it into space agree that when fully fuelled it felt like the rocket was alive – almost like an animal. Bill Anders, who flew the first manned Saturn V flight straight to the Moon on Apollo 8, described sitting inside this impossibly powerful rocket as "like being a rat in the jaws of a giant terrier!"

In the beginning

At each launch the man who had conceived this fire-breathing bird was there to reflect on his audacity. Wernher von Braun had been experimenting with rockets his entire life. After

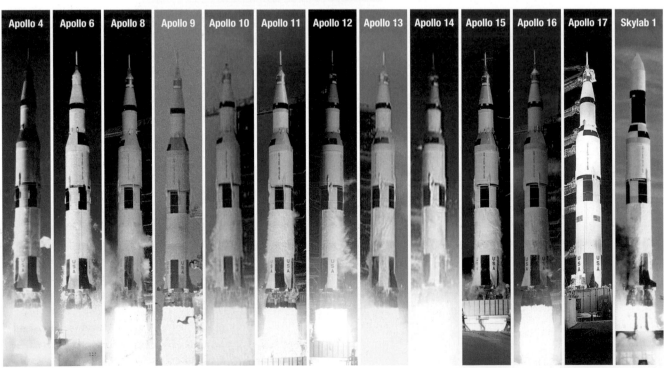

Apollo 4 · Apollo 6 · Apollo 8 · Apollo 9 · Apollo 10 · Apollo 11 · Apollo 12 · Apollo 13 · Apollo 14 · Apollo 15 · Apollo 16 · Apollo 17 · Skylab 1

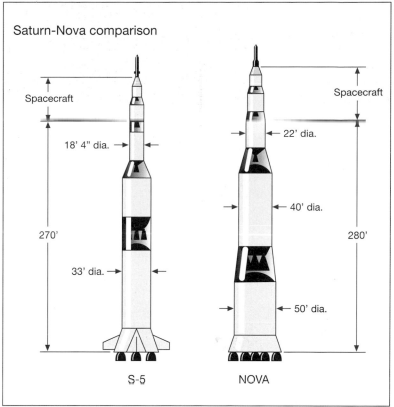

Saturn-Nova comparison

Spacecraft

18' 4" dia.

270'

33' dia.

S-5

Spacecraft

22' dia.

40' dia.

280'

50' dia.

NOVA

WWII, in the 1950s, and now working for the Army's Ballistic Missile Agency in America, he had succeeded in getting a liquid-fuelled rocket many hundreds of miles away from Earth. He had launched small WAC Corporal missiles from the tops of his larger V2 rockets, but although these early experimental multi-stage

ABOVE LEFT Dr Wernher von Braun inside the launch blockhouse, circa 1958. *(NASA)*

ABOVE Very early concept diagrams, circa 1959, for the Saturn V rocket (left) and the Nova C8 rocket (right). *(NASA/Matthew Marke)*

LEFT Dr Wernher von Braun is in his office, with an artist's concept of a lunar lander in the background, and models of Mercury-Redstone, Juno, and Saturn I. *(Marshall Space Flight Center)*

The basics of rocket science

It is the reaction principle which drives rocket motors forward by pushing matter under pressure in the opposite direction. This discovery is attributed to the Greek writer Hero in 62 AD. Hero's original reaction engine was a water-filled hollow metal sphere pivoted like a bicycle wheel on two free-rolling joints. A fire lit beneath the sphere would heat the water, pushing steam from the two jets and causing the device to spin. The force does not come from pushing on air, but from the combined momentum of all the molecules in the gas moving in one direction. According to Isaac Newton's third law the rocket's momentum in the opposite direction must match this. Typically the gas molecules in a modern rocket motor blow out the back of a rocket at between 5,000 and 10,000mph. The combined momentum of all these molecules is known as the rocket motor's specific impulse and can be thought of as a description of efficiency – like 'miles per gallon' for a car engine. To reach orbital speed this specific impulse or thrust needs to be applied for long enough to accelerate the rocket to a speed of 17,400mph.

Modern liquid-propelled rocket motors typically use a fuel and an oxidiser to achieve this. Using equations of momentum and Newton's laws of motion the exact power, and hence the size of a rocket needed to push its combined mass to orbital velocity, can be calculated. Due to the mass of propellant needed, a single-stage rocket is unable to achieve these speeds. With present-day technology, escape velocity can still only be reached through the use of multiple rocket stages, with smaller, lighter rockets riding on the top of larger ones, which fall away when spent to lighten the overall load.

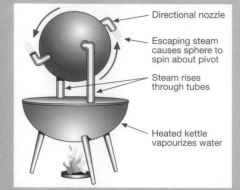

Directional nozzle

Escaping steam causes sphere to spin about pivot

Steam rises through tubes

Heated kettle vapourizes water

(Matthew Marke)

(Matthew Marke)

Fuel tank

Oxidizer tank

Fuel injector

Oxidizer pump

Oxidizer injector

Fuel pump

Cooling chamber

Combustion chamber

Combustion products

Nozzle

rockets had the thrust needed to reach these impressive altitudes, they lacked the greater speeds required to make it all the way into Earth orbit.

Employing the same multi-stage concept, with the first stage beefed up by four extra strap-on liquid rockets, the Soviet R7 launcher became the first rocket to reach orbital speed on 4th October 1957 when it placed the world's first artificial satellite, Sputnik 1, into space.

President Eisenhower, now realising that the future of the Cold War was going to be above the atmosphere, asked von Braun to start designing a new breed of American rocket, one which could close the embarrassing booster technology gap between the two nations and provide the potential for the US to launch a series of communications and spy satellites weighing over 9 tons.

Von Braun knew that the future of heavy-lift vehicles lay with the multi-stage liquid-fuelled rockets. The concept worked so well because, as the previous stage fell away and the rocket got lighter, the subsequent stages would need less power to achieve the speeds needed to reach orbit. Von Braun calculated that such a weight-efficient system could be harnessed to propel even the heaviest of manned spacecraft to orbital speeds and perhaps even fast enough to leave Earth's pull entirely, to head for the Moon. But, even with this multi-stage approach, existing US launchers would only be able to place a maximum of 1.4 tons into orbit. Von Braun would need a radically different sort of technology to reach the 9-ton target Eisenhower was demanding.

Desperate to achieve greater lift capability as quickly as possible, von Braun turned reluctantly to a concept called clustering. By strapping together existing booster rockets already developed for his Jupiter missile a new, more powerful launch vehicle he called the Super-Jupiter or 'Juno V' could be built quite quickly. Critics dubbed von Braun's relatively simple fast-track approach 'Cluster's Last Stand'.

This apparently straightforward solution was not as easy as it sounds. Frequencies of vibration created by engines operating so close together could easily interfere with each other. Using fewer, more powerful engines was preferable, but a new Air Force F-1 rocket

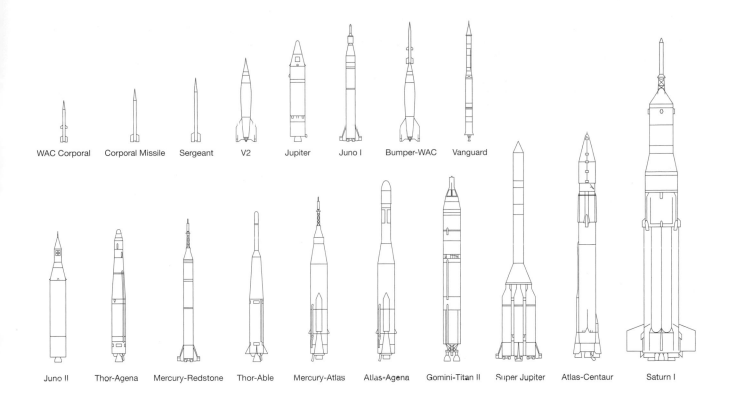

WAC Corporal Corporal Missile Sergeant V2 Jupiter Juno I Bumper-WAC Vanguard

Juno II Thor-Agena Mercury-Redstone Thor-Able Mercury-Atlas Atlas-Agena Gomini-Titan II Super Jupiter Atlas-Centaur Saturn I

engine, which promised over 1 million pounds of thrust, was still a long way from being ready to fly. So, for the new rocket's first stage, von Braun resorted to eight less powerful Rocketdyne H-1 engines, which he mounted together below eight propellant tanks from his Redstone rocket clustered around a central tank from a Jupiter rocket. For a second stage, he turned to an existing intercontinental ballistic missile technology from the Titan and Centaur series rockets, giving the new Juno V rocket the lift capabilities to achieve low Earth orbit that America needed. This was the country's first real space vehicle and official documents started to call it the 'Saturn' as 'the one after Jupiter' in the order of the planets from the Sun. The name had become official by February 1959.

The Army soon realised that it had no need for the sorts of Saturn super-boosters von Braun was now designing. Instead it transferred his team over to work for the newly formed NASA. Under this new management plans were drawn up for evolving the Saturn's cluster concept into an ultimate rocket with a clutch of the up-coming F-1 engines providing 6 million pounds of thrust. With a rocket like this NASA calculated that it could build a four-man space

station by 1961 and conduct a manned lunar landing by 1966 and even launch manned interplanetary trips by 1977. But in the summer of 1959, with no government approval for such missions and competing alternative rocket designs on NASA's books, like the giant Nova, the Saturn project came close to cancellation.

ABOVE Comparison of Western liquid-propelled rocket evolution from the 1940s to the 1960s. *(Matthew Marke)*

LEFT Von Braun briefs President Eisenhower at the front of the first stage of a Saturn 1 vehicle at the Marshall Space Flight Center on 8th September 1960. *(NASA)*

There were two things which kept it in the running. The Saturn concept was an evolution of existing clustered rocket technology and could be constructed using well-known concepts and designs. In contrast the new Nova rocket would require starting from scratch. And with NASA still debating the best way to land a man on the Moon, direct ascent, EOR, or LOR, the Saturn concept was, in the end, considered to be a more versatile option.

Aerospace engineer Abe Silverstein was asked to review the options and came up with three ideas. The Saturn A and B configurations would be fast-track solutions based on existing Titan, Centaur and Jupiter missile technology, whilst the ideal, though more ambitious, Saturn C series would be a brand new booster stack using the new F-1 and J-2 engine technologies and more powerful hydrogen-fuelled upper stages.

Silverstein felt that the Saturn C-5 was the only realistic rocket configuration for getting a

The Saturn options in 1960

Saturn A   A-1 – Saturn cluster lower stage, Titan second stage, and Centaur third stage (effectively a Juno V)
                  A-2 – Saturn cluster lower stage, proposed Jupiter cluster second stage, and Centaur third stage
Saturn B   B-1 – Saturn cluster lower stage, proposed Titan cluster second stage, proposed S-IV third stage and Centaur fourth stage
Saturn C   C1 – Saturn cluster lower stage, proposed S-IV second stage
                  C-2 – Saturn cluster lower stage, proposed S-II second stage, and proposed S-IV third stage
                  C-3, C-4, and C-5 – all based on different variations of a new lower stage using F-1 engines, variations of proposed S-II second stages, and proposed S-IV third stages.

The Saturn vehicle launch family as proposed in 1962. (Matthew Marke)

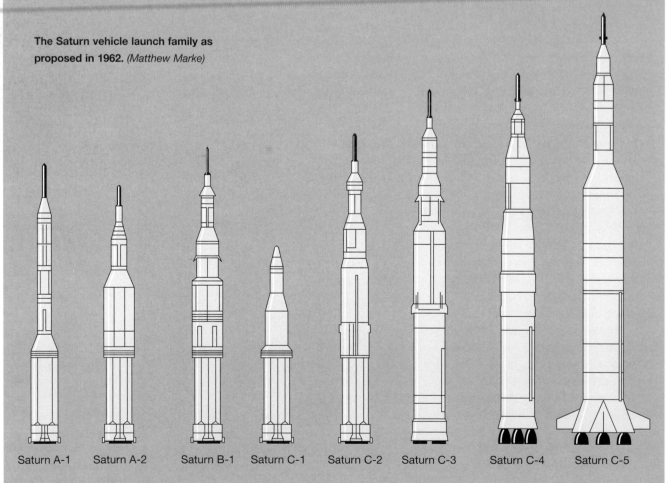

Saturn A-1   Saturn A-2   Saturn B-1   Saturn C-1   Saturn C-2   Saturn C-3   Saturn C-4   Saturn C-5

(Matthew Marke)

manned mission to the Moon. In January 1962 NASA confirmed the Saturn C-5 as its choice for the Moon rocket and gave it the new name 'Saturn V'. Its three new stages still only existed on paper and everyone knew that the Apollo spacecraft would be ready for testing in space long before the Saturn V would be ready to carry them there.

So, whilst the giant rocket went into development, NASA continued with the construction of the smaller C-1 (renamed Saturn 1) for use as a test vehicle. Its lower stage would be based on existing rocket tanks from the Redstone and Jupiter missiles.

Saturn 1

The first prototype, the Saturn 1, was composed of just two stages and stood 213ft tall. The first stage, designed and built by von Braun's team, was made of eight Redstone propellant tanks, four to carry liquid oxygen and four carrying RP-1 (a jet-fuel type of kerosene mix). These eight tanks were clustered around a central Jupiter rocket tank holding more liquid oxygen. All this propellant fed into eight H-1 Rocketdyne engines arranged in a central cluster of four and an outer square of four. The outer four corner engines were designed to gimbal so they could steer and guide the rocket in flight. Together at lift-off they could produce an unprecedented 1.5 million pounds of thrust, ten times more than the Jupiter-C rocket which had launched the first American satellite, Explorer 1, just three years before.

The second stage, called the S-IV (not to be confused with the S-IVB upper stage of the later Saturn V rocket), was a large liquid oxygen (LOX) and liquid hydrogen (LH$_2$) fuelled rocket. The engineering challenge of this ambitious cryogenic rocket stage was in storing the liquid hydrogen at −253°C. What made it doubly hard was that to save about ten tons of weight the two tanks storing the LOX and LH$_2$ shared a common joining wall or bulkhead. Storing them next to each other at vastly different temperatures with a single partition was not easy. The engineers achieved it by creating extra-thick aluminium walls and insulating them from the cold using special tiles bonded to the inside of the tank.

ABOVE Construction of the Saturn C-I in the Fabrication and Assembly Engineering Division at MSFC, composed of an S-I first stage, powered by eight H-1 engines, and a dummy S-IV second stage. *(NASA)*

ABOVE Saturn I S-I Stages in the MSFC building. *(NASA)*

Another key breakthrough for this rocket was something called the Instrumentation Unit – a ring-shaped structure fitted to the top of the S-IV stage. It carried an inertial-guidance

LEFT The NAA/ Rocketdyne H-1 rocket engine. *(NASA)*

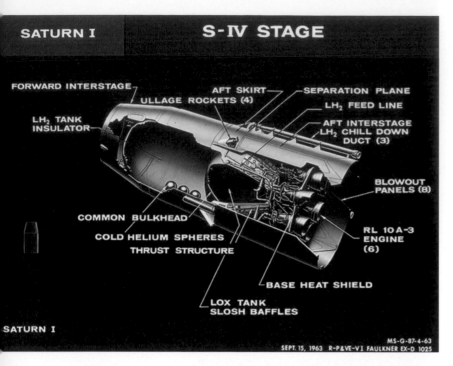

FORWARD INTERSTAGE
LH₂ TANK INSULATOR
AFT SKIRT
ULLAGE ROCKETS (4)
SEPARATION PLANE
LH₂ FEED LINE
AFT INTERSTAGE
LH₂ CHILL DOWN DUCT (3)
BLOWOUT PANELS (8)
RL 10 A-3 ENGINE (6)
COMMON BULKHEAD
COLD HELIUM SPHERES
THRUST STRUCTURE
BASE HEAT SHIELD
LOX TANK SLOSH BAFFLES

SATURN I

MS-G-87-4-63
SEPT. 15, 1963 R-P&VE-VI FAULKNER EX-D 1025

ABOVE Cutaway diagram of the Saturn I's upper S-IV stage. *(Alan Lawrie)*

BELOW The Marshall Space Flight Center's first Saturn I vehicle, SA-1, lifts off from Cape Canaveral, Florida, on October 27th, 1961. Weighing 460 tons at launch, this Block 1 first stage was powered by eight H-1 engines. The upper second stage (the S-IV) was a dummy. *(NASA/ALan Lawrie)*

system and a computer which controlled ascent through the atmosphere, sensing and compensating for any winds or loss of thrust during the flight. This cutting-edge on-board-control concept would prove a crucial feature of the larger Saturn V, enabling more reliable test flights and ultimately ensuring victory in the race to the Moon.

Above the Instrumentation Unit was a dummy third stage – providing an aerodynamic rocket cone to contain various different payloads.

After only two years of development, the first Saturn 1 had its maiden test flight on 27th October 1961. Only the first stage was live, carrying dummy upper stages, but the engineers who had worked on it could not suppress their excitement during countdown and ignition. They had only given the rocket a 75 per cent chance of making it off the pad and a 30 per cent chance of flying a complete mission. As the flight unfolded their whoops and cheers punctuated the communications loop recordings in the mission control room. This first Saturn flight was almost flawless – it soared to over 136 miles above the Earth.

It was only five months since President Kennedy's speech to Congress calling for a national effort to land a man on the Moon, and here, thanks to Eisenhower's and von Braun's foresight, was NASA's prototype Moon rocket already in flight. John Glenn was yet to fly his historic first American orbital mission, but this first Saturn rocket had already proved the value of clustered rocket engines – a technological breakthrough which would carry men on a flame to other worlds.

Nine more Saturn 1 flights before 1965 would pave the way for the Saturn 1B – the next stepping stone to the much larger Saturn V Moon rocket.

Saturn 1B

The Saturn 1B was first test flown in February 1966 using an improved, more powerful, version of von Braun's Saturn 1 first stage built by the Chrysler Corporation, and a new, improved second stage called the S-IVB, which was being manufactured by the Douglas

Aircraft Company (later the McDonnell Douglas Company). This historic flight also carried the new, unmanned, Block 1 Apollo Command and Service Modules into space for the first time on a mission called AS201. The S-IVB stage of this Saturn rocket would eventually become the third stage of the larger Saturn V Moon rocket and crucially could be switched off and restarted in space. It had started life as part of a rocket for use in an Earth Orbit Rendezvous scenario

for going to the Moon – but would also prove to be an essential feature for the Lunar Orbit Rendezvous concept which NASA eventually opted for. The S-IVB design was originally powered by six clustered RL-10 liquid hydrogen engines but for these Saturn 1B flights it would be powered by a single 200,000-lb thrust J-2 rocket engine built by Rocketdyne.

To restart the J-2 engine the liquid propellants had to be at the 'bottom' of the tanks, with gas above them. If they were not then the propellant pumps would suck up gas rather than liquid and the engine would fail to restart. To ensure that the liquid propellant was in the right end of the tank (a term called ullage) two small solid rockets housed in external pods were ignited moments before the J-2 engine was restarted to throw the rocket forward and force the propellant back and into the pumps.

The first Saturn 1B was launched on 26th February 1966, propelling its Apollo Command and Service Modules (CSM) payload to an altitude of almost 300 miles. Two more successful Saturn 1B flights, AS-202 and AS-203, took place in the summer of 1966; 202 carried an unmanned CSM on an important suborbital test flight. A fourth Saturn 1B flight carrying the Apollo 1 crew (AS-204) was planned for the end of 1966 – but problems with the Command Module slipped it into February 1967. And then, tragically, in a training exercise on the pad on 27th January, the Command Module caught fire on top of the rocket, killing the crew.

It was another year before AS-204 (later named Apollo 5) was re-flown. But this time the new Saturn 1B mission carried an unmanned

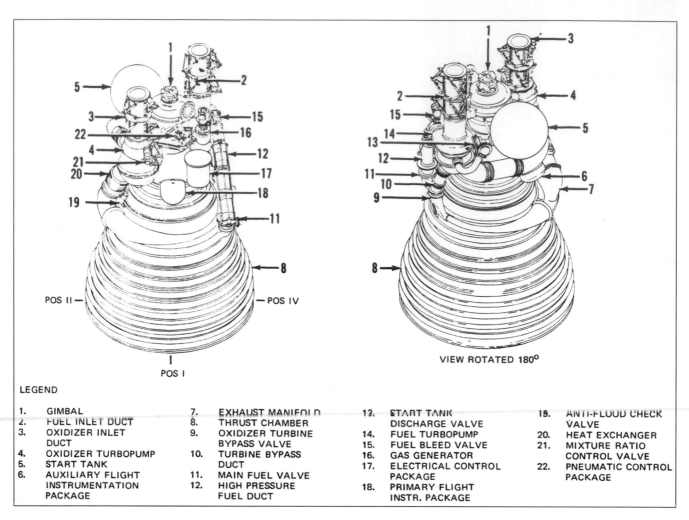

LEGEND

1. GIMBAL
2. FUEL INLET DUCT
3. OXIDIZER INLET DUCT
4. OXIDIZER TURBOPUMP
5. START TANK
6. AUXILIARY FLIGHT INSTRUMENTATION PACKAGE
7. EXHAUST MANIFOLD
8. THRUST CHAMBER
9. OXIDIZER TURBINE BYPASS VALVE
10. TURBINE BYPASS DUCT
11. MAIN FUEL VALVE
12. HIGH PRESSURE FUEL DUCT
13. START TANK DISCHARGE VALVE
14. FUEL TURBOPUMP
15. FUEL BLEED VALVE
16. GAS GENERATOR
17. ELECTRICAL CONTROL PACKAGE
18. PRIMARY FLIGHT INSTR. PACKAGE
19. ANTI-FLOOD CHECK VALVE
20. HEAT EXCHANGER
21. MIXTURE RATIO CONTROL VALVE
22. PNEUMATIC CONTROL PACKAGE

ABOVE The main components of the Rocketdyne J-2 liquid hydrogen rocket engine. *(NASA)*

RIGHT The Apollo 7 Saturn IB space vehicle is launched from the Kennedy Space Center's Launch Complex 34 at 11:03am on October 11th, 1968. A tracking antenna is on the left and a pad service structure on the right. *(NASA)*

Lunar Module into Earth orbit on its maiden space flight. By this time the fully stacked Saturn V Moon rocket had made its spectacular maiden flight carrying the unmanned Apollo 4 mission into space (*see page 56*).

The Saturn 1B would make one more vital milestone flight during the Apollo programme – carrying the first Apollo crew of Wally Schirra, Donn Eisle and Walt Cunningham into space aboard Apollo 7. It had been over 18 months since the Apollo 1 tragedy and half a million people turned up at the Cape to watch America return to manned spaceflight.

The Apollo 7 crew were the first astronauts to ride a Saturn rocket. Bizarrely the lift-off, they later recalled, was almost imperceptible. "We only knew [we had lifted off] … because the spacecraft clock began to tick off the elapsed time" recalled Walt Cunningham in his biography years later. But when it came to riding the Saturn through staging that was something else. Wally Schirra described it later as like "being in

ABOVE Apollo 4 is stacked in the VAB, prior to the first "all up" test flight of the Saturn V. *(NASA)*

On paper the three-stage concept for the Saturn V looked like this:

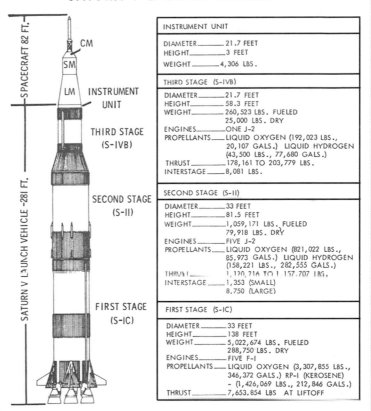

SATURN V LAUNCH VEHICLE

SPACECRAFT 82 FT.

SATURN V LAUNCH VEHICLE -281 FT.

CM
SM
LM — INSTRUMENT UNIT
THIRD STAGE (S-IVB)
SECOND STAGE (S-II)
FIRST STAGE (S-IC)

INSTRUMENT UNIT	
DIAMETER	21.7 FEET
HEIGHT	3 FEET
WEIGHT	4,306 LBS.

THIRD STAGE (S-IVB)	
DIAMETER	21.7 FEET
HEIGHT	58.3 FEET
WEIGHT	260,523 LBS. FUELED 25,000 LBS. DRY
ENGINES	ONE J-2
PROPELLANTS	LIQUID OXYGEN (192,023 LBS., 20,107 GALS.) LIQUID HYDROGEN (43,500 LBS., 77,680 GALS.)
THRUST	178,161 TO 203,779 LBS.
INTERSTAGE	8,081 LBS.

SECOND STAGE (S-II)	
DIAMETER	33 FEET
HEIGHT	81.5 FEET
WEIGHT	1,059,171 LBS. FUELED 79,918 LBS. DRY
ENGINES	FIVE J-2
PROPELLANTS	LIQUID OXYGEN (821,022 LBS., 85,973 GALS.) LIQUID HYDROGEN (158,221 LBS., 282,555 GALS.)
THRUST	1,120,216 TO 1,157,707 LBS.
INTERSTAGE	1,353 (SMALL) 8,750 (LARGE)

FIRST STAGE (S-IC)	
DIAMETER	33 FEET
HEIGHT	138 FEET
WEIGHT	5,022,674 LBS. FUELED 288,750 LBS. DRY
ENGINES	FIVE F-1
PROPELLANTS	LIQUID OXYGEN (3,307,855 LBS., 346,372 GALS.) RP-1 (KEROSENE) - (1,426,069 LBS., 212,846 GALS.)
THRUST	7,653,854 LBS AT LIFTOFF

NOTE: WEIGHTS AND MEASURES GIVEN ABOVE ARE FOR THE NOMINAL VEHICLE CONFIGURATION FOR APOLLO 11. THE FIGURES MAY VARY SLIGHTLY DUE TO CHANGES BEFORE LAUNCH TO MEET CHANGING CONDITIONS. WEIGHTS NOT INCLUDED IN ABOVE ARE FROST AND MISCELLANEOUS SMALLER ITEMS.

(NASA)

an erupting volcano with sparks and fire and smoke and debris all over the place".

Overall Wally confessed that riding this purpose-built space vehicle into orbit was far more comfortable than the converted intercontinental ballistic missiles, which he had previously ridden into space on his Mercury and Gemini flights. On a Mercury launch the astronaut pulled almost 10g, and in Gemini it was five or six, but the smooth Saturn 1B had achieved orbit without exposing its crew to more than 1g of extra load. Its ferocious forces had been immaculately tamed. But waiting in the wings there was an even bigger monster to ride – the Saturn V.

Saturn V

Work on the Saturn V had started in early 1963. Whilst test flights of the Saturn 1 and 1B were being undertaken to help develop the Apollo spacecraft, huge resources and effort were being thrown at this ultimate Moon rocket.

Despite the weight advantages gained through the Lunar Orbit Rendezvous technique for reaching the Moon, the Apollo spacecraft configuration would still weigh in at almost 100 tons. To lift this off the Earth and propel it to the Moon would require a rocket like no other. Each Saturn V would take a year to

Stage one (S-IC) would have a cluster of five F-1 engines. Each motor would produce as much thrust as an entire Saturn 1 rocket. On lift-off each would guzzle almost 3 tons of LOX and RP-1 propellant a second just to lift the enormous rocket off the pad.

Stage two (S-II) would also be powered by five smaller clustered J-2 engines running entirely on LOX and LH$_2$ propellant.

The third stage (S-IVB), which had already been flown on the Saturn 1B missions in a slightly different configuration, would use a single reusable J-2 engine also powered by cryogenic LOX and LH$_2$ propellants. Each of the three stages would present unique challenges to the engineers at the different companies which won the contracts to build them.

S-IC (BOEING)

BOTTOM OF SLOSH BAFFLE	248.00	
TOP ULLAGE ROCKET FAIRING MOTOR	178.68	7.213
TOP OF THRUST CONE	223.00	5.664
BOTTOM OF THRUST CONE	112.00	2.844
TOP FORWARD SKIRT	1541.00 39.141	-23.00 -0.584
LOWER SECTION OF FORWARD SKIRT	1420.30	36.075
RING SLOSH BAFFLES		
LOWER SECTION OF HELIUM BOTTLES (4)	946.50	24.041
TOP OF INTERTANK ASSEMBLY	865.20	22.484
FUEL VENT LINE	696.00	17.678
ACCESS DOOR (FAR SIDE)	794.18	20.172
LOX FILL & DRAIN (FAR SIDE)	776.18	19.715
LOX FILL & DRAIN (FAR SIDE)		
BOTTOM OF INTERTANK ASSEMBLY	628.80	15.971
SLOSH BAFFLES		
FUEL FILL & DRAIN	130.00	3.302
RETRO ROCKETS (2 EACH 4 PLACES)		
BOTTOM OF FUEL TANK	225.00	5.715
TOP OF HEAT SHIELD	112.00	2.844
BOTTOM OF F-1 ENGINE (5 PLACES)	-115.36	-2.930

3.723
5.664

NOTE: S-IC STAGE ROTATED 45° COUNTER CLOCKWISE FOR CLARITY

ISOMETRIC SCALE

POS II

POS III

S-IC

GIMBAL PLANE	100.00	2.540	
BOTTOM OF THRUST CONE			
BOTTOM ULLAGE R M FAIRING	-0.44	-.011	
J-2 ENGINES (5 PLACES)	0.00	0.000	
	-0.44	-0.584	
FLIGHT SEPARATION	1541.00 39.141	-23.00 -0.584	
S-II INTERSTAGE BOTTOM	1521.00	38.633	
LOX VENT	1511.75	38.398	
GOX LINE	1404.00	35.661	
Y RING			
PRESSURIZATION TUNNEL (2 PLACES)			
LOX FEED LINE TUNNEL (5 PLACES)			
Y RING	909.00	23.088	
BOTTOM OF LOX TANK	772.00	19.608	
TOP OF FUEL TANK	742.00	18.846	
FUEL PRESSURE LINE	692.80	17.576	
Y RING	605.00	15.367	
TOP OF ENGINE FAIRING	362.00	9.194	
TOP OF THRUST STRUCTURE	345.70	8.780	
INTERCONNECT LOX DRAIN	130.00	3.302	
BOTTOM OF ENGINE FAIRING	48.50	1.231	
BOTTOM OF THRUST STRUCTURE	116.00	2.946	
	100.00	2.540	

GIMBAL

THE BOEING COMPANY
SPACE DIVISION, LAUNCH SYSTEMS BRANCH
HUNTSVILLE, ALA. 35807
SATURN V APOLLO
FLIGHT CONFIGURATION
DRAWING ORIGINATED BY: HUNTSVILLE ENGINEERING
DATE: 1 JANUARY 1969
DRAWN BY: DON SPRAGUE
SHEET 1 OF 2   SATURN APOLLO 500 SERIES

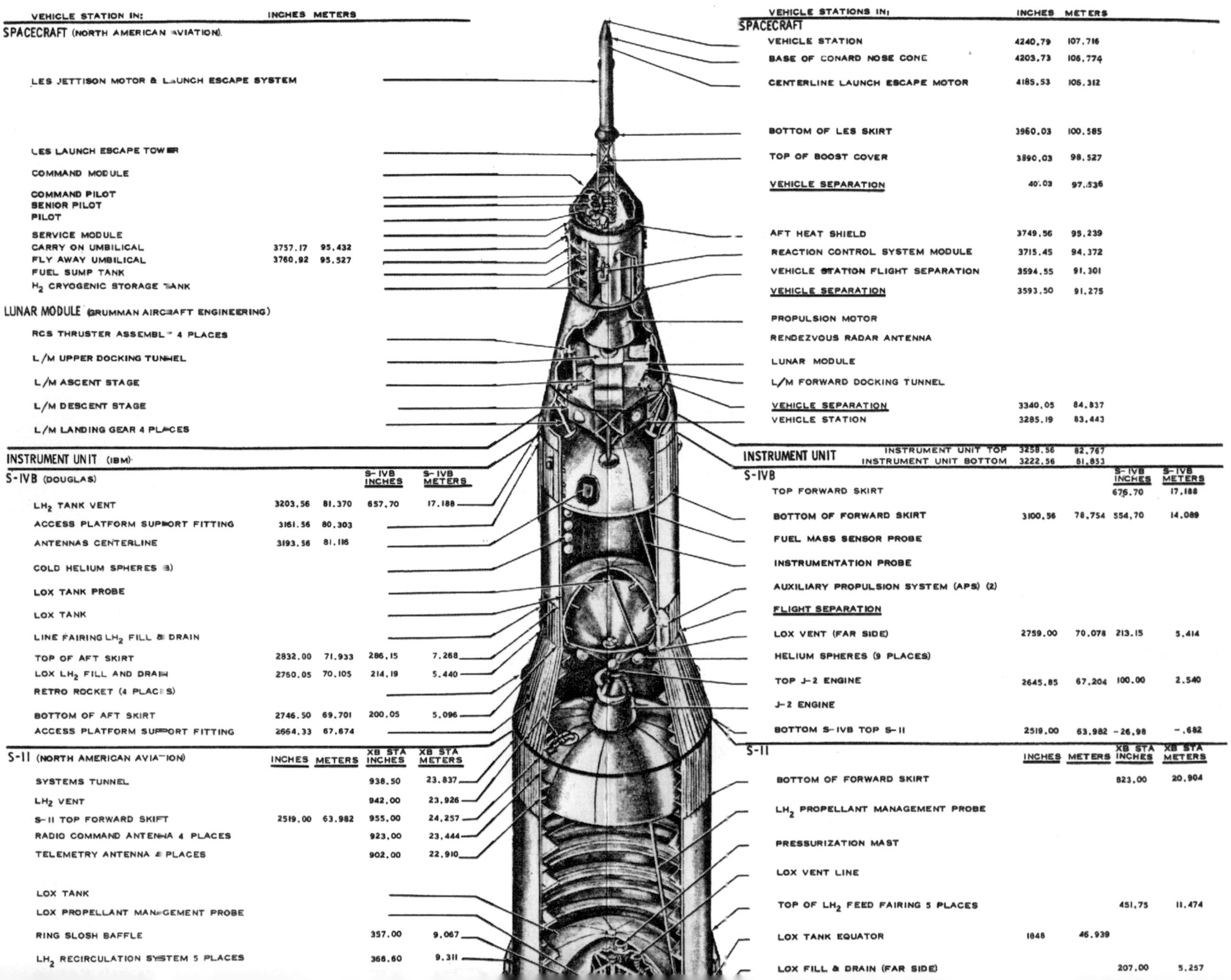
VEHICLE STATION IN: INCHES METERS
SPACECRAFT (NORTH AMERICAN AVIATION)
LES JETTISON MOTOR & LAUNCH ESCAPE SYSTEM
LES LAUNCH ESCAPE TOWER
COMMAND MODULE
COMMAND PILOT
SENIOR PILOT
PILOT
SERVICE MODULE
CARRY ON UMBILICAL 3757.17 95.432
FLY AWAY UMBILICAL 3760.92 95.527
FUEL SUMP TANK
H_2 CRYOGENIC STORAGE TANK
LUNAR MODULE (GRUMMAN AIRCRAFT ENGINEERING)
RCS THRUSTER ASSEMBLY 4 PLACES
L/M UPPER DOCKING TUNNEL
L/M ASCENT STAGE
L/M DESCENT STAGE
L/M LANDING GEAR 4 PLACES
INSTRUMENT UNIT (IBM)
S-IVB (DOUGLAS) S-IVB INCHES S-IVB METERS
LH_2 TANK VENT 3203.56 81.370 657.70 17.188
ACCESS PLATFORM SUPPORT FITTING 3161.56 80.303
ANTENNAS CENTERLINE 3193.56 81.116
COLD HELIUM SPHERES (3)
LOX TANK PROBE
LOX TANK
LINE FAIRING LH_2 FILL & DRAIN
TOP OF AFT SKIRT 2832.00 71.933 286.15 7.268
LOX LH_2 FILL AND DRAIN 2750.05 70.105 214.19 5.440
RETRO ROCKET (4 PLACES)
BOTTOM OF AFT SKIRT 2746.50 69.701 200.05 5.096
ACCESS PLATFORM SUPPORT FITTING 2664.33 67.674
S-II (NORTH AMERICAN AVIATION) INCHES METERS XB STA INCHES XB STA METERS
SYSTEMS TUNNEL 938.50 23.837
LH_2 VENT 942.00 23.926
S-II TOP FORWARD SKIRT 2519.00 63.982 955.00 24.257
RADIO COMMAND ANTENNA 4 PLACES 923.00 23.444
TELEMETRY ANTENNA 4 PLACES 902.00 22.910
LOX TANK
LOX PROPELLANT MANAGEMENT PROBE
RING SLOSH BAFFLE 357.00 9.067
LH_2 RECIRCULATION SYSTEM 5 PLACES 366.60 9.311
VEHICLE STATIONS IN: INCHES METERS
SPACECRAFT
VEHICLE STATION 4240.79 107.716
BASE OF CONARD NOSE CONE 4203.73 106.774
CENTERLINE LAUNCH ESCAPE MOTOR 4185.53 106.312
BOTTOM OF LES SKIRT 3960.03 100.585
TOP OF BOOST COVER 3890.03 98.527
VEHICLE SEPARATION 40.03 97.536
AFT HEAT SHIELD 3749.56 95.239
REACTION CONTROL SYSTEM MODULE 3715.45 94.372
VEHICLE STATION FLIGHT SEPARATION 3594.55 91.301
VEHICLE SEPARATION 3593.50 91.275
PROPULSION MOTOR
RENDEZVOUS RADAR ANTENNA
LUNAR MODULE
L/M FORWARD DOCKING TUNNEL
VEHICLE SEPARATION 3340.05 84.837
VEHICLE STATION 3285.19 83.443
INSTRUMENT UNIT
INSTRUMENT UNIT TOP 3258.56 82.767
INSTRUMENT UNIT BOTTOM 3222.56 81.853
S-IVB S-IVB INCHES S-IVB METERS
TOP FORWARD SKIRT 676.70 17.188
BOTTOM OF FORWARD SKIRT 3100.56 78.754 554.70 14.089
FUEL MASS SENSOR PROBE
INSTRUMENTATION PROBE
AUXILIARY PROPULSION SYSTEM (APS) (2)
FLIGHT SEPARATION
LOX VENT (FAR SIDE) 2759.00 70.078 213.15 5.414
HELIUM SPHERES (9 PLACES)
TOP J-2 ENGINE 2645.85 67.204 100.00 2.540
J-2 ENGINE
BOTTOM S-IVB TOP S-II 2519.00 63.982 -26.98 -.682
S-II INCHES METERS XB STA INCHES XB STA METERS
BOTTOM OF FORWARD SKIRT 823.00 20.904
LH_2 PROPELLANT MANAGEMENT PROBE
PRESSURIZATION MAST
LOX VENT LINE
TOP OF LH_2 FEED FAIRING 5 PLACES 451.75 11.474
LOX TANK EQUATOR 1848 46.939
LOX FILL & DRAIN (FAR SIDE) 207.00 5.257

(NASA)

ABOVE The Saturn V first stages, S-1C-10, S-1C-11, and S-1C-9, are in the horizontal assembly area, ready for the installation of the engines (five F-1 engines) at Michoud Assembly Facility (MAF). *(NASA)*

ABOVE RIGHT The S-IC stage being erected for final assembly of the Saturn V launch vehicle for the Apollo 8 mission (AS-503), photographed in the Vehicle Assembly Building (VAB) high bay at the Kennedy Space Center. *(NASA)*

build and would have a lifetime of just minutes. From the handling of the massive quantities of volatile propellant needed to power it, to the containment and precision control of its engines' enormous forces, the sheer scale of the Saturn V was stunning. Even the infrastructure needed to handle it, like the giant cathedral-like VAB hangar needed to stack it or the fuel guzzling 150 gallon per mile crawler vehicle required to transport it to the pad, was off the scale of conventional aerospace engineering.

The first stage

The first stage of the giant rocket would be the most powerful. It needed to provide the

initial thrust to lift the fully fuelled 3,000-ton rocket, from rest on the pad to a speed of over 5,300mph and a height of around 35 miles. With five F-1 engines clustered together at its base it would pack an incredible 7.5 million pounds of thrust for the first 2½ minutes of its flight. In those first minutes it would burn the best part of an Olympic size pool of liquid oxygen and kerosene propellant.

Although the S-1C was the largest and most powerful of the Saturn V stages, its manufacturer, Boeing, had relatively few problems. This was largely because its design was quite traditional, simply scaling up existing technologies. The 138ft-long stage was composed of two gigantic 33ft-wide

RIGHT Boeing's S-1C (first) stage for the Saturn V. *(NASA)*

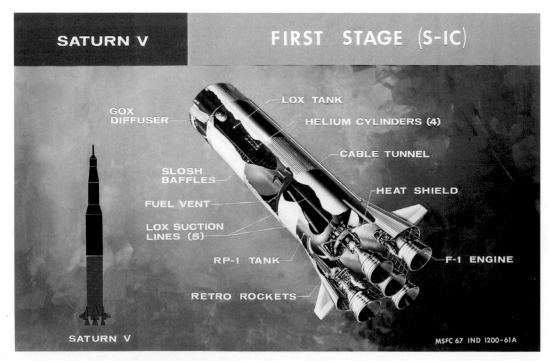

SATURN V — FIRST STAGE (S-IC)

GOX DIFFUSER
LOX TANK
HELIUM CYLINDERS (4)
CABLE TUNNEL
SLOSH BAFFLES
HEAT SHIELD
FUEL VENT
LOX SUCTION LINES (5)
RP-1 TANK
F-1 ENGINE
RETRO ROCKETS
SATURN V
MSFC 67 IND 1200-61A

propellant tanks arranged one above the other. The lower tank held 800,000 litres of refined jet aircraft grade kerosene fuel known as RP-1. The upper tank stored 1.3 million litres of super-chilled LOX held at −183 °C. The explosive power of liquid oxygen, in which anything would burn, was something everyone working on the programme was aware of, and not even as much as a fingerprint was allowed to contaminate the inside of the tanks it was stored in.

Five enormous, insulated ducts ran down through the RP-1 fuel tank to feed the five F-1 engines mounted at the base. Five of these 1.5-million-pound thrust F-1 motors were needed to power the first stage of the Saturn V. This simplified the clustering configuration and the gimballed steering. Despite their awesome statistics the F-1 engines' lifetime from ignition to running out of propellant was only a little over 2½ minutes. But containing and controlling such immense force, even for so short a time, was one of the toughest engineering challenges of the Apollo programme.

The F-1 engine

The engineers responsible for breathing life into the F-1 engine concept worked for Rocketdyne, a division of North American Aviation. The years between Apollo's

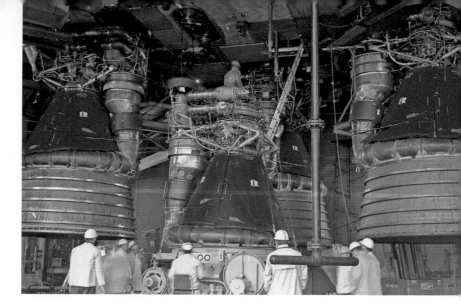

conception in 1962 and their deadline for man-rating the engine for safety in 1966 were the toughest that Rocketdyne had experienced. And whilst there were no fatal accidents, the tensions and stresses of these delivery dates took their toll on the team.

The performance of the F-1 was ahead of its time. It remains the most powerful rocket engine ever conceived and built, although the Russian-designed RD-170 that came a generation later did approach its output. In operation, a single engine could produce a force that could lift 680 tons of mass. Test stands which could contain this force had to be constructed on an unprecedented scale. Giant flame buckets beneath the engine bells were

ABOVE Five F-1 engines are installed on the base of the S-1C stage for the Saturn V. (NASA)

LEFT Rocketdyne's mighty F-1 engine – the most powerful single-nozzle liquid-fuelled rocket engine ever used in service. (NASA)

RIGHT Test firing of an F-1 engine at Edwards Air Force Base. *(NASA)*

BELOW The main components of Rocketdyne's legendary F-1 engine. *(NASA)*

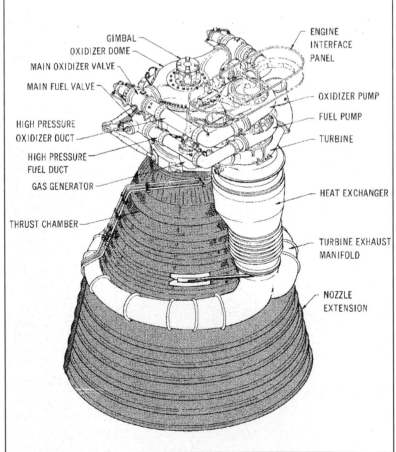

GIMBAL
OXIDIZER DOME
MAIN OXIDIZER VALVE
MAIN FUEL VALVE

HIGH PRESSURE OXIDIZER DUCT
HIGH PRESSURE FUEL DUCT
GAS GENERATOR

THRUST CHAMBER

ENGINE INTERFACE PANEL

OXIDIZER PUMP
FUEL PUMP
TURBINE

HEAT EXCHANGER

TURBINE EXHAUST MANIFOLD

NOZZLE EXTENSION

needed to deflect the thrust outwards to stop it blasting away the foundations.

Those who experienced the ground tests never forgot them. Witnesses described their internal organs shaking from over a mile away as 15 tons of LOX-charged kerosene fuel exploded out of the five engine bells each second. Inside the blockhouse, from where these S-1C stage tests were run, those in charge could barely believe the energy they were unleashing. The knowledge that they could control 180 million horsepower with the push of a button left many of them tingling with excitement and fear.

For the tests Rocketdyne acquired a boulder-strewn area in the Mohave Desert, north of Los Angeles, to be as far away from civilisation as possible. But, despite its distance from anyone else, certain weather conditions would still trap the shock waves from the test firings and funnel them along the ground for tens of miles, shattering windows and pulling plaster from ceilings in the nearest towns. It was not surprising that Saturn stage one test firings attracted almost as much interest as a space flight, often making the national news!

These experimental firings quickly revealed that simply scaling up the design of contemporary engines was not always guaranteed to work. Injecting so much propellant each second into a huge chamber almost 3ft wide could lead to destructive high frequency instabilities in the combusting fluid and disastrous effects on the engines. On 28th June 1962, combustion instability destroyed an F-1 engine in a catastrophic incident which also wrecked the test stand.

Without computers to model the problem the only way to learn if it had been cured was to do repeated tests, which became all the more costly when instability randomly recurred, quickly destroying the engines again. After losing two more F-1 rocket motors in early 1963 NASA and Rocketdyne came up with a new method of testing them using small bombs detonated in the engine bells to trigger the instability on cue. This way they could better study how quickly the oscillations were dampened down by their modified engine designs and they were also ready to shut an engine down quickly, before it blew up, if the problem persisted.

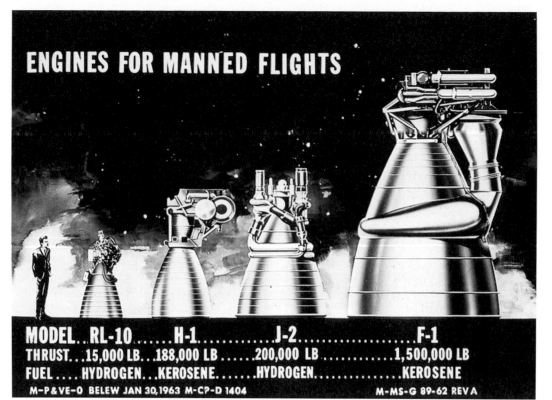

ENGINES FOR MANNED FLIGHTS

MODEL	RL-10	H-1	J-2	F-1
THRUST	15,000 LB	188,000 LB	200,000 LB	1,500,000 LB
FUEL	HYDROGEN	KEROSENE	HYDROGEN	KEROSENE

M-P&VE-O BELEW JAN 30,1963 M-CP-D 1404   M-MS-G 89-62 REV A

LEFT Comparison of the manned flight engines in use during the Apollo programme. *(NASA)*

BELOW LEFT Copper baffles, positioned on the face of the injector inside the F-1 engine bell, were used to solve a combustion instability problem. *(Alan Lawrie)*

BELOW First-stage separation during the launch of Apollo 11. The S-IC has dropped away, and the S-II stage has ignited to continue the journey to orbit. *(NASA)*

The solution they discovered lay in the way the propellant was injected into the combustion chambers. By 1965, after two and a half years of testing, the engineers had a fix. By introducing a series of copper baffles on the face of the injector, the destructive oscillations would dampen themselves down within 400 milliseconds, thought to be safe enough for manned flight. The triumph of the F-1 rocket engine was a crucial breakthrough for the Saturn V and essential to the success of the whole Apollo programme.

The second stage

As the mighty S-1C first stage finished its job at an altitude of 220,000 feet, and dropped away,

RIGHT Cutaway
diagram of the Saturn
V's second stage – the
S-II, built by North
American Aviation.
(NASA)

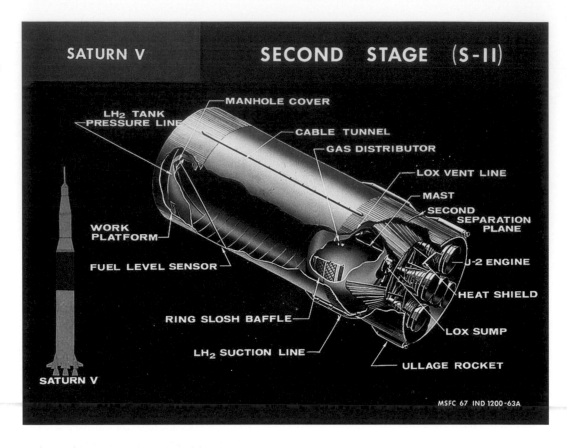

SATURN V

SECOND STAGE (S-II)

LH$_2$ TANK PRESSURE LINE

MANHOLE COVER

CABLE TUNNEL

GAS DISTRIBUTOR

LOX VENT LINE

MAST

SECOND SEPARATION PLANE

J-2 ENGINE

WORK PLATFORM

FUEL LEVEL SENSOR

HEAT SHIELD

LOX SUMP

RING SLOSH BAFFLE

LH$_2$ SUCTION LINE

ULLAGE ROCKET

SATURN V

MSFC 67 IND 1200-63A

stage two would carry the remaining 1,000 tons of rocket and spacecraft (now just a third of its launch mass) up to 610,000 feet and a speed of over 4 miles each second. Although superficially quite straightforward in design – consisting of just a couple of propellant tanks stacked one above the other – stage two with its entirely cryogenic propellant (LOX and LH$_2$) proved to be the hardest of the three Saturn V stages to develop and build.

To feed the five hungry J-2 engines at its base with enough propellant, this second stage would have to be the same width as the first stage (32.8 feet) and not much shorter in length (81.6 feet) – making it the largest cryogenic rocket ever built. It was so large that it needed to be shipped from Los Angeles, where it was built, through the Panama Canal, to the test and launch facilities on the east side of the Gulf of Mexico.

North American Aviation (which was also building the Command Module) had won the contract to construct the S-II. But the company's jubilation at bidding successfully for this prestigious job was short-lived. Since it was the last stage to be designed and

built, any late stage reductions in mass of the Saturn V, required to compensate for weight gains in the Apollo spacecraft designs, were automatically passed on to the S-II engineers at North American to solve. Losing tens of tons of mass out of an already finely balanced precision machine was never going to be easy but having to lose it from the largest cryogenic rocket in history left the team at North American wondering if they had bitten off more than they could chew!

For the S-II, carrying super-chilled liquid hydrogen alongside the liquid oxygen (as with the development of the S-IV and S-IVB stages), the most obvious way to lose weight and height was to fit the two tanks together into a single structure with a common bulkhead. Insulating the super-chilled liquid hydrogen at –253°C against the comparatively warm liquid oxygen (at –183°C) and the ambient outside temperature had been achieved on the S-IVB stage with a slightly thicker aluminium metal wall. But weight was so crucial on the S-II stage that thicker metal sheeting was not an option for the North American engineers. A new approach to insulation was needed.

The S-II team came up with a novel honeycomb insulation material, but the sticking processes they used to hold it in place at first did not prove adequate. When the liquid propellants were pumped into the tanks any pockets of air trapped in the bonding glue would freeze, loosening the honeycomb coating and causing it to lift off during testing. Even applying the honeycomb under vacuum conditions did not solve the problem.

In desperation the North American engineers turned to a rather unconventional group of specialists near their southern Californian Seal Beach factory. The local surfers, some of whom were also engineers, were experts at working with honeycomb – they built their surfboards out of it. So a group of them were hired to help at the factory and, together with the aerospace engineers, they came up with an arrangement of grooves within the insulation. Any air gaps present during the bonding were purged with helium gas which, unlike air, would not freeze once the tanks were filled with the cryogenic propellants. The new 'Beach Boys' team provided an invaluable solution to the second stage common bulkhead problem, even if there

RIGHT The second stage for Apollo 13. This photo shows the S-II-8 stage at North American's Seal Beach plant on 5th May 1968, being prepared for LH_2 feedline and engine installation. *(Alan Lawrie)*

BELOW The Saturn V S-II (second) stage for the Apollo 6 mission being lowered atop the S-IC (first) stage during the final assembly operations in the Vehicle Assembly Building (VAB) at the Kennedy Space Center. *(NASA)*

was a big absentee problem when the surf was up!

The common bulkhead solution saved an impressive 3.6 metric tons of weight, and reduced the overall height of the S-II stage. But the programme still demanded further weight reductions, and the easiest way to achieve them was to reduce the thickness of the tank walls themselves by chemically etching their aluminium. But with every micron of metal removed the rocket also lost structural integrity. The safety margin was eventually crossed when two prototype stage two tanks, filled with water to test their strength, failed without warning, bursting catastrophically like flimsy paper bags and spilling hundreds of thousands of gallons of water out into the test area. Storing highly volatile, explosive liquid oxygen and hydrogen in such a fragile container was never going to be an option.

Perhaps it was an impossible job to achieve this miraculous rocket stage with such little mass. But the tenacious engineers refused to quit and eventually found a structure which was both light and strong enough for the job. The thin aluminium skin they employed grew

The J-2 and liquid hydrogen

While the F-1 used conventional kerosene-based jet-engine-type fuel, the J-2 engines, also built by Rocketdyne, harnessed the power of the more exotic liquid hydrogen, which nearly doubled their efficiency. The mounting of the engines on this stage was similar to those on the first stage – with one central fixed engine and four corner engines which could gimbal to provide steering. Together they could lift 520 tons of mass (over a million pounds).

They burned in space with a clean flame – their ignition is barely visible on the archive film footage, in contrast to the dirty kerosene flame of the first-stage F1 engines. Despite being more efficient, however, they could not match the raw power levels attained by the F-1, making them more suitable for an upper stage. A single engine could lift over 100 tons and most significantly for Apollo the single J-2 third-stage motor could be restarted in space.

(Alan Lawrie)

(Alan Lawrie)

stronger when chilled by the liquid hydrogen. It was said of the finished structure that it was so thin a workman was able to hear a washer the size of a penny sliding around inside. Incredibly the total weight of the gigantic empty rocket stage was less than 10 per cent of its fully fuelled weight.

Separation of the first and second stages

To provide room for the five J-2 engine bells a spacing ring was inserted between the first and second stages. The ring also housed up to eight 219,000-pound solid-rocket ullage motors which were fired just after the first stage was jettisoned, to provide an extra kick – forcing the propellant to the bottom of the second-stage tanks and into the pumps to the J-2 engines. The 'inter-stage ring', as it was called, was jettisoned 30 seconds after the first stage, in what the rocket scientists referred to as 'a two

plane separation'. A similar, although tapering second inter-stage ring joined the top of stage two to the bottom of the narrower third stage and remained attached to the second stage on separation.

The third stage

The smallest Saturn V stage, the S-IVB, had the job of propelling Apollo into and out of Earth orbit and on to a trajectory to take it towards the Moon. A single restartable J-2 engine would be charged with this task. Four solid-rocket ullage motors were arranged around its circumference to be fired just before ignition, forcing the propellant floating inside the tanks to the bottom and into the engine pumps.

The S-IVB rocket had been flying as a second stage of the Saturn 1B rocket for some years and only required slight modification by the McDonnell Douglas Aircraft Company to work with the rest of the Saturn V. The overall

ABOVE An S-IVB, Saturn V final stage is winched onto its test stand. *(NASA)*

RIGHT View from onboard the top of the second stage (S-II) of Apollo 3's Saturn 1B rocket, watching the third stage J-2 engine ignite, after a brief fire of three ullage motors mounted around the edge of the stage. *(NASA/Footagevault)*

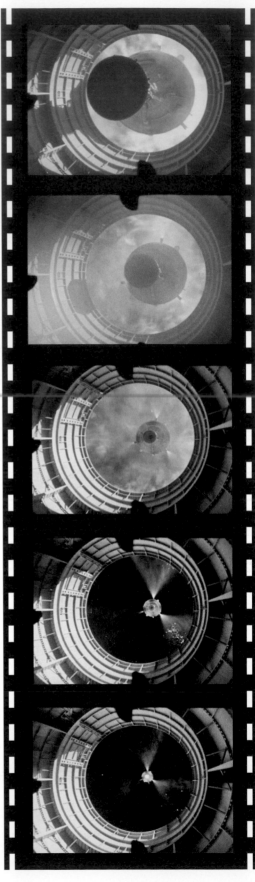

length of the stage was 59ft with a 21½ft-diameter tank section, and although it was the smallest Saturn V stage, it was the largest rocket McDonnell Douglas had ever worked on.

The most important stage

Early on in the design planning of the Saturn V it was decided that the rocket should carry its own autonomous guidance system. The equipment needed for this was housed in a 21½ft-diameter 3ft-high ring called the Instrumentation Unit, positioned at the top of the S-IVB stage. It housed a computer and a gyroscopically stabilised guidance platform. In emergencies the Saturn could still be controlled from the Mission Commander's joystick inside the Command Module at the top of the stack, but the Saturn's own guidance system was programmed to control the sequences needed to run the entire flight from before launch all the way through translunar injection, diagnosing problems and changing systems to compensate in real time, whilst transmitting a 'running commentary' to the ground.

The onboard computer was in fact three computer processors all working in parallel for safety. If any one of them deviated from the pre-programmed flight plan the other two would take control. This crucial design feature meant that a whole raft of systems could go down and the rocket could continue to fly. Even at 99.99 per cent reliability the 5,600,000 parts in a Saturn V could be expected to have 560 failures. But with luck the Instrumentation Unit could still adjust the flight profile to compensate for any of these failures – making sure the rocket reached orbit.

IBM's breakthrough prompted von Braun to call the Instrumentation Unit 'the Saturn's most critical stage'. This single design feature allowed the Saturn V to accomplish something called 'the all-up test' where all three stages were test flown together for the first time. It also gave NASA the confidence to send men to the Moon on the first manned Saturn V flight, and only the third ever Saturn V launch.

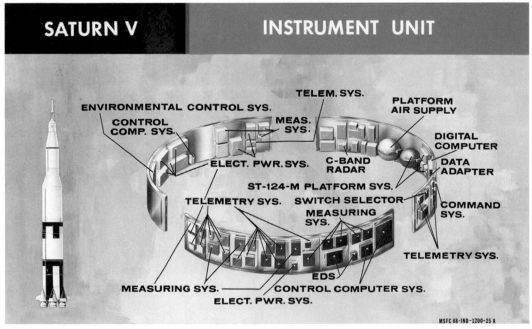

ABOVE This photograph was taken during the final assembly operation of the Saturn V launch vehicle for the Apollo 4 (SA-501) mission. The Instrumentation Unit (IU) is being hoisted to be mated to the S-IC/S-II assembly in the Vehicle Assembly Building high bay at the Kennedy Space Center. *(NASA)*

LEFT The Instrumentation Unit – dubbed the Saturn V's most important stage. *(NASA)*

Apollo 4

The first fully stacked Saturn V rolled out onto the gravel track leading to Launch Complex 39 on 26th August 1967. At the pad it was lowered onto pedestals and locked down ready for fuelling. After two further months of tests propellants started to be pumped into the rocket on 6th November. This task required almost 90 cautiously driven truckloads of liquid oxygen and 28 trucks of liquid hydrogen. The kerosene was brought in equally gingerly in 27 separate rail cars.

Finally, on 9th November, after more than half a decade of exhausting development and testing, the Saturn V was ready for its first unmanned flight. As the count reached nine seconds, the kerosene and liquid oxygen started to rattle down the pipes towards the five main engines. It ignited inside the centre engine bell first, and then opposing corner F-1 engine pairs at 300-millisecond intervals. Frozen moisture from the Florida air, stuck in frosted sheets to the skin of the super-chilled upper stages, began to fall in large white slabs towards the fire pit beneath. As the rising horsepower climbed towards 160 million, the rocket began to strain at the colossal locks holding it down. The Instrumentation Unit, sensing that the F-1s had reached maximum power, initiated release and the hold-down arms swung back in a blizzard of ice and fire. Shock waves from the five screaming F-1 engines reverberated across the launch centre – buffeting the VAB and the press and VIP stands four miles away and leaving commentators speechless.

Released for their first flight, the gyros in the Instrumentation Unit began sensing that the rocket was no longer fixed to the Earth and immediately began to gimbal the engines, balancing the pencil-like rocket and keeping it upright. It took 12 seconds to clear the tower, yawing away further for safety as it passed the top. A second later it began to roll and pitch onto the correct course, the four corner engines gimballing outwards for stability.

All-up testing

Early in the Apollo programme NASA realised that it would have to accelerate the development of the Saturn V drastically in order to meet the deadline of placing a man on the Moon by the end of the decade. Von Braun's original plans for his test flights called for at least ten unmanned flights before anyone would muster the courage to launch a human crew. Even ten was far fewer than the Mercury and Gemini rockets had flown before risking a human life. But the brilliant engineer and Apollo manager George Mueller felt a bolder programme of manned test flights was essential if America was to beat the Russians.

At Mueller's insistence the first flight of each stage would take place at the same time in a complete stack. The flight became known as 'an all-up test'. Even with the Instrumentation Unit managing things it was a high-risk strategy. Any major failing on a single stage could mean losing the other two stages and setting the programme back months.

Dr George Mueller follows the progress of the Apollo 11 Mission. *(NASA)*

By the time it had reached a height of 6,500 feet it was travelling at over 1,100mph. The F-1 engines continued to push up to 38 miles high, before cutting off. Six hundred milliseconds later separation occurred and eight solid rocket motors fired briefly to push stage one away. Thirty seconds later the inter-stage ring tumbled away and the launch escape tower on the top of the Command Module was jettisoned. Stage two kicked in for the next 6½ minutes; lifting what remained of the stack to 108 miles high and 17,400mph. Once more, the Instrumentation Unit, detecting that the stage two tanks were almost empty, initiated another staging sequence and handed the baton to the S-IVB to carry the spacecraft all the way into Earth orbit.

The Saturn V's maiden flight had worked perfectly. A correspondent writing from Cape Kennedy the next day summed up the triumph, declaring "American spacemen stood a giant step closer to the Moon today ..."

RIGHT The Apollo 11 Saturn V space vehicle climbs towards orbit after lift-off from Pad 39A at 9:32am EDT. In 2½ minutes of powered flight, the S-IC booster lifted the vehicle to an altitude of about 39 miles, some 55 miles downrange. (NASA)

'… we shall send to the Moon a giant rocket more than 300 feet tall – made of new metal alloys some of which have not been invented, capable of withstanding heat and stresses greater than have ever been experienced before, fitted with a precision better than the finest watch, carrying all the equipment for propulsion, guidance, control, communications, food and survival on an untried mission to an unknown celestial body and then returning it safely to Earth, re-entering the atmosphere at speeds of over 25,000 miles per hour, causing heat about half that on the temperature of the Sun …'

Chapter 2

The Command and Service Modules

It is November 1967 and the first Apollo spacecraft to reach space is in a parking orbit 115 miles above the Earth. There is no one on board this prototype Apollo Command and Service Module and the only sounds to be heard are the low drone of the environmental-control life-support systems and the whir of an automatic film camera controlled from the ground. Engineers are scanning their screens back at mission control in Houston checking for any tell-tale signs of a breach in the spaceship's integrity. They know that soon a similar craft will have to carry three men all the way to the Moon and back.

A powerful engine at the bottom of the Service Module ignites, sending the spacecraft out 11,000 miles from Earth and into interplanetary space. It drifts there, immersed in the vacuum and soaked in solar radiation for 4½ hours as telemetry signals record the cabin environment. Pleasingly for the engineers who built it there is no degradation in conditions onboard. But the ultimate test is yet to come. Attitude thrusters tip the spacecraft's nose down towards the Earth and the Service Module engine fires again, accelerating the craft to 25,000 mph to simulate a return from the Moon. The Service Module is jettisoned soon afterwards and the capsule starts to enter the high atmosphere. At these speeds, travelling almost seven miles every second, it is the fastest re-entry ever attempted.

Cameras pointing out of the window record the tremors and the growing howl of the air. Blunt end forward, the capsule's underbelly is now glowing white hot – heated to over 5,000°C by the compression wave of air trapped ahead of it. This extreme heat strips electrons from the atoms in the atmosphere turning them into dazzling ribbons of white and orange plasma. The capsule's heat shield starts to disintegrate as it is designed to do, fragments streaming off into the thin atmosphere. Down below in the Pacific Ocean recovery crews on the US Navy aircraft carrier *Bennington* scan the sky for a glimpse of the three orange and white parachutes which will signify its safe return.

LEFT The Apollo 9 Command/Service Modules photographed from the Lunar Module, 'Spider', on the fifth day of the Apollo 9 Earth-orbital mission. The docking mechanism is visible in the nose of the Command Module, 'Gumdrop'. The object jutting out from the Service Module aft bulkhead is the high-gain S-Band antenna. *(NASA)*

A new kind of spacecraft

The Apollo Command Module had to be a craft that the astronauts could really fly and it needed to be built by a team with a track record in this area. Since 1955 a company called North American Aviation had been building NASA's X-15 rocket plane. Whilst the X-15 was not designed to travel at orbital speed it could reach an altitude of over 60 miles – which technically was the edge of space. Some of the astronauts (including Neil Armstrong and

Joe Engle) had piloted the X-15 and had a high regard for the designers at North American. And on that basis NASA picked North American Aviation to build its new Apollo Spacecraft.

It would be far more complex than anything the company had tried to manufacture before. The capsule would need to be a self-contained biosphere – a miniature world which could provide everything three men would need for up to two weeks away from the Earth, on a half-million-mile flight to the Moon and back. Their ambition was to achieve this with 100 per cent

reliability without the craft weighing the same as a small building. The engineers would have just six years to accomplish this. It would prove to be the toughest and most costly challenge that the Apollo programme faced.

Two spacecraft in one

All the basic requirements for three men for two weeks – power, food, water, air, temperature regulation, waste disposal and hygiene facilities – would need to be carried on board, making it potentially a very heavy spacecraft. With the further requirements of a craft needed to fly to the Moon and back, such as propulsion, celestial guidance and navigation, deep space communication and an Earth landing system including a heat shield and parachutes, the mass of the vehicle became so great on paper that during re-entry at 25,000mph it would simply burn up.

The solution to this problem came from the fact that not everything required to get the crew to the Moon needed to be returned to Earth. The Gemini spacecraft had first pioneered the concept of a separate 'Service Module' (SM) or trailer slung behind or beneath the capsule to support the men on board. A similar service module design seemed like a sensible idea for Apollo as well. This could be discarded minutes before reaching the Earth, leaving the smaller, lighter conical capsule known as the 'Command Module' (CM) to make a re-entry on its own. Together the two Apollo spacecraft would

LEFT A Gemini capsule being tested in the Unitary Plan wind tunnel. *(NASA)*

ABOVE The Apollo Command Module – Ameriica's first three-man spacecraft – would sit right at the apex of the Saturn V stack. *(NASA)*

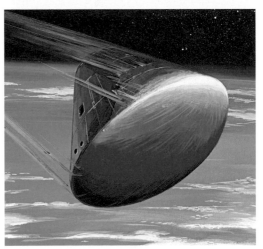

ABOVE Artist's impression of the moment of jettison of the Service Module from the Command Module – prior to re-entry. *(NASA)*

LEFT Artist's impression of the blunt-ended Command Module making a re-entry. *(NASA)*

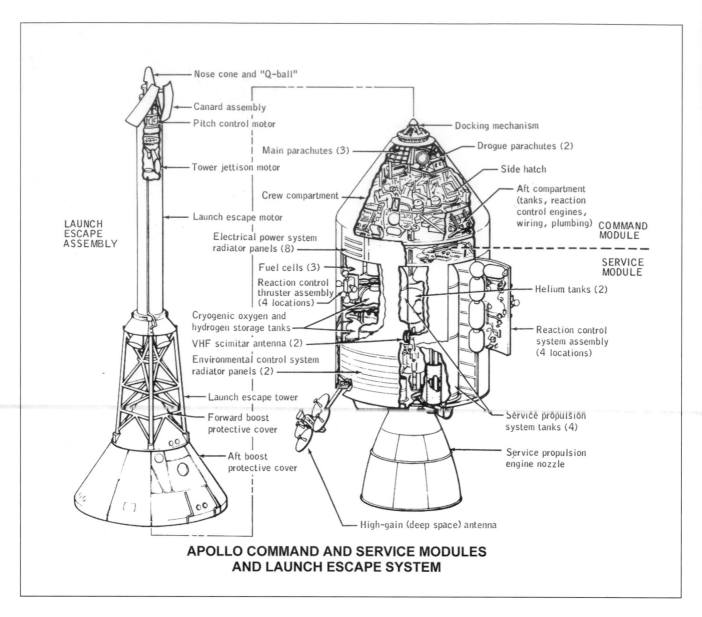

Nose cone and "Q-ball"

Canard assembly

Pitch control motor

Main parachutes (3)

Tower jettison motor

Crew compartment

Launch escape motor

Electrical power system
radiator panels (8)

Fuel cells (3)

Reaction control
thruster assembly
(4 locations)

Cryogenic oxygen and
hydrogen storage tanks

VHF scimitar antenna (2)

Environmental control system
radiator panels (2)

Launch escape tower

Forward boost
protective cover

Aft boost
protective cover

LAUNCH
ESCAPE
ASSEMBLY

Docking mechanism

Drogue parachutes (2)

Side hatch

Aft compartment
(tanks, reaction
control engines,
wiring, plumbing)

COMMAND
MODULE

SERVICE
MODULE

Helium tanks (2)

Reaction control
system assembly
(4 locations)

Service propulsion
system tanks (4)

Service propulsion
engine nozzle

High-gain (deep space) antenna

**APOLLO COMMAND AND SERVICE MODULES
AND LAUNCH ESCAPE SYSTEM**

ABOVE The full
configuration of the
Command and Service
modules, showing
the SPS engine and
the launch escape
assembly (on the left)
which is secured to
the apex of the CM
during launch. *(NASA)*

become known as the Command and Service
Modules or CSM.

Command Module

The blunt-ended, conical Command Module
(CM) was constructed from two shells
separated by insulation material. The inner airtight pressure shell was built from a lightweight
double-skinned aluminium alloy and the outer
skin from a steel honeycomb substructure
onto which was bonded fibreglass honeycomb
whose cells were filled with an epoxy resin. This
outer layer acted as a full wrap-around heat
shield and micro-meteorite protection layer. This

heat shield protection would be thickest at its
base where the most severe heat of re-entry
would be focused. The outer skin would
also accommodate small rocket thrusters,
communications antennae and a couple of
ports from which to expel waste water
and urine.

The top of the cone housed a removable
docking mechanism to mate with the lunar
lander. This precisely engineered mechanical
device had to have the refinements of a Swiss
watch and yet be strong enough to absorb
the momentum of a rolling railway carriage.
On top of this the mechanism also had to
be removable, to provide astronaut access
between the two spacecraft once they had

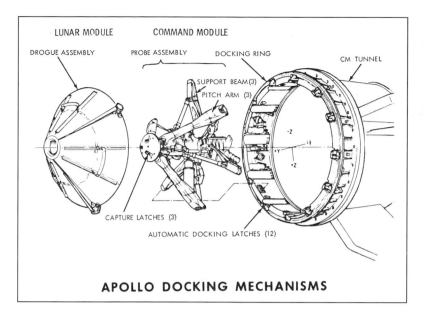

LUNAR MODULE   COMMAND MODULE

DROGUE ASSEMBLY   PROBE ASSEMBLY   DOCKING RING   CM TUNNEL

SUPPORT BEAM (3)

PITCH ARM (3)

-Z

+Y

+Z

CAPTURE LATCHES (3)

AUTOMATIC DOCKING LATCHES (12)

APOLLO DOCKING MECHANISMS

LEFT The docking mechanism – known as the 'probe and drogue' assembly – housed in the apex of the CM. *(NASA)*

ABOVE A view of the probe and drogue assembly on the nose of the CM during the flight of Apollo 17. *(NASA)*

BELOW LEFT The main components of the Apollo Command Module pressurised crew cabin and heat shields. *(Matthew Marke)*

BELOW The inside of Command Module 'America' (CM-114) – from Apollo 17 – currently on display at the Johnson Space Center visitors' centre. *(Duncan Copp)*

docked. The section around the docking tunnel also carried the Earth Landing System (ELS), including the drogue and main parachutes and their pyrotechnic deployment charges.

The lower part of the Command Module, forming the wider base of the cone, was mostly occupied by the pressurised crew compartment and housed all the electronic equipment they needed to operate and fly the spacecraft.

The crew compartment

A glance inside the Apollo Command Modules housed in museums today (*see Appendix*) suggests that they were cramped and cluttered places to live in for ten days; but in the zero gravity of a space flight the crews found them relatively spacious compared to a Gemini or Mercury capsule. The actual space available to float around in was 210 cubic feet, which was equivalent to being inside a large family car.

There was also the luxury of five windows, a circular one 9 inches in diameter in the main hatch door, two large ones 13 inches square either side of the hatch, and two triangular windows 13 x 8 inches in size facing forward. All five windows were made with triple layers of glass, the outer one almost ¾ inch thick. The glass was designed to filter out infrared and ultra-violet light and could withstand temperatures of 1,500°C. Some missions used windows made from quartz which transmitted UV light to allow UV photography.

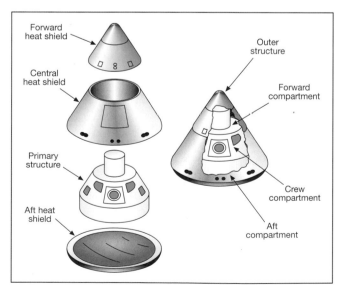

Forward heat shield

Central heat shield

Primary structure

Aft heat shield

Outer structure

Forward compartment

Crew compartment

Aft compartment

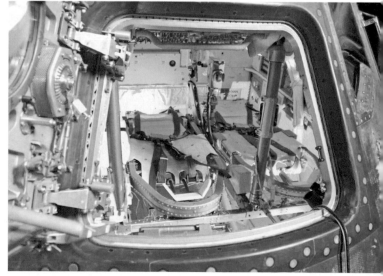

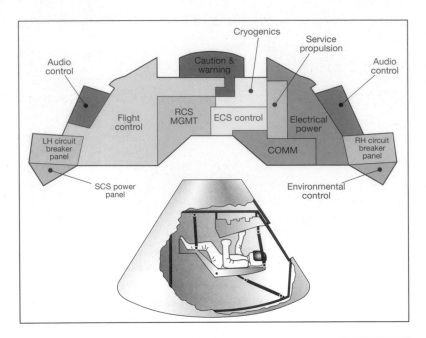

Audio control

Cryogenics

Caution & warning

Service propulsion

Audio control

Flight control

RCS MGMT

ECS control

Electrical power

LH circuit breaker panel

COMM

RH circuit breaker panel

SCS power panel

Environmental control

APOLLO COMMAND MODULE INTERIOR

LEFT SIDE

CABIN HEAT EXCHANGER SHUTTER (ECS)

PRESSURE SUIT CONNECTORS (3) (ECS)

CABIN PRESSURE RELIEF VALVE CONTROLS (ECS)

OXYGEN SURGE TANK (ECS)

CABIN TEMP CONTROL PANEL (ECS)

POTABLE WATER SUPPLY PANEL (ECS)

GMT CLOCK & EVENT TIMERS

CONTROL PANEL (G&C)

RATE & ATTITUDE GYRO ASSEMBLY (SCS)

POWER SERVO ASSEMBLY (G&C)

COMMAND MODULE COMPUTER (G&C)

WATER / GLYCOL CONTROL VALVES (ECS)

SCS MODULES

ECS PACKAGE

CO_2 ABSORBER CARTRIDGE STOWAGE (ECS)

OXYGEN CONT PANEL

RIGHT SIDE

DATA STORAGE EQUIP.

G & C OPTICS

VACUUM CLEANER STOWAGE

CONTROL PANEL (G & C)

WASTE MGMT CONTROL PANEL

SCS MODULES

MASTER EVENT SEQUENCE CONTROLLERS & SCIENTIFIC EQUIPMENT (BEHIND PANELS)

CO_2 ABSORBER CARTRIDGE STOWAGE (ECS)

LEFT Layout of the main instrument panel in the Apollo Command Module. **Refer to the illustration on pages 66–67 for more details.** *(Matthew Marke)*

During major manoeuvres the crew would lie on three couches. At the foot of the couches was an area called the lower equipment bay, which housed, amongst other things, the main communications and the guidance, navigation and control systems (GNCS), including a sextant (optical alignment system – OPS) and the Apollo guidance computer (AGC).

The main display console (MDC), housing the majority of the flight controls and instruments was positioned immediately in front of the couches, in easy reach of the crew. Constructed around the entrance to the docking tunnel, it held around 400 different instruments, switches, circuit breakers, warning lights and alarms. More control switches and circuit breakers were mounted to the sides of the couches.

Every other available space around the cabin was occupied by stowage bays and lockers to house food supplies, clothing, cameras, medical and hygiene kits, survival gear, waste-management containers and the bulky lithium hydroxide canisters needed for CO_2 removal. The lockers on either side of the lower bay were reserved for moon rock samples on the return journey.

During launch the Commander in charge of the mission (CDR) would sit in the left couch in reach of the majority of the flight instruments. The Command Module Pilot (CMP) would sit next to him in the centre couch, with his head close to the spacecraft's main hatch and his feet in the lower instrument bay. The Lunar Module Pilot (LMP) would take the right couch, from where the spacecraft systems could be monitored. During certain flight procedures, such as re-entry, the CMP would switch seats with the CDR. During much of their time in space the centre couch would be collapsed giving more room to move around and helping access to the lower instrument bay.

LEFT Left and right sides of the Apollo Command Module, showing simplified interior layout of equipment and controls. *(NASA/Frank O'Brien)*

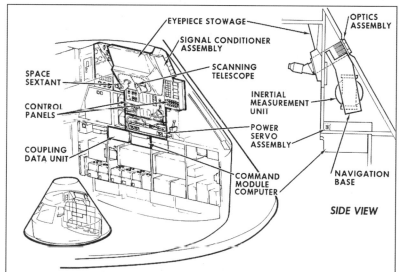

EYEPIECE STOWAGE

SIGNAL CONDITIONER ASSEMBLY

SCANNING TELESCOPE

SPACE SEXTANT

INERTIAL MEASUREMENT UNIT

CONTROL PANELS

POWER SERVO ASSEMBLY

COUPLING DATA UNIT

COMMAND MODULE COMPUTER

OPTICS ASSEMBLY

NAVIGATION BASE

SIDE VIEW

ABOVE LEFT The Apollo 8 capsule being hoisted on to the recovery ship following splashdown on 27th December 1968. *(NASA)*

ABOVE A 'pilot's-eye' view inside the Apollo Command Module, showing the left-hand seat controls and main instrument panel *in situ*. *(Smithsonian Institution)*

LEFT The Command Module sextant assembly and Guidance and Navigation Control Systems (GNCS) equipment. *(NASA/Scott Schneeweig)*

BELOW The Apollo Command Module main instrument panel – see illustration on pages 66–67 for more details. *(Smithsonian Institution)*

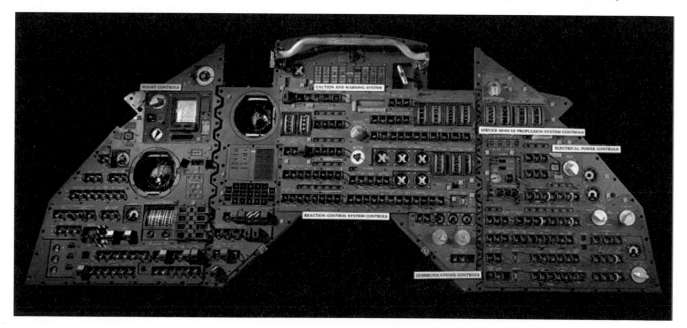

Detailed illustration showing the layout of an
Apollo Command Module's main control panel.
Flight control was managed from the left side,
whilst electrical power and SPS was managed
from the right. RCS management, environmental
control and cryogenics was operated from the
centre controls. *(NASA/Frank O'Brien)*

APOLLO COMMAND MODU

IN CONTROL PANEL

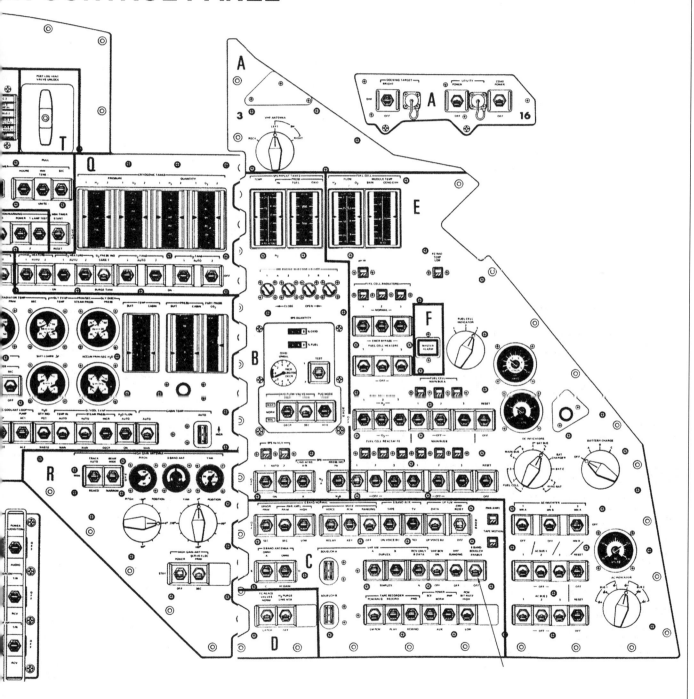

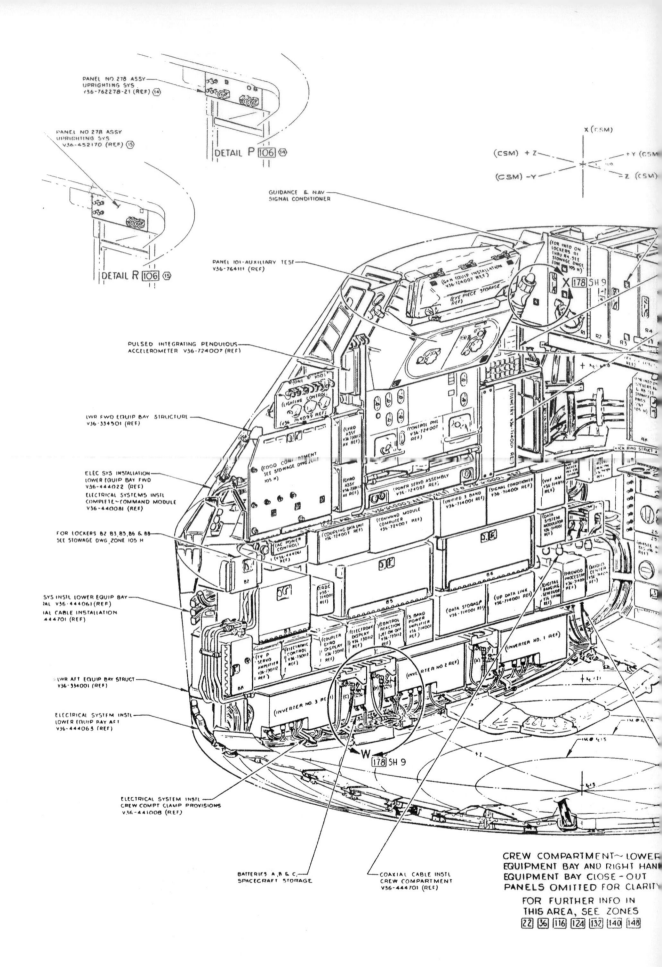

PANEL NO 278 ASSY
UPRIGHTING SYS
V36-762278-21 (REF) (14)

PANEL NO 278 ASSY
UPRIGHTING SYS
V36-452170 (REF) (15)

DETAIL P 106 (14)

DETAIL R 106 (15)

GUIDANCE & NAV
SIGNAL CONDITIONER

X (CSM)

(CSM) +Z

(CSM) -Y

+Y (CSM)

-Z (CSM)

PANEL 101-AUXILIARY TEST
V36-764111 (REF)

(FOR INFO ON
LOCKERS R1
THRU R4, SEE
STOWAGE DWG,
ZONE 105 H)

PULSED INTEGRATING PENDULOUS
ACCELEROMETER V36-724007 (REF)

X 178 SH 9

LWR FWD EQUIP BAY STRUCTURE
V36-334501 (REF)

ELEC SYS INSTALLATION
LOWER EQUIP BAY FWD
V36-444022 (REF)
ELECTRICAL SYSTEMS INSTL
COMPLETE~COMMAND MODULE
V36-440081 (REF)

FOR LOCKERS B2,B3,B5,B6 & B8
SEE STOWAGE DWG, ZONE 105 H

SYS INSTL LOWER EQUIP BAY
AL V36-444061 (REF)
AL CABLE INSTALLATION
444701 (REF)

LWR AFT EQUIP BAY STRUCT
V36-334001 (REF)

ELECTRICAL SYSTEM INSTL
LOWER EQUIP BAY AFT
V36-444063 (REF)

ELECTRICAL SYSTEM INSTL
CREW COMPT CLAMP PROVISIONS
V36-441008 (REF)

BATTERIES A,B & C
SPACECRAFT STORAGE

COAXIAL CABLE INSTL
CREW COMPARTMENT
V36-444701 (REF)

W 178 SH 9

CREW COMPARTMENT~LOWER
EQUIPMENT BAY AND RIGHT HAN
EQUIPMENT BAY CLOSE-OUT
PANELS OMITTED FOR CLARITY
FOR FURTHER INFO IN
THIS AREA, SEE ZONES
22 36 116 124 132 140 148

STOWAGE DWG

FOI-100512 (AX)(REF) – (12)
FOI-100513 (AX)(REF) – (13)
FOI-100514 (AX)(REF) – (14)
FOI-100515 (AX)(REF) – (15)

RETAINER DWG

V36-630015 (REF) – (12)
V36-630016 (REF) – (13) (14)

SEE RETAINER DWG, ZONE 105 G

DISPLAYS AND CONTROLS KEYBOARD
V36-772400 (REF)

ELECTRONIC SYSTEMS
INSTL COMPLETE
V36-700001 (REF)

INNER M. AT Xc:80.75

CONTINUED IN ZONE 153 G, SH 8

LOCKER R5, SEE STOWAGE DWG, ZONE 105 H

ELECTRICAL SYS RH FWD V36-442061 (REF)
CREW COMPT ELEC COMPLETE V36-440081 (REF)

PANEL 229 AUXILIARY "C" CIRCUIT BREAKER
V36-762029 (REF)

ELECTRICAL CONNECTOR PANEL (REF)

DISPLAYS & CONTROLS INSTL RH EQUIP
BAY V36-762012 (REF)

CKT BKR MODULE V36-752521 (REF)

PANEL NO 278 ASSY, UPRIGHTING
SYS V36-762278-11 (REF)

LUNAR DOCKING EVENTS CONTROLLER
'A' & 'B'

INNER M. AT Xc:42.665

PYRO CONTINUITY VERIFICATION BOX

EARTH LANDING SYS CONTROLS 'A' & 'B'

CURRENT LIMITER OPERATIONAL
V36-752521 (REF)

INSTRUMENTATION COMPLETE
V36-750906 (REF)

ELEC RH AFT V36-442062 (REF)

INNER M. AT Xc:14.07

GRD SPT EQUIP GROUND TEST PLUGS

PYRO BATTERIES

1.6 STR

SIZE	CODE IDENT NO	
E	03953	
SCALE NONE	PAGE 11-10	SHEET 6

LEFT Detailed engineering drawing (by hand) showing the arrangement of stowage items lining the interior of the Command Module. Everything not only had to fit in, but it had to be accessible during flight, after the main control panel and crew couches were also inserted (see page 70 overleaf). (NASA/Frank O'Brien/ Scott Schneeweis)

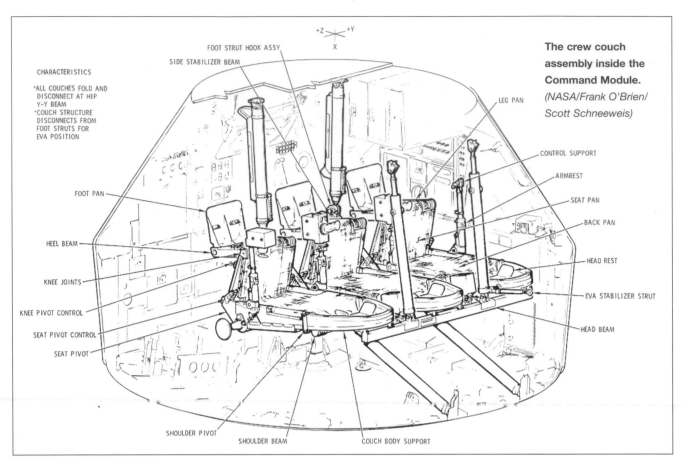

CHARACTERISTICS

*ALL COUCHES FOLD AND
DISCONNECT AT HIP
Y-Y BEAM
*COUCH STRUCTURE
DISCONNECTS FROM
FOOT STRUTS FOR
EVA POSITION

FOOT STRUT HOOK ASSY
SIDE STABILIZER BEAM

+Z — +Y
X

LEG PAN

CONTROL SUPPORT
ARMREST
SEAT PAN
BACK PAN
HEAD REST
EVA STABILIZER STRUT
HEAD BEAM

FOOT PAN
HEEL BEAM
KNEE JOINTS
KNEE PIVOT CONTROL
SEAT PIVOT CONTROL
SEAT PIVOT

SHOULDER PIVOT
SHOULDER BEAM
COUCH BODY SUPPORT

**The crew couch
assembly inside the
Command Module.**
*(NASA/Frank O'Brien/
Scott Schneeweis)*

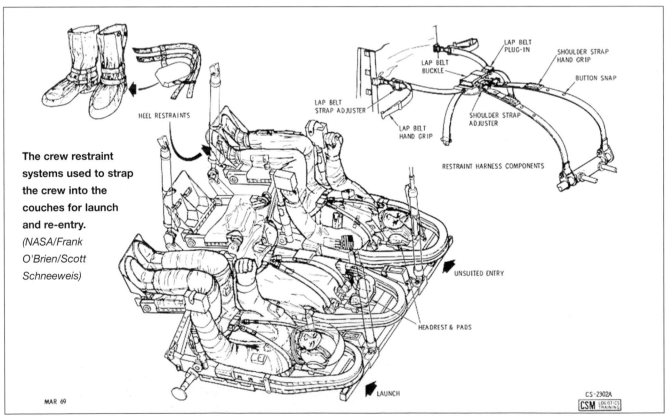

HEEL RESTRAINTS

**The crew restraint
systems used to strap
the crew into the
couches for launch
and re-entry.**
*(NASA/Frank
O'Brien/Scott
Schneeweis)*

LAP BELT
PLUG-IN
LAP BELT
BUCKLE
SHOULDER STRAP
HAND GRIP
BUTTON SNAP

LAP BELT
STRAP ADJUSTER

LAP BELT
HAND GRIP

SHOULDER STRAP
ADJUSTER

RESTRAINT HARNESS COMPONENTS

UNSUITED ENTRY

HEADREST & PADS

LAUNCH

MAR 69

CS-2302A
CSM LOGISTICS TRAINING

Launch Escape Tower (LET)

With a human crew on board an escape system became an important consideration during launch on top of the Saturn V. And in the absence of individual ejector seats, as the Gemini capsules had carried, a relatively safer system for ejecting the entire Apollo capsule from the rocket was developed. To achieve this a truss structure topped by a slender tower was added to the apex of the Command Module. This tower housed a powerful solid rocket motor capable of lifting 66 tonnes of weight. The system could be triggered by an abort handle on the mission commander's side, or automatically by the onboard computer. But it would be a rough ride. The harsh 7g acceleration of the rocket motor would need to last for eight seconds to pull them a safe distance away from the rocket before the re-entry parachute system deployed to bring them back to Earth. The system was designed to protect the crew from 5 minutes before launch through to 3½ minutes into the flight, the most dangerous part of the ascent.

After this time, following ignition of the second stage, at 295,000 feet when parachutes were no longer of use above most of the atmosphere, another smaller 31,500-lb thrust rocket motor in the top of the tower would jettison the truss and the shroud, exposing the docking mechanism in the top of the spacecraft.

Heat shield

At the opposite end to the LET was a blunt surface, designed with one overriding consideration: to survive the fiery heat of re-entry as the CM slammed back into the atmosphere. The Apollo spacecraft would be travelling faster at re-entry than any craft before it, generating enough heat energy to vaporise the entire spacecraft several times over. To prevent this, a special kind of shield was used which slowly charred and burnt away taking the heat with it in a process called ablation. It was built in three sections: an upper wrap-around cone shape called the apex cover which would be jettisoned at 24,000 feet to uncover the parachutes, a larger conical section around the main part of the spacecraft called the forward

heat shield and a more substantial 'aft heat shield', up to 2.5 inches thick.

The physics and engineering of re-entry had been pioneered in the 1950s when the study of nuclear warhead delivery from intercontinental ballistic missiles travelling out of the atmosphere became important. After initially attempting a solution which tried to absorb the heat, using beryllium and copper, Cold War research turned to ablative materials which would burn away in a controlled manner taking the heat with them.

Atmospheric heating and re-entry

Frictional heating was not just a problem during re-entry. During the acceleration after launch through the thicker, lower atmosphere, the apex of the Command Module would also be exposed to aerodynamic heating and needed protection by an additional cork and fibreglass shroud attached to the launch escape tower.

The far more intense re-entry heating is often mistakenly thought to be something to do with friction with the passing air. In fact the extra heating during re-entry is more comparable to the heat that builds up in a valve on a bicycle pump as air is compressed into a tyre. When any gas is compressed the amount of energy it holds in a given volume rises. When the air in front of a blunt hypersonic craft cannot move aside fast enough it becomes compressed and so heats up for the same reason.

During re-entry the speeds, and therefore the compression, are so great that the temperatures can quickly rise into the thousands of degrees, approaching the same sort of temperature as on the surface of the Sun (5,500°C). The advantage that a blunt shape has in this process over a more streamlined form is that by creating this compressed layer of air ahead of it, the main part of the craft is separated from the hottest and most damaging heat.

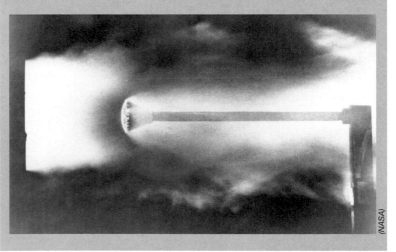

(NASA)

**Launch, escape
and Earth-landing
systems for the Apollo
Command Module.**
(NASA)

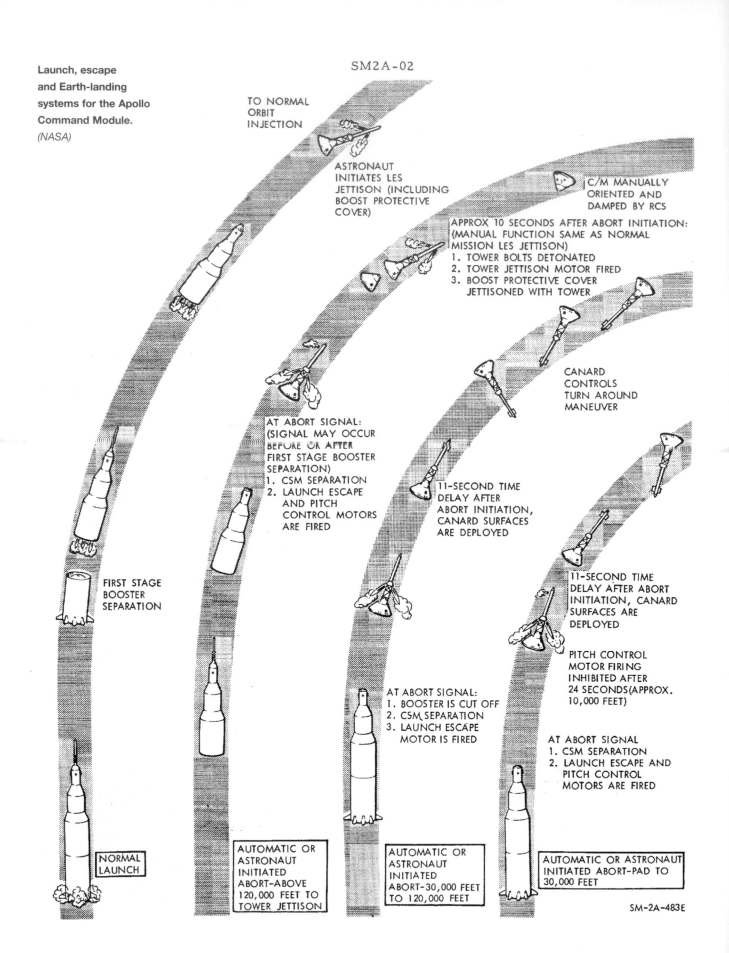

TO NORMAL
ORBIT
INJECTION

ASTRONAUT
INITIATES LES
JETTISON (INCLUDING
BOOST PROTECTIVE
COVER)

C/M MANUALLY
ORIENTED AND
DAMPED BY RCS

APPROX 10 SECONDS AFTER ABORT INITIATION:
(MANUAL FUNCTION SAME AS NORMAL
MISSION LES JETTISON)
1. TOWER BOLTS DETONATED
2. TOWER JETTISON MOTOR FIRED
3. BOOST PROTECTIVE COVER
   JETTISONED WITH TOWER

CANARD
CONTROLS
TURN AROUND
MANEUVER

AT ABORT SIGNAL:
(SIGNAL MAY OCCUR
BEFORE OR AFTER
FIRST STAGE BOOSTER
SEPARATION)
1. CSM SEPARATION
2. LAUNCH ESCAPE
   AND PITCH
   CONTROL MOTORS
   ARE FIRED

11-SECOND TIME
DELAY AFTER
ABORT INITIATION,
CANARD SURFACES
ARE DEPLOYED

11-SECOND TIME
DELAY AFTER ABORT
INITIATION, CANARD
SURFACES ARE
DEPLOYED

FIRST STAGE
BOOSTER
SEPARATION

PITCH CONTROL
MOTOR FIRING
INHIBITED AFTER
24 SECONDS (APPROX.
10,000 FEET)

AT ABORT SIGNAL:
1. BOOSTER IS CUT OFF
2. CSM SEPARATION
3. LAUNCH ESCAPE
   MOTOR IS FIRED

AT ABORT SIGNAL
1. CSM SEPARATION
2. LAUNCH ESCAPE AND
   PITCH CONTROL
   MOTORS ARE FIRED

NORMAL
LAUNCH

AUTOMATIC OR
ASTRONAUT
INITIATED
ABORT-ABOVE
120,000 FEET TO
TOWER JETTISON

AUTOMATIC OR
ASTRONAUT
INITIATED
ABORT-30,000 FEET
TO 120,000 FEET

AUTOMATIC OR ASTRONAUT
INITIATED ABORT-PAD TO
30,000 FEET

SM-2A-483E

FROM NORMAL ENTRY OR
ABORT ABOVE 120,000 FEET

AT APPROXIMATELY
24,000 FEET:
1. TOWER BOLTS DETONATED
2. TOWER JETTISON MOTOR FIRED
3. BOOST PROTECTIVE COVER
   JETTISONED WITH TOWER
4. APEX COVER JETTISONED 0.4 SECONDS
   AFTER BOOST PROTECTIVE COVER

AT APPROXIMATELY 24,000 FEET
PLUS 0.4 SECONDS
APEX COVER JETTISONED

DROGUE CHUTES DEPLOY
(REEFED) 1.6 SECONDS
AFTER APEX COVER
JETTISONED

DROGUE CHUTES FULLY OPENED
AFTER BEING REEFED FOR 8 SECONDS

APEX COVER
JETTISONED 0.4
SECONDS AFTER
LES TOWER
JETTISON

DROGUE CHUTES DEPLOYED
(REEFED) 2 SECONDS AFTER
LES TOWER JETTISON

DROGUE CHUTES
RELEASED AND
PILOT CHUTE
MORTARS FIRED
TWELVE SECONDS
AFTER DROGUE
CHUTE
DEPLOYMENT
OR AT
APPROXIMATELY
10,000 FEET

3-SECOND TIME DELAY AFTER
CANARD DEPLOYMENT:
1. TOWER BOLTS DETONATED
2. TOWER JETTISON MOTOR
   FIRED
3. BOOST PROTECTIVE COVER
   JETTISONED WITH TOWER

MAIN CHUTES EXTRACTED
& DEPLOYED TO A REEFED
CONDITION

MAIN CHUTES FULLY
OPENED AFTER BEING
REEFED FOR 8 SECONDS

NOTE: SATURN V BOOSTER
        SHOWN IN DIAGRAM.

MAIN CHUTES RELEASED
AFTER TOUCHDOWN

SM-2A-473F

The Avco Corporation from Massachusetts manufactured the shield for the Apollo Command Module. Its outer ablative surface was made from a fibreglass honeycomb filled with a phenolic epoxy resin. For complete protection it was crucial that no air bubbles got trapped in the resin, so it was applied carefully by hand into each of the more than 300,000 individual honeycomb cells. Quality controllers scrutinised each packet of resin and any imperfections were painstakingly drilled out and refilled. Beneath this fibreglass resin layer was another honeycomb of brazed stainless steel which had been shown to work well on the Mercury re-entry flights.

Guidance and navigation system

The Apollo Guidance Navigation and Control System (GNCS) had three main sub-systems; the Apollo Guidance Computer (AGC), the Inertial Measurement Unit (IMU) and the optical system, consisting of the sextant and the telescope. These were stationed at the foot of the middle couch to provide easy access for their principal user, the Command Module Pilot. Two computer interfaces, known as DSKYs, were fitted in the main display console and the lower instrument bay, close to the sextant. See Chapter 3 for more information.

Earth landing system

Without wings, or rudders, the blunt conical shape of the Command Module looks incapable of any sort of steerable flight through the Earth's atmosphere, and yet that is exactly what it could do. Unlike the first generation of US and Soviet spacecraft which flew pre-determined ballistic trajectories with no ability to steer towards a landing site, the Gemini, Apollo and Soyuz spacecraft pioneered controlled flight without wings, perfecting it to the point where they could make pinpoint landings.

This level of control was achieved in the Apollo CM by carefully designing the capsule so that, fully loaded, its centre of gravity was slightly off the mid-line towards the crew's feet, causing the capsule to hang in the air during free fall at a slightly cocked angle. This tilt gave the craft a slight aerodynamic lift, in effect turning it into a crude wing. By rolling the capsule to the left or right, using small reaction control system (RCS) rocket thrusters mounted around the craft, this lifting force could be pointed in different directions to steer the Command Module left or right and up or down. Such control could even be used to accomplish small adjustments to the craft's speed by forcing it deeper into the thicker

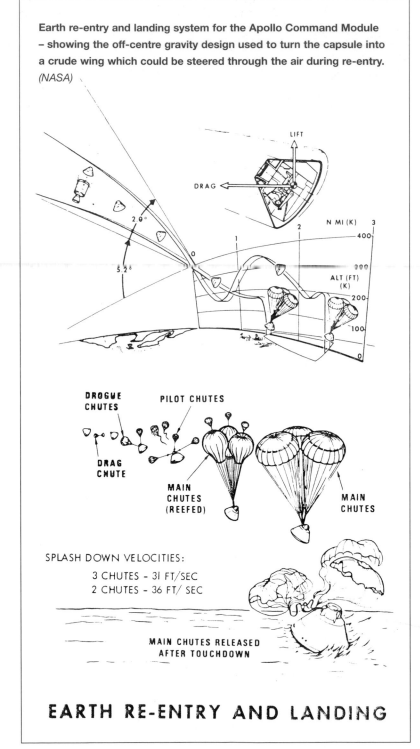

Earth re-entry and landing system for the Apollo Command Module – showing the off-centre gravity design used to turn the capsule into a crude wing which could be steered through the air during re-entry. (NASA)

atmosphere to slow down more quickly.

These motors, mounted flush with the capsule's outer surface and clustered into two groups of four nozzles on opposite sides of the craft, could also be used to perform small pitch and yaw moves to dampen any oscillations. This phase of the flight could be handled by the Command Module Pilot, although the primary method was intended to be through the autopilot.

Parachutes

Ask any re-entry systems engineer what the most crucial factor in returning to Earth is and they will answer that there are three things 'parachutes, parachutes, parachutes'. The sight of those international orange and white 'canopies of reassurance' as Apollo 11 CMP Michael Collins called them, warmed the hearts of everyone involved in a mission, not least the astronauts themselves.

NASA had been developing parachutes for returning spacecraft since the days of its Mercury flights, but the heavier Apollo craft would be the ultimate test of this relatively new application of canopy technology. The Army had been air-dropping trucks and heavy equipment using clusters of parachutes since World War II. It had achieved the reliability needed by bundling so many chutes together

that even if half of them failed there was still enough margin for the rest of the chutes to land the kit safely. But this sort of approach, where extra weight was not an issue, was never going to be applicable to the mass-obsessed Apollo programme. The Command Module's more minimal chute specification would have to work perfectly first time, without such safety margins.

Testing of the early designs began in a giant vertical wind tunnel. Once the shape

ABOVE High-angle view of Spacecraft 012 Command Module, during preparation for installation of the crew compartment heat shield. *(NAA/NASA)*

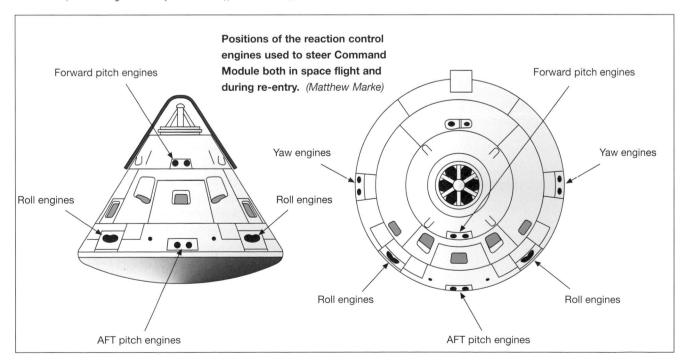

Positions of the reaction control engines used to steer Command Module both in space flight and during re-entry. *(Matthew Marke)*

Forward pitch engines

Roll engines

Yaw engines

Roll engines

AFT pitch engines

Forward pitch engines

Yaw engines

Roll engines

Roll engines

AFT pitch engines

and size were confirmed a programme of full-size capsule drop tests from the backs of open aircraft were performed. Over a six-year period the North American Aviation parachute engineers performed 137 drops.

A returning Apollo capsule would deploy its first two 16.5-foot-diameter drogue chutes by pyrotechnic charge whilst still 25,000 feet up and travelling at 320mph. Then, at 10,000 feet and still travelling at over 160 mph, the drogues would be discarded and the three main chutes would be released by another series of pyrotechnic mortars. For a safe landing, at least two of these giant canopies would need to survive these unprecedented speeds without

shredding in order to slow the capsule to less than 20mph for splashdown.

Each of the three main chutes was made of half an acre of lightweight nylon rip-stop fabric. It took two million stitches to put them together and attach the mile and a half of suspension lines needed to anchor them to the Command Module. The women who constructed them in NAA's Downey factory needed to pack them under hydraulic presses to get them to fit around the outside of the docking tunnel at the top of the capsule. By the time they were fitted they had been squeezed to the density of maple wood!

Splashdown or crunch down?

Landing in water at speed is like hitting concrete. And even with a sophisticated and reliable clutch of parachutes fully unfurled to slow you down it remains a potentially dangerous way of making a landing. To study these potential dangers NAA conducted extensive drop tests into a giant pool, constructed at the back of its factory at Downey, California.

NAA engineers would pour out of their offices to come and watch these brief, but satisfying tests. They were heavily instrumented and filmed from every angle to analyse the capsule's performance. During one splashdown test the spacecraft landed with its typically spectacular bow wave surge. But then, to the horror of the CM team and others from NAA and NASA watching, it began to list over as it filled with water and quickly sank.

The spacecraft's belly flop had cracked the heat shield's outer skin, allowing water to flood in. The thought of losing an entire crew in front of the world's press in this way after a successful Moon mission was too awful to comprehend. It was a dark day for the engineers responsible who now had to strengthen the CM's outer skin without adding significant weight.

Even with a stronger hull, no one was entirely happy with a water landing during Apollo. The ocean with its waves and storms was an unpredictable place to return to. Modifications of the splashdown were considered – slicing into the water like a diver rather than belly flopping – and inflatable bags were eventually

BELOW The Apollo 15 Command Module 'Kitty Hawk', with Astronauts David R. Scott, Alfred M. Worden and James B. Irwin aboard, nears a safe touchdown in the mid-Pacific Ocean to end their lunar landing mission. Although causing no harm to the crewmen, one of the three main parachutes failed to function properly. The splashdown occurred at 3:45:53pm on 7th August 1971, some 330 miles north of Honolulu, Hawaii. *(NASA)*

added to the capsule's collar to right the craft should it tip over in the swell. Such careful plans paid off and no one was ever lost or injured at sea during an Apollo splashdown, even when one of the three parachutes failed during Apollo 15's return to Earth.

Early on in the Command Module's development there had also been a concern that during a launch abort on the Saturn V the capsule might end up making an emergency landing on dry land; which was not something it was designed to do safely. A programme of drop tests from the back of a crane driving down a test track showed just how problematic a hard landing would be. In test after test the prototype capsules tumbled end over end, their docking towers and heat shields wrecked by the fall. By 1964, NAA studies had demonstrated that these problems of a hard landing were very nearly insurmountable.

Impacting the ground without the use of retro rockets was almost certainly going to injure the crew and so a small extra rocket motor was included in the launch escape tower to force an escaping CM to head out east into the Atlantic Ocean in case of a stationary or near-stationary activation from on or near the pad.

Service Module

Attached by a fairing to the bottom of the Command Module's heat shield for the entire journey to the Moon and back, right up to re-entry, was the Service Module (SM). It was 12 feet 10 inches in diameter and 24 feet 7 inches high and made of 1-inch thick walls of aluminium alloy honeycomb panels. The SM was divided up inside into six longitudinal compartments. Four of them carried the 16

ABOVE AND BELOW LEFT The Command Module's 'first flight' during moving drop tests from a mobile crane – to test the stability of the capsule during a hard landing with horizontal velocity. *(NASA/ Footagevault)*

RIGHT The supply 'trailer' or Service Module – designed to provide oxygen, water, electrical power and propulsion for the Command Module. (NASA)

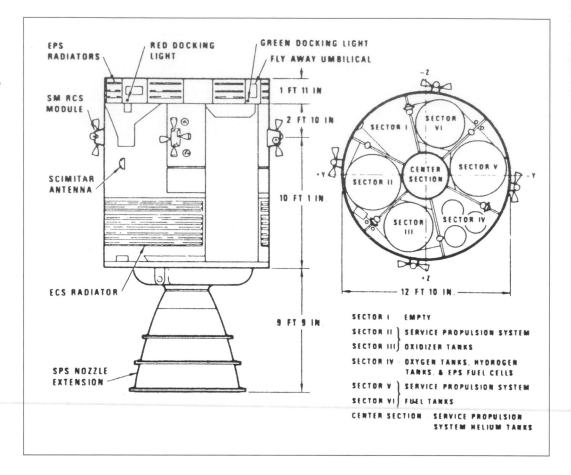

EPS RADIATORS
RED DOCKING LIGHT
GREEN DOCKING LIGHT
FLY AWAY UMBILICAL
SM RCS MODULE
SCIMITAR ANTENNA
ECS RADIATOR
SPS NOZZLE EXTENSION
1 FT 11 IN
2 FT 10 IN
10 FT 1 IN
9 FT 9 IN

-Z
SECTOR I
SECTOR VI
+Y
SECTOR II
CENTER SECTION
SECTOR V
-Y
SECTOR III
SECTOR IV
+Z
12 FT 10 IN.

SECTOR I   EMPTY
SECTOR II } SERVICE PROPULSION SYSTEM
SECTOR III } OXIDIZER TANKS
SECTOR IV OXYGEN TANKS, HYDROGEN TANKS, & EPS FUEL CELLS
SECTOR V } SERVICE PROPULSION SYSTEM
SECTOR VI } FUEL TANKS
CENTER SECTION SERVICE PROPULSION SYSTEM HELIUM TANKS

BELOW Service Module configurations for Block I and Block II Service Module. (NASA/Frank O'Brien)

tons of propellant needed for the Service Propulsion System (SPS) engine. The fifth housed the fuel cells and their reactants needed for electrical power and the plumbing for the life-support systems, water management, air and temperature regulation equipment. The sixth was left empty until later flights, when it was used to carry the SIM (Scientific Instrument Module) a bay of equipment for lunar observations.

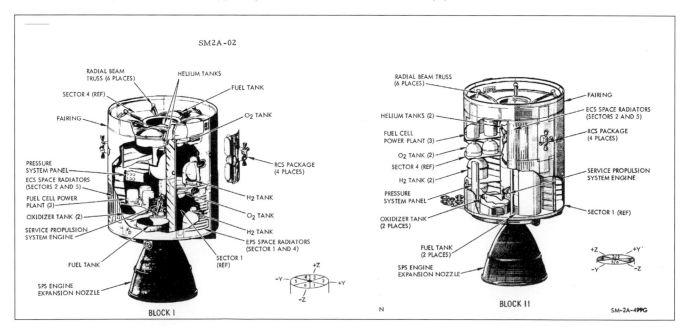

SM2A-02

RADIAL BEAM TRUSS (6 PLACES)
HELIUM TANKS
SECTOR 4 (REF)
FUEL TANK
FAIRING
O2 TANK
PRESSURE SYSTEM PANEL
ECS SPACE RADIATORS (SECTORS 2 AND 5)
FUEL CELL POWER PLANT (3)
RCS PACKAGE (4 PLACES)
OXIDIZER TANK (2)
SERVICE PROPULSION SYSTEM ENGINE
H2 TANK
O2 TANK
FUEL TANK
H2 TANK
EPS SPACE RADIATORS (SECTOR 1 AND 4)
SECTOR 1 (REF)
SPS ENGINE EXPANSION NOZZLE
BLOCK I

RADIAL BEAM TRUSS (6 PLACES)
FAIRING
HELIUM TANKS (2)
ECS SPACE RADIATORS (SECTORS 2 AND 5)
FUEL CELL POWER PLANT (3)
RCS PACKAGE (4 PLACES)
O2 TANK (2)
SECTOR 4 (REF)
H2 TANK (2)
SERVICE PROPULSION SYSTEM ENGINE
PRESSURE SYSTEM PANEL
OXIDIZER TANK (2 PLACES)
SECTOR 1 (REF)
FUEL TANK (2 PLACES)
SPS ENGINE EXPANSION NOZZLE
BLOCK II
SM-2A-499G

Oxidizer tank

Helium isolation
valves

Regulators

Test
port

Oxidizer
servicing
port

Relief
valve

Check valve

Helium
tank

Engine

Propellant
isolation valves

Fuel servicing
port

Quad

Fuel
tank

Quad D
+Y/-Y

Quad B
+Y/-Y

Quad C
+P/-P

Quad A
+P/-P

The Service Module also carried most of the deep space communications and all the smaller thrust engines for attitude control. Fully laden it weighed 51 tons. During the mission its services would be connected to the Command Module by an umbilical arm which would be severed by a guillotine prior to re-entry. Three explosive charges would then release stainless steel tension ties which held the two modules together.

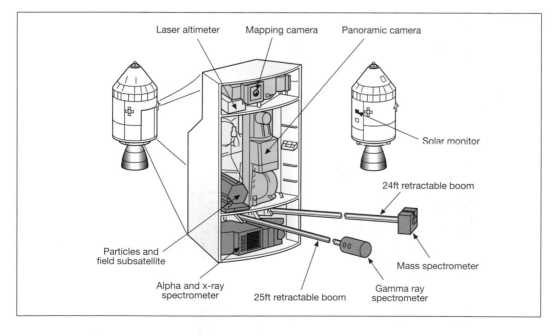

Laser altimeter

Mapping camera

Panoramic camera

Solar monitor

24ft retractable boom

Mass spectrometer

Particles and
field subsatellite

Alpha and x-ray
spectrometer

25ft retractable boom

Gamma ray
spectrometer

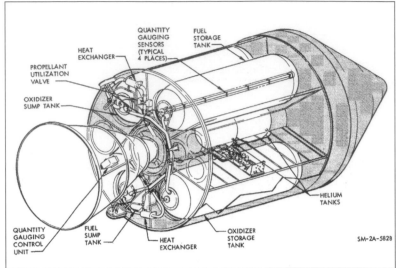

SM-2A-5828

ABOVE LEFT Apollo 15 CSM 'Endeavor' orbits above the moon with SIM Bay visible. *(NASA)*

ABOVE Details of the Service Propulsion System (SPS) engine and fuel tanks. *(NASA/ Frank O'Brien)*

LEFT SPS quantity gauging and propellant utilisation systems – showing where the data from these systems is displayed inside the crew cabin on the main console. *NASA/ Frank O'Brien)*

OPPOSITE Details of the SPS plumbing – showing the gauging systems and helium pressurisation design. *(NASA/Frank O'Brien)*

Service Propulsion System (SPS)

The far end of the Service Module was dominated by a large engine bell, which would be used for all the major manoeuvres after trans-lunar injection (TLI) and jettison of the S-IVB third stage. Most critically this would include slowing down the spacecraft to place it into lunar orbit and later, after the mission's exploration of the lunar surface, setting it back on a course for Earth.

Without the luxury of a backup system the SPS had to work first time for these mission-critical moments. Simplicity was the key to its reliability and so hypergolic fuels (dimethyl hydrazine propellant with a nitrogen tetroxide oxidiser) which would explode on contact with

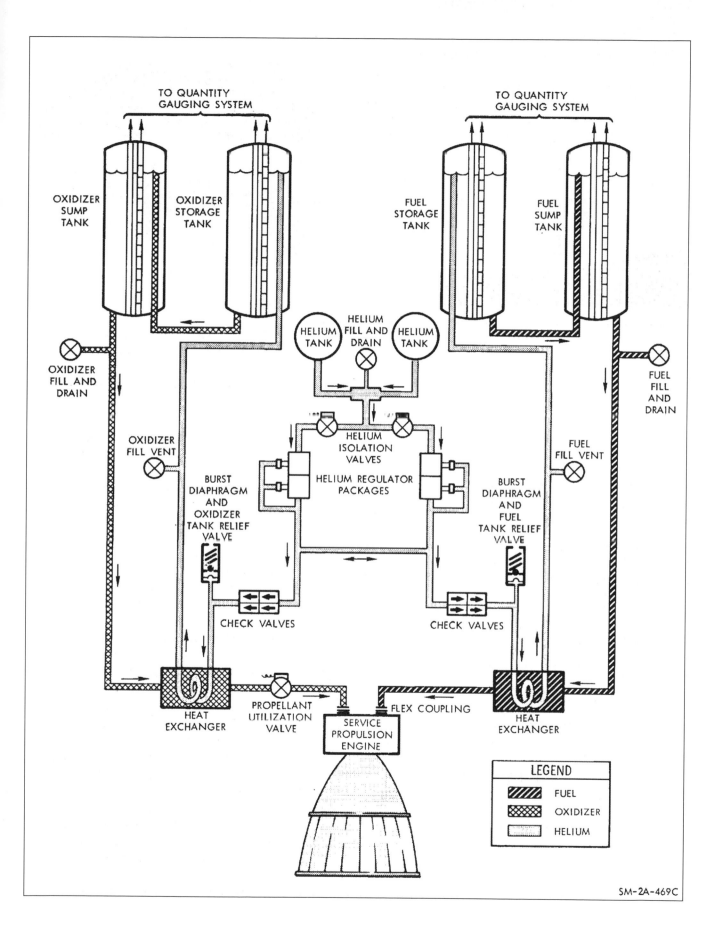

TO QUANTITY
GAUGING SYSTEM

TO QUANTITY
GAUGING SYSTEM

OXIDIZER
SUMP
TANK

OXIDIZER
STORAGE
TANK

FUEL
STORAGE
TANK

FUEL
SUMP
TANK

HELIUM
TANK

HELIUM
FILL AND
DRAIN

HELIUM
TANK

OXIDIZER
FILL AND
DRAIN

FUEL
FILL
AND
DRAIN

OXIDIZER
FILL VENT

HELIUM
ISOLATION
VALVES

FUEL
FILL VENT

BURST
DIAPHRAGM
AND
OXIDIZER
TANK RELIEF
VALVE

HELIUM REGULATOR
PACKAGES

BURST
DIAPHRAGM
AND
FUEL
TANK RELIEF
VALVE

CHECK VALVES

CHECK VALVES

HEAT
EXCHANGER

PROPELLANT
UTILIZATION
VALVE

FLEX COUPLING

HEAT
EXCHANGER

SERVICE
PROPULSION
ENGINE

LEGEND

▨	FUEL
▨	OXIDIZER
☐	HELIUM

SM-2A-469C

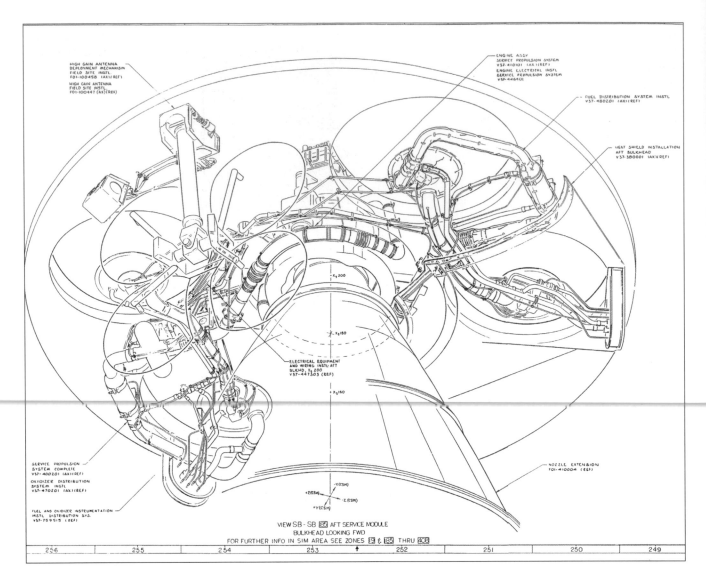

Labels on the engineering drawing:

HIGH GAIN ANTENNA
DEPLOYMENT MECHANISM
FIELD SITE INSTL
FOI-100458 (AXII REF)
HIGH GAIN ANTENNA
FIELD SITE INSTL
FOI-100447 (AXII REF)

ENGINE ASSY
SERVICE PROPULSION SYSTEM
VS7-410101 (AXII REF)
ENGINE ELECTRICAL INSTL
SERVICE PROPULSION SYSTEM
VS7-446401

FUEL DISTRIBUTION SYSTEM INSTL
VS7-480201 (AXII REF)

HEAT SHIELD INSTALLATION
AFT BULKHEAD
VS7-380001 (AXII REF)

ELECTRICAL EQUIPMENT
AND WIRING INSTL, AFT
BLKHD, X₄ 200
VS7-447303 (REF)

SERVICE PROPULSION
SYSTEM COMPLETE
VS7-400201 (AXII REF)
OXIDIZER DISTRIBUTION
SYSTEM INSTL
VS7-470201 (AXII REF)

FUEL AND OXIDIZER INSTRUMENTATION
INSTL DISTRIBUTION SYS.
VS7-759515 (REF)

NOZZLE EXTENSION
FOI-410004 (REF)

VIEW SB - SB AFT SERVICE MODULE
BULKHEAD LOOKING FWD
FOR FURTHER INFO IN SIM AREA SEE ZONES 13 & 188 THRU 408

| 256 | 255 | 254 | 253 | 252 | 251 | 250 | 249 |

ABOVE Engineering drawing (by hand) showing details of the Service Propulsion System from the aft of the Service Module.
(NASA/Frank O'Brien)

each other were used to eliminate the need for an ignition system. The need for mechanical pumps was eliminated by pressurising the tanks with inert helium gas. Even the moving parts of the 'on' switch were replaced with a single valve opened by a small explosive device.

The constant-thrust SPS engine was manufactured by a company called Aerojet General and, like the J-2 engine in the Saturn S-IVB stage, it was also restartable. With 20,500 pounds of thrust, originally defined by the power needed to lift a CSM off the Moon, this rocket motor was larger and more powerful than many upper stages of other launch vehicles. Like all the other Saturn engines the SPS engine could also be gimballed to help steer the spacecraft and make mid-course corrections en route to the Moon. It was

controlled by the Command Module's Guidance and Navigation System.

Electrical power

A reliable supply of power was crucial to maintain all the life-support systems of the Command Module. Most robotic missions to the inner solar system rely on solar power – generated from panels – but the size of the solar panels needed for the power requirements of an Apollo spacecraft would have made them unwieldy, particularly during the engine-burn accelerations when mechanical stresses could have damaged them.

Batteries were also an option, as they had been during the Mercury and Gemini missions, but they were heavy and unreliable in a space environment and unable to supply power for missions of up to two weeks. So for the primary power source the engineers decided on fuel cells. They had been tested on Gemini flights and were considered suitable for Apollo.

Developed and manufactured by the Pratt and Whitney Aircraft Division, the Apollo fuel cells produced plenty of electricity (over 1 kilowatt per cell) and, as a useful by-product, drinking water. Fifty to sixty gallons could be made during a single mission and passed forward through the umbilical connection to the Command Module's environmental system to be used for cooling electrical systems and as drinking and washing water for the crew and to rehydrate their food.

As an extra power source during busy parts of the mission, and for the brief period when the Service Module was jettisoned, before re-entry, the Command Module carried a set of five silver oxide–zinc batteries.

Life-support systems

A scuba diver commonly uses a tank of air in 60 minutes. In Apollo an equivalent amount of oxygen was made to last for 15 hours. Oxygen was not simply inhaled once and then discarded. The exhaled gas was 'scrubbed' with lithium hydroxide canisters to eliminate its CO_2, before being pumped back into the cabin to be re-breathed.

The same life-support system also maintained the cabin at the right pressure, removed moisture and odours, provided hot and cold water and a circulating coolant to keep all the electronic gear and the atmosphere at the proper temperature in the weightless environment of space. All this was achieved by an Environmental Control System (ECS) manufactured by Hamilton Standard, which was not much bigger than a domestic air conditioner, located on the left side of the equipment bay, below the left couch.

One of the main weight savings when it came to maintaining this breathable, shirt-sleeve atmosphere was achieved by using a single gas – oxygen. On Earth only about a fifth of the atmospheric pressure of 14.7 pounds

LEFT Apollo fuel cell. *(Ken Thomas/Hamilton Standard)*

per square inch is oxygen. A pure oxygen atmosphere required to keep the crew healthy inside the spacecraft therefore only needed to be around 5psi. This was found to provide the same concentration of oxygen in the blood as at sea level. This lower-pressure cabin environment in turn required a much lighter, thinner hull wall to contain it against the vacuum of space.

However, one consequence of this decision was that on the pad before launch, at sea level, the spacecraft atmosphere would need to be pumped up to at least 14.7psi to balance the outside atmospheric pressure. It was a decision which everyone at NASA would live to regret when, in January 1967, in this high-pressure oxygen environment, the Apollo 1 crew were asphyxiated when a ferocious fire took hold as they sat inside the spacecraft while they were rehearsing for the first manned Apollo flight.

Apollo 1 Fire

Apollo 1 was slated to be the first manned flight of a so called 'Block 1' prototype Apollo CSM in Earth orbit and was originally scheduled for the end of 1966, but delays at North American Aviation had pushed the launch back to February 1967. Three weeks before their flight, on 27th January 1967, Mercury astronaut veteran Gus Grissom and his crew of rookie astronaut Roger Chaffee and America's first space walker Ed White were in their seats on the launch pad, on top of a Saturn rocket, conducting what a 'Count Down Demonstration Test' to verify all the spacecraft and rocket procedures up to ignition. As a test of the hull, to look for leaks in the Command Module, the pure oxygen inside the spacecraft had been pumped up to 16psi.

At 18.30 a glitch in the capsule's electrical systems was detected by launch control. It probably caused a spark down by the astronaut's feet and in the pure oxygen environment it quickly started a fire. Under these conditions everything inside the cabin was highly flammable. Even aluminium burns in high-pressure pure oxygen. Within seconds the temperatures and pressures had risen so high inside the capsule that the inward-opening hatch could not be opened. The crew died of asphyxiation due to smoke inhalation whilst still trapped inside their spacecraft.

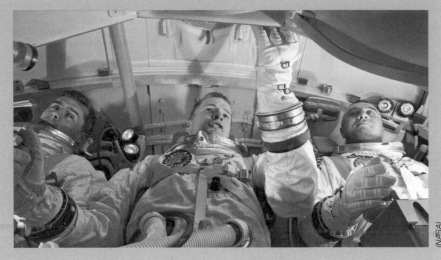
(NASA)

Changes after the fire

The inquiry which followed the Apollo 1 disaster was unable to pinpoint the exact cause of the fire, but it did identify deficiencies in the spacecraft's design and North American's workmanship and quality control. Spacecraft design changes focused on removing flammable material, re-routing wire bundles and using better insulation on the wires so that they would not burn. Most important of all was the encasement of all wiring and tubing in metal trays to prevent future damage if they were stepped on by crew or ground crew. Debris nets and hook and eye fastening fabric were significantly reduced, but despite their best efforts the engineers could not make the entire Command Module cabin fireproof in a launch-pad atmosphere of 16psi oxygen. A different approach was needed.

The legendary engineer Max Faget came up with the winning idea: launch with an atmosphere that was 60 per cent oxygen and 40 per cent nitrogen, and then slowly bleed out the nitrogen during ascent, to convert the cabin to a pure oxygen environment by the time orbit had been reached, when the oxygen pressure would be down to 5psi. To prevent the crew from getting the bends during this relatively rapid decompression they would pre-breath pure oxygen from the time they suited up three or more hours before launch, to flush dissolved nitrogen out of their blood. It was a delicate balance between medical requirements on the one hand, avoiding the bends, and flammability problems on the other.

Temperature regulation

When fully powered-up the electrical equipment in a Command Module could quickly raise the temperature on board and the challenge for the engineers became keeping the inside of the spacecraft cool. The electrical heat could be channelled away through heat sinks and into pipes containing water and glycol which carried it into two large radiators embedded in the Service Module's skin, from where it was radiated out into space. Should the heat be needed to keep the inside of the spacecraft warm at some points in the mission, for example when the spacecraft entered the shadow of the Moon, then this heat-shedding process was automatically slowed down.

To supplement the radiator system, a second process kicked in to feed the water/glycol

mixture through a series of metal plates, chilled by evaporating water directly into the vacuum of space. This evaporator, or 'the boiler' as the crew called it, worked by the controlled exposure of liquid water to space through a porous stainless steel plate peppered with ultra-fine holes. As the water boiled away quickly into the vacuum it took the excess heat from the spacecraft with it.

The outside of a spacecraft facing the Sun will grow hot as it absorbs energy, radiating some back into space until it reaches an equilibrium at around 200°C. The other side of the spacecraft facing deep space and out of the Sun's light will simply radiate any heat it has out to dark space and will chill down to −150°C. Such temperature differences caused problems of their own. The heat shield, if exposed to prolonged cold, was known to develop cracks and the RCS engines could freeze up or become over pressurised if left in the sunlight. A reflective Mylar covering on the outer skin was one way to tackle these problems, but on a three-day journey heat outside could still accumulate and cause problems.

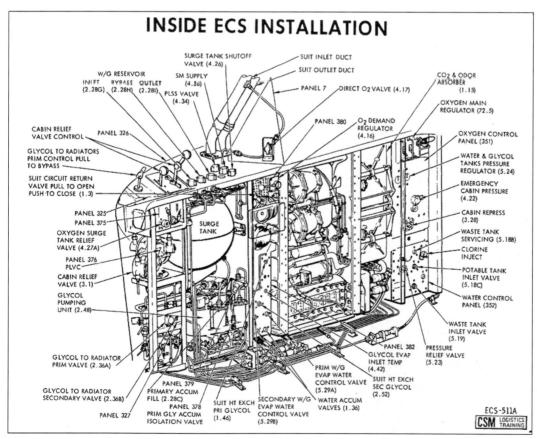

RIGHT Configuration of equipment inside the CM's Environmental Control System. *(NASA/Scott Schneeweis)*

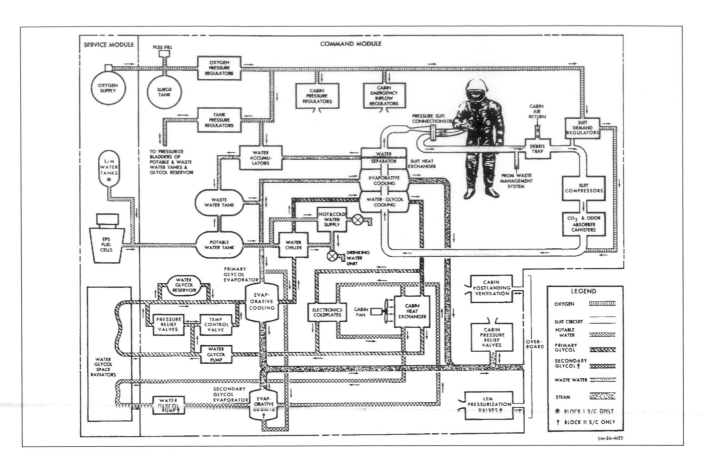

SERVICE MODULE | COMMAND MODULE

ABOVE Flow diagram showing the temperature regulation plumbing for the Command Module, including its connection to the pressure suits for removing body heat during launch and re-entry. *(NASA/Scott Schneeweis)*

A solution was eventually found, without adding a single ounce in weight. The idea was called Passive Thermal Control (PTC) and it involved programming the attitude-control system to rotate the spacecraft very slowly (about once every 20 minutes) in what the astronauts referred to as 'barbecue mode'. This simple 'rotisserie' solution prevented any single part of the spacecraft from being exposed to prolonged heating or cooling from the Sun and the shade.

Food

Early space missions had been plagued by bland dehydrated, unappetising food pastes served from a tube, but by the time the Apollo crews were flying things had improve markedly. The Apollo 11 crew, for example, had more than 70 food items from which to plan daily menus before the flight. Some were dehydrated, but others were wet-packed or spoon-and-bowl food products. Alan Bean, the Apollo 12 LMP famously ate spaghetti for lunch every day on Earth and for his flight to the

Moon he had requested that spaghetti also be included so he could become the first person to eat it on the Moon!

Food rehydrating water, like the drinking water, came from the Service Module's fuel cell by-product water. It was dispensed from three places inside the Command Module – a trigger operated drinking water dispenser and two more water spigots located at the food preparation station: one to dispense hot (68.3°C) and the other cold (12°C) water in 1-ounce units.

After water was squirted into the food bags through a hole, the contents were kneaded for about three minutes. The neck of the bag or a corner was then cut off and the meal could be squeezed directly into the astronaut's mouth. After a meal germicide pills attached to the outside of the bags were placed inside to prevent fermentation, and the bags were rolled up and stowed in the waste-disposal compartments.

As well as the rehydration items, Apollo main meals often resembled an in-flight meal of today, with a peel-back lid. They were stored in a freezer, and heated up using a small electrical food warmer.

APOLLO XI (ARMSTRONG)

MEAL	DAY 1*, 5	DAY 2	DAY 3	DAY 4
A	Peaches Bacon Squares (8) Strawberry Cubes (4) Grape Drink Orange Drink	Fruit Cocktail Sausage Patties** Cinn. Tstd. Bread Cubes (4) Cocoa Grapefruit Drink	Peaches Bacon Squares (8) Apricot Cereal Cubes (4) Grape Drink Orange Drink	Canadian Bacon and Applesauce Sugar Coated Corn Flakes Peanut Cubes (4) Cocoa Orange-Grapefruit Drink
B	Beef and Potatoes*** Butterscotch Pudding Brownies (4) Grape Punch	Frankfurters*** Applesauce Chocolate Pudding Orange-Grapefruit Drink	Cream of Chicken Soup Turkey and Gravy*** Cheese Cracker Cubes (6) Chocolate Cubes (6) Pineapple-Grapefruit Drink	Shrimp Cocktail Ham and Potatoes*** Fruit Cocktail Date Fruitcake (4) Grapefruit Drink
C	Salmon Salad Chicken and Rice** Sugar Cookie Cubes (6) Cocoa Pineapple-Grapefruit Drink	Spaghetti with Meat Sauce** Pork and Scalloped Potatoes** Pineapple Fruitcake (4) Grape Punch	Tuna Salad Chicken Stew** Butterscotch Pudding Cocoa Grapefruit Drink	Beef Stew** Coconut Cubes (4) Banana Pudding Grape Punch

*Day 1 consists of Meal B and C only
**Spoon-Bowl Package
***Wet-Pack Food

Toilet stops

Just as it was in the 1960s, the question still most commonly asked of astronauts is 'How do you go to the bathroom in space?' Back then the answer might at one time have been 'You don't!'

Despite the range of food items available for Apollo astronauts, much of their diet was designed to minimise the production of solid human waste. The spacecraft engineers had initially felt optimistic that the entire 10-day voyage to the Moon and back could be carried out without a single bowel movement! Human test subjects who tried these early low-waste diets became so constipated that, after a 14-day trial, their first bowel movement reportedly felt like delivering a baby!

There was no avoiding the fact that waste management on Apollo was going to be as essential as water, air or food. On the long-duration Gemini flights astronauts had collected and stored their solid waste in faecal bags. They were made with a peel-away circular cover which exposed adhesive to attach to an astronaut's buttocks He then defecated straight into the bag whilst his colleague politely looked the other way. After he had cleaned up he added a sachet before sealing the bag. The final unpleasant task was to knead the bag until the sachet inside split and spread through the contents. The bags were sealed in another bag in the hope that, if the spacecraft was depressurised, the bag would not burst. Smells were not as easy to capture, but to help with the overall spacecraft environment; the faecal bags were stored in a container on the right-hand side of the cabin, from where odours could be vented out into space.

Compared to solid-waste management urination was relatively easy. If an astronaut was wearing a pressure suit the urine would be collected in a bag worn under the suit. A valve allowed the bag to be drained from outside without removing the suit. If, as was more normal, he was just wearing a mission tunic, he would pass water by rolling a condom over his penis to pass the urine down a tube and into a bag. The contents of the bag could be simultaneously dumped

ABOVE A four-day menu sample for Apollo 11 Commander Neil Armstrong. Note that on day 5 the menu cycles back round again to the items scheduled for day 1. *(NASA)*

OVERLEAF Human waste disposal systems on board the Apollo Command Module. *(NASA/Scott Schneeweis)*

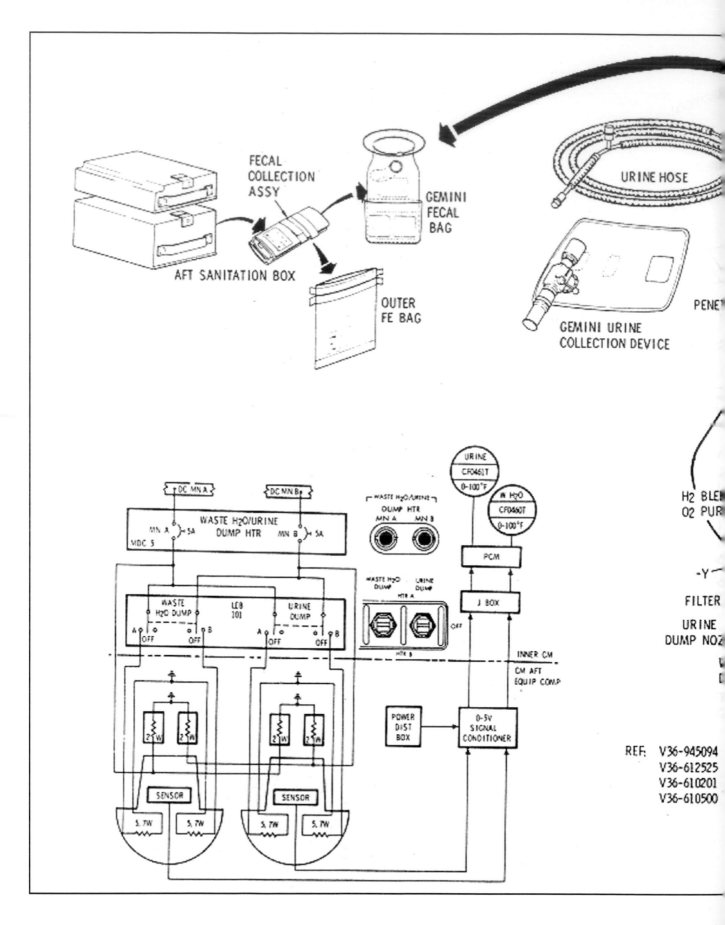

FECAL COLLECTION ASSY

GEMINI FECAL BAG

AFT SANITATION BOX

OUTER FE BAG

URINE HOSE

GEMINI URINE COLLECTION DEVICE

PENET

H2 BLE
O2 PUR

-Y

FILTER

URINE
DUMP NOZ

URINE
CF0461T
0-100°F

IN H2O
CF0460T
0-100°F

DC MN A   DC MN B

WASTE H2O/URINE
DUMP HTR

MN A ─ 5A   MN B ─ 5A

VDC 5

WASTE H2O/URINE
DUMP HTR
MN A   MN B

WASTE
H2O DUMP

LEB
101

URINE
DUMP

A   B   A   B

OFF   OFF   OFF   OFF

WASTE H2O
DUMP   URINE
DUMP

HTR A

OFF

HTR B

PCM

J BOX

INNER CM

CM AFT
EQUIP COMP

21 W   21 W   21 W   21 W

SENSOR   SENSOR

5.7W   5.7W   5.7W   5.7W

POWER
DIST
BOX

0-5V
SIGNAL
CONDITIONER

REF: V36-945094
      V36-612525
      V36-610201
      V36-610500

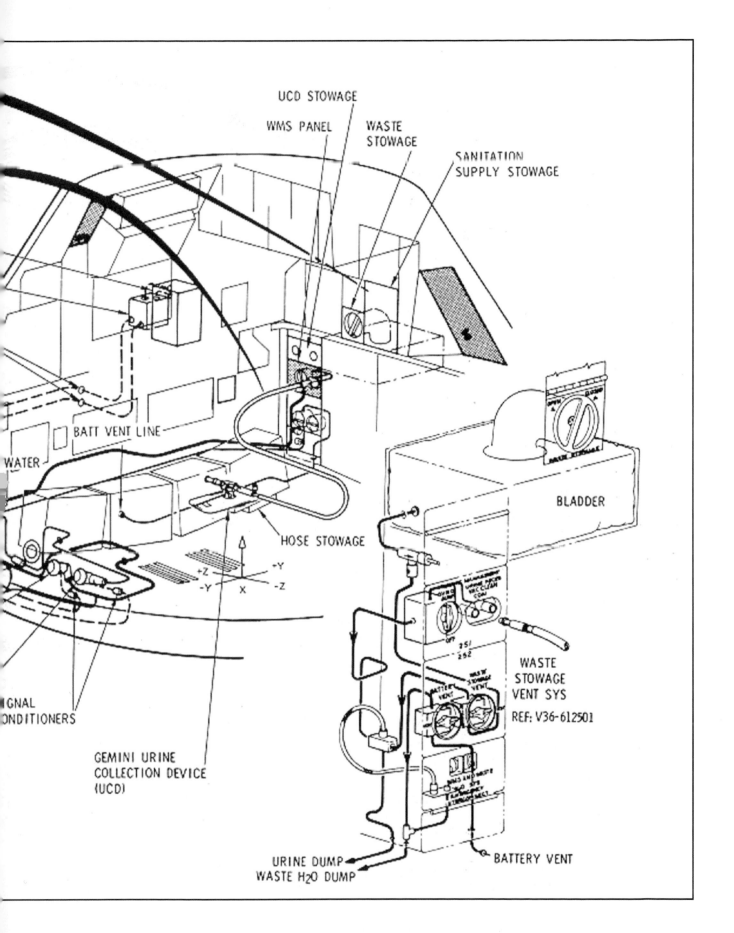

UCD STOWAGE

WMS PANEL

WASTE STOWAGE

SANITATION SUPPLY STOWAGE

BATT VENT LINE

WATER

HOSE STOWAGE

+Z
-Y +Y
X -Z

BLADDER

WASTE STOWAGE VENT SYS

REF: V36-612501

IGNAL ONDITIONERS

GEMINI URINE COLLECTION DEVICE (UCD)

URINE DUMP
WASTE H₂O DUMP

BATTERY VENT

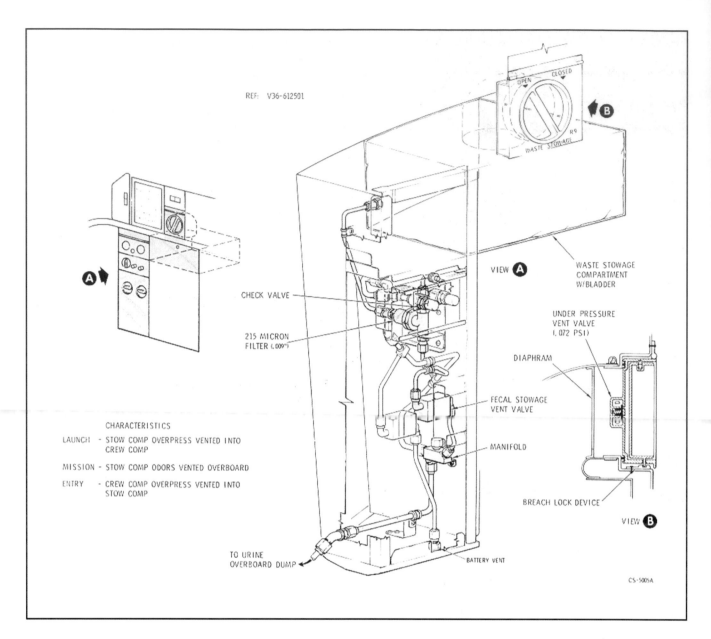

REF: V36-612501

OPEN CLOSED
R9
WASTE STOWAGE

VIEW **B**

WASTE STOWAGE
COMPARTMENT
W/BLADDER

VIEW **A**

CHECK VALVE

215 MICRON
FILTER (.009")

UNDER PRESSURE
VENT VALVE
(.072 PSI)

DIAPHRAM

FECAL STOWAGE
VENT VALVE

MANIFOLD

BREACH LOCK DEVICE

VIEW **B**

CHARACTERISTICS

LAUNCH - STOW COMP OVERPRESS VENTED INTO
CREW COMP

MISSION - STOW COMP ODORS VENTED OVERBOARD

ENTRY - CREW COMP OVERPRESS VENTED INTO
STOW COMP

TO URINE
OVERBOARD DUMP

BATTERY VENT

CS-5005A

ABOVE Controls and plumbing for the urine management system onboard the Command Module. *(NASA/Scott Schneeweis)*

directly into space through a valve, to the right of the lower equipment bay, which prevented direct exposure to the vacuum. As the liquid sprayed out into space it would often freeze into a cloud of sparkling ice crystals which Apollo 7 Commander Wally Schirra dubbed the 'Constellation Urion'.

Personal hygiene

Washing and personal hygiene was performed with the warm water from the food preparation area, and a wet towel or cleansing cloth rub. The cloths contained a germicide and were typically used after meals or

a toilet visit. On Apollo 17 Harrison Schmitt even managed to wash his hair by adding water to one of these towels. Curiously an unexpected benefit of the 100 per cent oxygen atmosphere was that oral hygiene was never as much of an issue as it can be on Earth, but crews carried both toothpaste and toothbrushes just in case they needed them. A special digestible chewing gum was also an option to keep their mouths feeling fresh.

Shaving was not just a matter of hygiene, as stubble also had an impact on communications. The microphones inside astronauts' helmets could catch on whiskers, making conversations sound scratchy, so crews on early Apollo

missions were encouraged to shave. The Apollo 10 crew wet-shaved with cream and a razor, which they preferred to the mechanical razors which had a tendency to scatter the dry whisker clippings out into the cabin. Subsequent missions tried variations of the wet and dry shaves. But not all astronauts chose to shave. Michael Collins returned from Apollo 11 with a moustache and the crew of Apollo 15 went ten days without shaving. Harrison Schmitt also returned from the Moon with a good growth of beard on Apollo 17.

To the Moon

By October 1968, less than two years after the disastrous Apollo 1 fire, the most magnificent flying machine yet devised had risen from the ashes. It was ready for its maiden manned voyage into space. Operating like a miniature planet for the 11-day Apollo 7 flight, it would pave the way for Apollo 8, two months later, when CM-103 would transport the first humans in history to another world. Over the next four years eight more Apollo Command Modules would fly a total of 24 Americans to the Moon and safely back to Earth. They are the only pieces of Moon shot hardware to have reached lunar orbit and returned to Earth and rest today in museums around the world as an ultimate monument to mankind's greatest adventure.

FAR LEFT The crew shave during various Apollo missions – from top to bottom; John Young (Apollo 10), Tom Stafford (Apollo 10), John Young (Apollo 10), Mike Collins (Apollo 11), Alan Shepard (Apollo 14). *(NASA/Footagevault)*

LEFT Crewmen aboard the *USS Iwo Jima*, prime recovery ship for the Apollo 13 mission, hoist the Command Module aboard ship. The Apollo 13 crewmen were already aboard the *Iwo Jima* when this photograph was taken. *(NASA)*

(NASA/Alan Lawrie)

(NASA)

Fuel cells and Apollo 13

The principle of the fuel cell was invented in the 19th century, but was not developed seriously until after World War II. They work like batteries using chemical reactions to generate electricity. But, unlike a battery, as long as the reactants are constantly replenished the cell will make electrical power. The chemical reaction which generates the electricity involves two hydrogen atoms combining with one oxygen atom making water and releasing two electrons which create the electrical potential.

Storing the oxygen and hydrogen needed to power them inside a spacecraft required new advances in leak-proof insulated containers. The engineers got so good at it that if a car tyre leaked at the same rate as these tanks, it would take 30 million years to go flat! Under zero gravity the oxygen in these tanks will tend to settle into layers of different densities, making it hard to assess how full the tanks actually are. So a small fan inside each tank was employed to stir up the contents and homogenise it before the volume of its contents was measured.

At 02:08 UT on 14th April 1970, with Apollo 13 over 200,000 miles from home, Mission Control requested that the Command Module Pilot, Jack Swigert, stir the tanks in the Service Module. This routine request would lead to the most famous space event in history.

As Swigert stirred the oxygen in tank number 2, it caused further damage to an already damaged heating element in the tank and ignited wiring insulation. Fed by the liquid oxygen, a fire quickly took hold, raising the pressure and rupturing the tank with such force that it blew one side of the Service Module right off and damaged the only remaining oxygen tank (number 1). With no power, air or propulsion left in the CSM one of the greatest stories of human survival began. The engineering ingenuity which eventually triumphed against the odds to bring the crew safely back to Earth became known as NASA's finest hour and was vividly portrayed in Ron Howard's 1995 film *Apollo 13*.

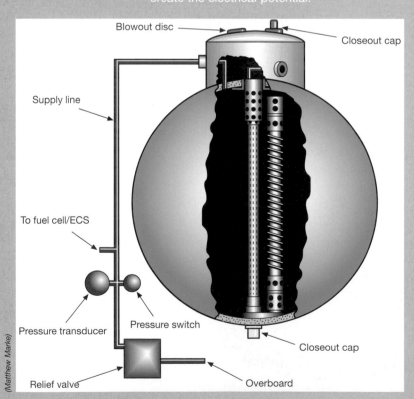

(Matthew Marke)

Blowout disc

Closeout cap

Supply line

To fuel cell/ECS

Pressure transducer

Pressure switch

Relief valve

Overboard

Closeout cap

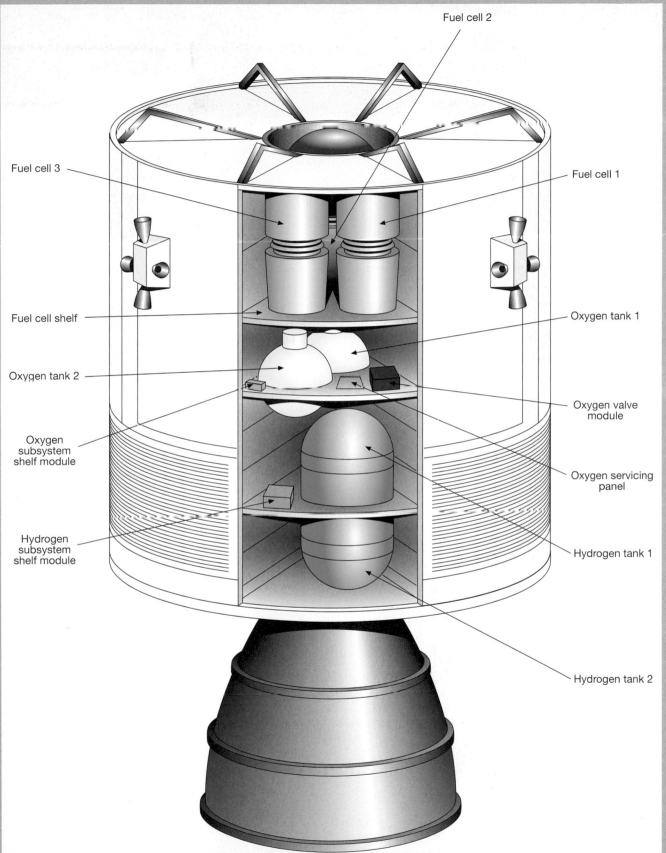

Fuel cell 2

Fuel cell 3

Fuel cell 1

Fuel cell shelf

Oxygen tank 1

Oxygen tank 2

Oxygen valve module

Oxygen subsystem shelf module

Oxygen servicing panel

Hydrogen subsystem shelf module

Hydrogen tank 1

Hydrogen tank 2

(Matthew Marke)

Chapter 3

The guidance, navigation and control system

It is July 1969 and two small computers designed and programmed at the MIT labs in Massachusetts and manufactured by Raytheon are in orbit around the Moon. They barely have enough memory to store the sort of tiny thumbnail jpeg image we email freely today and yet they are managing the entire landing of the Apollo Lunar Module.

Slowly the spacecraft moves away from the mother ship which has carried it from Earth and at just the right moment a pre-determined combination of electrical signals sent by the computer ignites the descent engine. The electronic equipment is alive, focused on one single objective: landing on the Moon. Without warning, inside the cabin the computer display suddenly flashes up an error message. Those in mission control hear the tension in Neil Armstrong's voice. "Program alarm … its a 1202 … Give us a reading on the 1202 Program Alarm!"

In Cambridge, Massachusetts, a group of engineers, also listening to the voice loop, jump out of their skins. They are the men and women from MIT's Instrumentation Lab and they are only too aware that in the next few moments the success or failure of the entire Apollo programme will be decided by the performance of the machine they have spent the last eight years designing and programming.

The lynchpin of Apollo

If there was one part of Apollo that was more important, more complex, and more demanding than any other it was the Primary Navigation and Guidance System (PNGS – pronounced 'pings'). The

LEFT Interior view of the Apollo 11 Lunar Module 'Eagle' showing astronaut Buzz Aldrin, the Lunar Module Pilot, during the lunar landing mission. This picture was taken by astronaut Neil Armstrong, Commander. *(NASA)*

95

entire challenge of landing on the Moon would hang upon this system's performance. With pin-point accuracy it had to guide the spacecraft across 250,000 miles of empty space, achieve a precise orbit around the Moon, land on its surface within a few yards of a pre-designated spot, guide the Lunar Module from the surface to a rendezvous in lunar orbit, fly the Command Module back across the quarter-million-mile void to hit the Earth's atmosphere within a carefully defined 'window' and finally land it as close as possible to a recovery ship in the middle of the Pacific Ocean. And all this when computers were still in their infancy and more likely to occupy a room the size of a tennis court than be the size needed to fit inside a spacecraft.

Tough as all this sounded, back in 1961 when Kennedy's challenge was laid down, guidance and navigation was something that America excelled at. And this technological lead over the Russians was, in large part, down to the work of a man called Charles Stark Draper.

Draper's interest in guidance and navigation went back to the 1930s when he had cut his aeronautical engineering teeth working on instrumentation for early aeroplanes. By the 1950s, and now based at the Massachusetts Institute of Technology in Cambridge, Draper was working on a new concept called inertial guidance. In 1955 his new gyroscopically stabilised inertial-guidance system had successfully navigated an aircraft from Bedford, Massachusetts, near Boston on the east coast, to Los Angeles on the west coast of the United States, without external intervention. It landed within 2,500 feet of the target point which was not bad for a flight of almost 3,000 miles. The next day Draper stood up at a conference on inertial guidance in LA to declare that he had achieved it!

Draper's team at MIT's Instrumentation Lab would go on to create the guidance systems for the Polaris missile and by the late 1950s they were also looking beyond the Earth, studying how they would guide a spacecraft carrying a camera the 100 million miles to Mars to take photographs and then return them to Earth.

To make this mind-boggling journey they came up with an onboard light sensor which could measure the angle between stars and planets to keep track of its position and velocity. Controlling it was a revolutionary 4 kilobyte micro-computer which fitted into a box half a foot square and weighed just 20 pounds. Its data and programmes were woven into its solid state hardware, and the novel device could even slow down its performance to save power when it was not busy. Although this was then just a feasibility study, ten years later many of these concepts would feature in the guidance system which would help to fly men to the Moon.

In recognition of the importance that NASA placed on guidance and navigation, and how impressed it was by Draper's track record in this area, the very first Apollo contract went to MIT's Instrumentation Lab.

A new integrated guidance system

Apollo's guidance system would be based on the inertial-guidance devices Draper had developed for the Polaris missile. Cold War paranoia meant that such an autonomous onboard guidance system was thought essential to prevent the Russians from interfering with the mission. The other main element needed to keep track of where they were was a sighting system for the astronauts to check their position manually by charting star positions, just as the Mars probe had been designed to do.

During 1962, as the technical nature of the system became clearer, the need for some sort of small computer also emerged, to help the crew keep track of their progress and make navigation calculations. Arguments about the details of the computer raged for a while between NASA, North American (builders of the Command Module), Grumman (builders of the Lunar Module) and MIT. But, in January 1964, NASA declared that the two guidance computers for the CM and the LM would be identical.

During the early 1960s rapid technological advances in a number of fields allowed NASA to start tracking spacecraft from Earth with great precision. Measurements of the Doppler shifts of signals bounced off a spacecraft could pinpoint its position to within 33ft and its velocity to within 1½ft per second. Such accuracy meant that navigation could be reliably conducted from the ground. This progress, and a rethink by NASA about the reality of Soviet interference with a peaceful Apollo mission, effectively meant MIT's navigation system could be relegated to a secondary role for most of the flight.

The onboard navigation system would of course still be important when the spacecraft was out of contact from Earth on the far side of the Moon, and it would be used throughout the flight as a complimentary data source to check against the ground-tracking system. Initially, this change of priorities came as a disappointment to the MIT team and its goal of autonomous operation.

But then, in the summer of 1964, things at MIT started to a get a whole lot more interesting again. Honeywell had been commissioned to

build an analogue flight-control computer for Apollo to manage the main engines and the reaction control system – but this design meant duplicating certain guidance equipment. NASA decided it was more sensible to merge the two computers and do the job digitally with the MIT computer taking on the task of controlling the entire flight of the spacecraft as a complete digital autopilot system.

This new decision suddenly increased the whole scope of MIT's role in the programme. Overnight the lab's machine suddenly became much more than a navigation and guidance device to get them from the Earth to the Moon and back. It would now be a complete

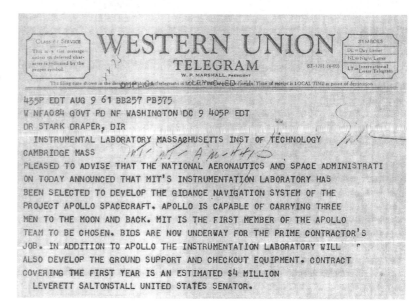

ABOVE The first Apollo contract awarded goes to MIT's Instrumentation Lab to develop the guidance and navigation system – considered to be the single most important element needed to deliver Kennedy's goal. *(The Charles Stark Draper Laboratory, Inc)*

LEFT A cartoon created by MIT at the time to illustrate just how essential their guidance, navigation and control system was going to be to help the crew avoid being overworked. *(MIT Library)*

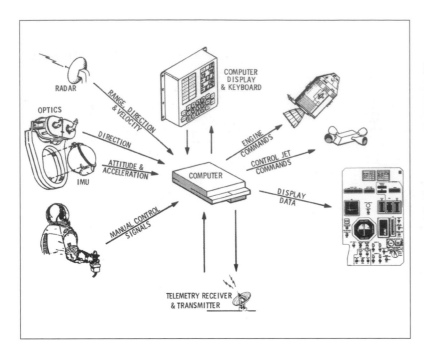

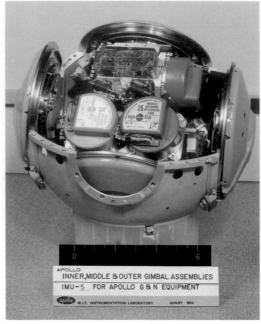

ABOVE Schematic view of the Guidance, Navigation and Control System. *(MIT Library)*

ABOVE RIGHT The Inertial Measuring Unit (IMU). *(The Charles Stark Draper Laboratory, Inc)*

BELOW Key elements of a three-plane IMU. *(The Charles Stark Draper Laboratory, Inc)*

digital fly-by-wire system – the first of its kind – controlling the attitude and trajectory of the Command Module by managing the Reaction Control System thrusters and the main Service Propulsion System engine. On the Lunar Module it would now also have to run the complex engines and the changing flight characteristics of this unique spacecraft from undocking, through descent, landing and lift-off to rendezvous.

Apollo's new Guidance, Navigation and Control (GN&C) system now consisted of three main components – the inertial measurement unit, the optical star-sighting device (or sextant/scan telescope) and a computer to integrate

it all together. There were just two years left before the first scheduled manned Apollo flights, but far from being daunted by the task at hand, most of the young men and women at the lab were just excited to be doing it.

Inertial Measurement Unit

A key part of each GN&C system was the mechanical sensor which could detect the inertial motion of the spacecraft. It was called the Inertial Measuring Unit (IMU) and was a direct descendant of the invention which a decade earlier had guided Draper's aircraft from coast to coast.

The Apollo IMU consisted of a set of three orthogonally arranged (at 90 degrees to each other) swivelling gimbals which carried spinning gyroscopes to hold them in position as the spacecraft's motion and orientation changed. The fixed reference that the platform remained locked to was termed 'inertial space' – which distinguished it from previous Earth-bound references which typically measured an aircraft's orientation relative to the ground surface beneath.

Inertial space was essentially pegged to the star positions which, like everything else on Apollo, went by an acronym – in this case REFSMMAT, standing for Reference to Stable

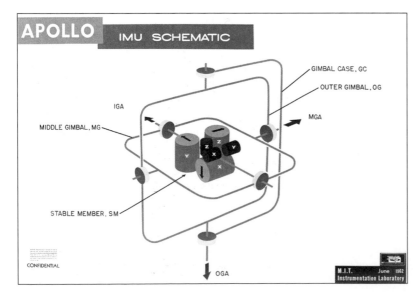

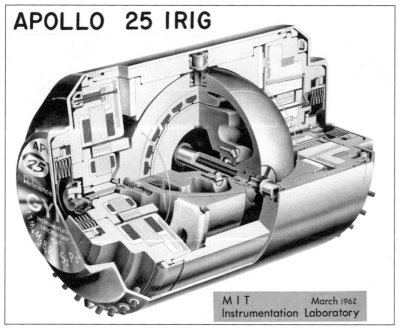

APOLLO 25 IRIG

MIT March 1962
Instrumentation Laboratory

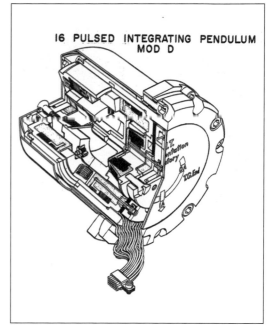

16 PULSED INTEGRATING PENDULUM
MOD D

Roll Axis

Outer gimbal

Middle gimbal
resolver

Case structure

Middle
gimbal

25 IRIG

16 PIPA

Yaw
Axis

Pitch Axis

Stable member
(inner gimbal)

25 IRIG
gyroscope

Outer gimbal
torque motor

16 PIPA
accelerometer

Middle gimbal
torque motor

APOLLO — INERTIAL
MEASURING UNIT, BLOCK II
CUTAWAY.
DSR 55-238 DWG 106646
GEO.T. BERNARD 7-26-66

ABOVE LEFT An Apollo 25 IRIG – the gyro component which held each arm of the IMU fixed in inertial space. *(The Charles Stark Draper Laboratory, Inc)*

ABOVE A Pulsed Integrating Pendulous Accelerometer (PIPA) – the component mounted on each arm which senses the motion of the spacecraft in each direction – needed to compute the mission's state vector. *(The Charles Stark Draper Laboratory, Inc)*

RIGHT Labelled diagram of an Apollo IMU. *(The Charles Stark Draper Laboratory, Inc)*

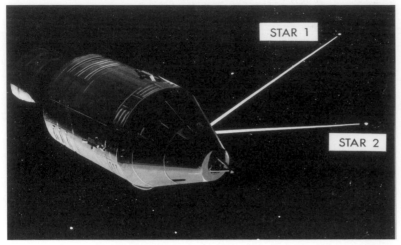

STAR 1

STAR 2

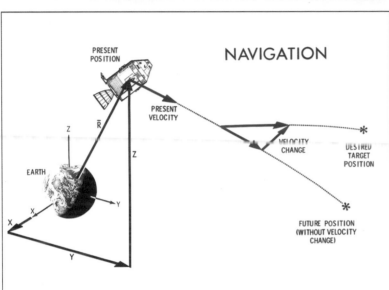

NAVIGATION

PRESENT POSITION

PRESENT VELOCITY

VELOCITY CHANGE

DESIRED TARGET POSITION

FUTURE POSITION (WITHOUT VELOCITY CHANGE)

EARTH

Z $\bar{R}$

Z

X   X   Y

Y

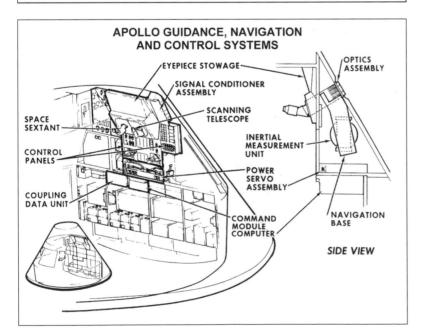

APOLLO GUIDANCE, NAVIGATION AND CONTROL SYSTEMS

EYEPIECE STOWAGE

SIGNAL CONDITIONER ASSEMBLY

SCANNING TELESCOPE

SPACE SEXTANT

CONTROL PANELS

COUPLING DATA UNIT

COMMAND MODULE COMPUTER

INERTIAL MEASUREMENT UNIT

POWER SERVO ASSEMBLY

OPTICS ASSEMBLY

NAVIGATION BASE

SIDE VIEW

Member Matrix. The platform would initially be aligned with the stars manually using a sextant and then periodically re-aligned (*see below*).

Sensors on each axis measured three angles which described the direction the spacecraft was orientated in with respect to the fixed stars. Accelerometers (known as Pulsed Integrating Pendulous Accelerometers – PIPA) mounted along each axis would sense the magnitude and direction of the craft's acceleration in each direction. Together these data provided an important piece of information called the 'state vector' which described both the vehicle's velocity and where it was in space relative to the fixed star positions at any time. Knowing where you are and where you want to get to as well as how fast and in what direction you are moving, would provide the basic information needed to calculate each engine burn and course correction.

Whilst the spacecraft's attitude could be expressed relative to inertial space, the astronauts were more comfortable with a more 'pilot-friendly' visualisation of their orientation and so an instrument called the Flight Director/ Attitude Indicator (FDAI) was developed. It looked like the artificial horizon indicator found in an aircraft cockpit and the crew called it their '8-ball'. For safety there were two 8-balls on the CM and LM instrument panel, displaying the current attitude as pitch, yaw and roll angles, and a representation of the Earth's or the Moon's horizon.

Gimbal lock

Red shading on the 8-ball represented orientations that the spacecraft should avoid to prevent any two of the IMU's three axes lining up in a single plane. If they became aligned it would reduce the capacity that the platforms had for full free movement, resulting in the gimbals becoming locked to the movement of the spacecraft rather than remaining independent from it. If the orientation of the spacecraft got too close to this gimbal lock danger zone, the IMU could be realigned to a new star reference to keep the platforms moving freely. Another IMU in the Saturn V's guidance system had a fourth gimbal axis to avoid the possibility of gimbal lock and the inertial system on the Gemini spacecraft also carried a fourth axis. But on Apollo the fourth gimbal had been shed to save weight and size and increase simplicity and hence reliability.

Gimbal lock was to be avoided, as it resulted in a loss of known orientation and onboard position data, and required time consuming realignment of the unit and a resetting of the entire guidance and navigation system. But avoiding it in flight would, in the end, use more fuel, increase software complexity and crew workload. The three-gimbal Apollo IMU was an extra burden the astronauts were never entirely comfortable with.

(Bruce Yabro Smithsonian Institution)

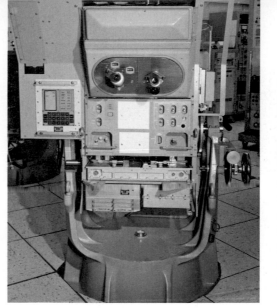

LEFT A ground-based mock-up of the Apollo GNCS in the MIT lab. The unit carries the sextant and wide-field telescope optics, the computer processor racks (gold) and the control panel and DSKY needed to link it all together. *(The Charles Stark Draper Laboratory, Inc)*

The sextant

Impressive as the precision of the IMU was, perfect friction-free ball-bearings for the gyroscopes were never going to be possible. Consequently the platform would drift slightly over time with respect to the stars, and periodically during a flight it would need to be realigned with the star positions to bring it back on course. The technology did exist to allow such star alignment to be done automatically – but for reasons of Apollo deadlines it was decided to let the astronauts perform the task manually using an onboard sextant to measure angles between key stars from which to triangulate their position.

Pointing a sextant out of an airtight spacecraft was never going to be straightforward. To maximise the accuracy of the optics MIT favoured a retractable submarine-periscope-style design with a heat-resistant cap to protect it during launch and re-entry. North American (builders of the Command Module) and the astronauts were concerned that should this mechanical retraction system fail it would compromise the heat shield. In the end NASA decided that a fixed heat-resistant window for the sextant to look out of would be safer than a breach in the heat shield, even if it compromised the optical quality of the instrument.

To hold the spacecraft steady during star sightings the digital autopilot would be called upon to maintain its orientation in a flight configuration called minimum 'deadband'. Computer Program 52 would then be selected

Celestial navigation and all balls

With practice an astronaut could achieve star-position accuracies to hundredths of a degree. The computer carried a look-up table in its memory, listing the angles between 37 bright stars, and after a second star had been manually aligned it would display the accuracy of the astronaut's work.

Despite problems of solar glare bleaching out stars and distracting reflections from the Earth and the Moon, astronauts would routinely make a perfect sighting – resulting in a '00000' error reading which they triumphantly referred to as 'all balls'. This level of accuracy was not only a tribute to the dedication of the astronauts but also the sextant's builders at Kollsman Instrument. Kollsman had a long history of designing and building aviation instruments, and had been making Sun- and star-tracking instruments for Air Force bombers since the 1950s.

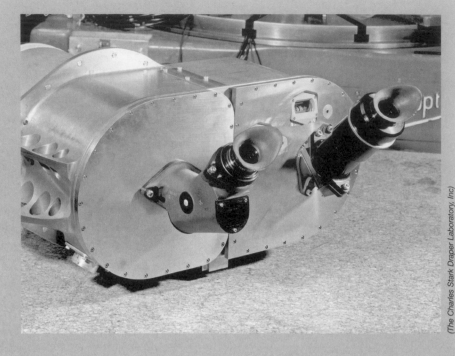

(The Charles Stark Draper Laboratory, Inc)

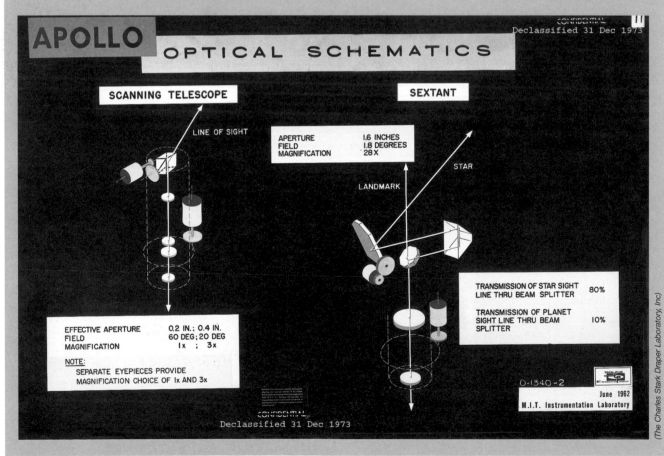

(The Charles Stark Draper Laboratory, Inc)

to do the actual realignment of the IMU. The Command Module pilot would then move the wide-angle scanning telescope towards a specific star and then line it up in the crosshairs of the main 28x magnification sextant. Pressing a button would then tell the computer the star's exact position compared to where the IMU had drifted to. These angles were displayed on the DSKY and recorded how much the platforms needed to be rotated to move back into correct alignment. Before an Apollo flight crews started training for this task in planetariums, and later on a simulator which had been mounted on the roof of the Instrumentation Lab at MIT, overlooking the Boston skyline.

The computer

Completing the Guidance and Navigation system, knitting all this together, was a finely tuned computing machine (the Apollo Guidance Computer – AGC) designed to interface between the crew and the other flight systems on each spacecraft. To simplify things, it was decided early on that the Command Module and the Lunar Module computers would have the same design, with different software running on them to achieve the different mission objectives.

Before the time of Apollo computers had traditionally been cumbersome, heavy devices which often filled entire rooms with racks of power-hungry valve-based electronics. By the start of the 1960s the MIT team had already had some success at miniaturising computers – using new integrated silicon circuit technology to replace cumbersome computer valves. But quite how small they could make the Apollo computer no one knew. So, when North American Aviation, the builders of the Command Module called at the start of the Apollo programme to ask how much space was needed for the computer, MIT was not sure.

To be on the safe side the computer designers asked for a cubic foot, thinking initially that this would be plenty. But a few years later, when NASA had asked for the computer to serve as an autopilot as well as a guidance and navigation system, the MIT team began to wish they had asked for double this space. Even with the

ABOVE Charles Draper sits inside his simulator, built on the roof of the MIT labs to help train astronauts in celestial navigation before a mission. *(Theodore Polumbaum/The Charles Stark Draper Laboratory, Inc)*

LEFT An artist's impression of how the simulator worked – providing the astronauts with experience of taking star readings from inside the CM as they would have to do *en route* to the Moon. *(The Charles Stark Draper Laboratory, Inc)*

potential for miniaturisation offered by integrated circuits, folding a powerful, reliable flight computer system into one cubic foot was going to require a lot of imagination and ingenuity.

Their first prototype computer called MOD3 – termed a breadboard design because it included on it room to expand and experiment – was a long way off fitting into one cubic foot. The logic circuits it was built from were all assembled using transistor switches and together they occupied a space the size of four refrigerators along one wall of a room in the Instrumentation Lab.

Transistors, developed at the Bell Labs in 1948 to switch and amplify electronic signals, had started to be used in military equipment in the 1950s and were soon being collected together and mounted on a single piece of semiconductor material making what was termed an integrated circuit (IC) or microchip. In 1962 MIT took large quantities of these novel ICs, manufactured by a company called Fairchild Semiconductor, to build a new version of its MOD3 computer. The new miniature version was working by 1963 and was christened the Apollo Guidance Computer (AGC). The new IC-based computer was twice as fast as a design which used individual transistors and half the size and weight. It also fitted into the allocated one cubic foot volume.

To force the manufacturers to learn how to perfect the manufacturing process NASA

purchased more than 1 million silicon chips between 1962 and 1967. Many were never used in building the Apollo computer systems, but this apparently extravagant policy was responsible for kick-starting the semiconductor industry and a technological revolution we are still living through today.

The software

The word 'software' was hardly known at the time and a software requirement barely featured in the original contract for the Apollo GN&C system. The original contract given to MIT had pointed out in a very low-key way that the lab would also write the programmes to run on the system. Inevitably, at the start of the job, the bulk of the lab's efforts were devoted to hardware and in the absence of any software decisions from NASA, little if any programming was done for the first five years. Any software development which was done at this time was on navigation and guidance to support orbital test flights. However, by 1967, as the immensity of the programming challenge became evident, software had become the lab's biggest task. It would take 350 man-years in 1968 alone to pull the design together!

Back in 1961 NASA was engrossed in running Mercury, Gemini and Apollo in parallel and had not paid a lot of attention to what MIT was doing in this area. For the first year the method of reaching the Moon was still undecided and nobody had a clear idea what the computer should be doing, so the software engineers were free to write almost anything they liked – and much of it was made up as they went along.

From the beginning software programmes had been written onto punch cards and carried over (without dropping them and losing their precise

BELOW MOD3 – MIT's first prototype 'breadboard' computer.
(The Charles Stark Draper Laboratory, Inc)

BELOW RIGHT The final Apollo GNCS computer fitted into a cubic foot. The DSKY keyboard interface is on the right.
(The Charles Stark Draper Laboratory, Inc)

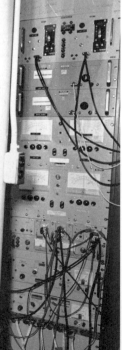

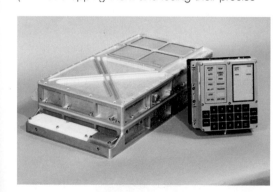

order) to a couple of large mainframe computers. The lab's IBM 360 and a Honeywell mainframe were programmed with the universal laws of physics, the mathematics of the Earth–Moon system, the dynamics of the spacecraft and even a simulation of an actual astronaut's behaviour. Endless 'electronic' Moon shots were simulated around the clock on these supercomputers of their day, to test each bit of new code. There were no screens to display results. Instead they were churned out of a continuous line printer in the corner of the room. Programmers would return to pick up their results after each simulation run. If the print-out was just a few pages long they knew it had probably worked, but if it was two feet thick, it was a sign that the code needed some more work!

The software was written into the AGC's scarce memory at a very basic binary 'assembly' or 'machine language' level, using about 40 instructions. A slightly higher-level language called 'Interpreter', which allowed the computer to interpret mathematical functions associated with guidance and control, was also used. A small, but surprisingly sophisticated operating system or master programme called the 'Executive' managed the programmes allocating time to each as it was called up. Several programmes would typically be running on the AGC at the same time, with the computer multi-tasking between them.

Both the Interpreter language and the Executive master programme had been devised by a young PhD mathematician called Hal Laning, a veteran of the ground-breaking Whirlwind computer and one of the inventors of the higher-level language which evolved into FORTRAN. Using erasable memory Laning's system could run seven programmes simultaneously – saving information from each to allow them to resume at a later time when their turn came round again. The genius of Laning's design came from a novel prioritising system which assigned a level of importance to each programme and then allowed interrupts by programmes of higher priority or importance.

So, for example, during landing, if the computer got too busy, then a task like managing the descent engine with a higher pre-assigned importance would be prioritised over a less vital task like updating the display

LEFT 'Software' engineer Margaret Hamilton with a pile of print-out results from simulations, circa 1969. *(MIT Library)*

screen in the LM's cabin. Hal's interruptible queuing system lay at the heart of the reliability of the AGC and ultimately kept the Lunar Module running during Apollo 11's first landing on the Moon, when it became over-loaded with programme requests during its descent.

Whilst early flight software was customised for individual unmanned missions, later programmes for each spacecraft became more generic and were named with Sun themes to go with Apollo the Sun God, like Eclipse, Sunrise, Sunburst, Corona and so on. The final Command Module programme was called Colossus and that for the Lunar Module Luminary.

BELOW Hal Laning – inventor of the interruptible executive design for the Apollo computer, which allowed it to prioritise jobs during the flight. *(The Charles Stark Draper Laboratory, Inc)*

Computer memory and information storage

Today, we are comfortable about expressing memory and disk space in terms of 'bytes', where each byte is made up of 8 bits. In contrast the unit of memory in the AGC was the 'word' (byte was never used), which was made up of 15 bits for memory storage and one extra bit for an error detection code called 'parity'.

When MIT began the work on the computer, it was thought that 4 kilobytes of read only memory (ROM) and 512 bytes (or 0.5 kilobytes) of erasable random access memory (RAM) would be adequate. But as the software grew the need for more ROM to store it doubled three times to 8, 16 and then 32KB. The final memory specifications of the AGC were 36,864 Bytes (36KB) of ROM and 2,048 Bytes (2KB) of erasable memory.

The computer's programmes were not stored on a hard disk in the modern style but in ROM which was fabricated by weaving a copper wire either through or around a tiny magnetic core. If a wire passed through a core it represented a '1' and around it was a '0'.

In this way the software was painstakingly woven together by a team of women weavers at a factory. The team at MIT called it the 'LOL method' standing for the Little Old Ladies who threaded the cores in the Raytheon Factory. Painstakingly, core by core, wire by wire, bit by

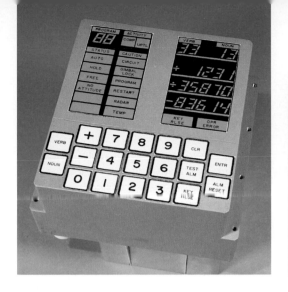

bit, the software programmes were woven into the hardware. The end result was tough and spaceflight environment-resistant, and could be wrapped carefully into a relatively tiny space on board the spacecraft.

The first 'breadboard' designs looked like tangled pieces of rope so the team dubbed them 'rope memory'. The flight-ready memory was packaged more neatly into a set of six small modules which would be mounted in the AGC. It took about six weeks to manufacture a rope, and so all programming had to be stopped six months prior to a mission, to allow time for manufacture and then testing before flight. Once the rope module had been produced alterations to the code were impossible.

The computer's 2KB RAM needed to write and read live mission data and was also fabricated from cores in this way, with the '1's and '0's written temporarily to each core by using a high enough current to flip the core's magnetic direction between clockwise and counter-clockwise, and read using a second lower-powered pulse of current to sense this magnetic field direction. To make the most of this very limited erasable memory different programmes running at different times used the same blocks of memory in a sort of 'time-share' way – overwriting each other as they ran.

Operating the computer

When describing the user interface for the AGC it is helpful to compare it to a modern computer system in a car rather than a personal desktop or laptop computer with a QWERTY keyboard. Like a car's trip computer whose menu settings are called up with a simple keypad and displayed on a flat LCD display the AGC also

had a simple digital display and keypad known as the DSKY (pronounced diss-key). By entering different two-figure-number commands various engine pre-settings and flight routines could be initiated, or different display modes called up. The computer actually did its calculations in binary numbers but it then converted the results it displayed on the DSKY into base 10 imperial units for the astronauts to appreciate better.

To control the computer, enter data and view results, three different types of number could be entered; Programs, Verbs and Nouns. A programme number (entered after Verb 37 to change the programme) would call up a piece of software which would do anything from managing the Lunar Module's engines during ascent or rendezvous (Program 12), to setting up its inertial platform with Program 52 (known as 'doing a P52'). Verb numbers would tell the computer to carry out a specific instruction and 'noun' numbers would specify the details of that instruction. So, for example, if the astronauts

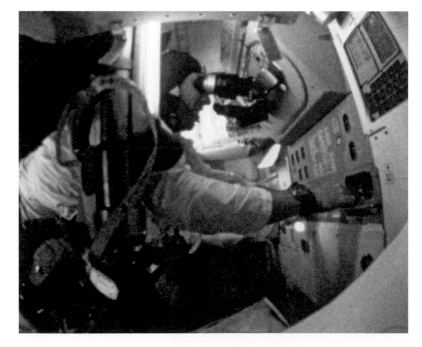

wanted to see how fast they were climbing during lift-off, then by first pressing 'Verb' and typing '06' (06 = Display Data) the crew could ask the computer to display a value, and then by pressing 'Noun' and entering the number '62' the computer would know they wanted to see values of their speed, their height and how fast the height was changing.

An identical DSKY display at Mission Control in Houston could also be used to control the computer remotely. Although the verb/noun system was powerful it was also a cumbersome way of issuing instructions – with anything from 30–130 key presses needed to align the Inertial Measurement Unit (IMU), and over 10,000 needed to fly to the Moon and back. But after some initial resistance, the astronauts appreciated its versatility, and some even grew fond of it.

In addition to the ten number keys and the Program, Verb and Noun keys, the DSKY also had a plus and a minus key, a CLR (clear), a PRO (proceed), a RSET (reset), a KEY REL and an ENTR (enter) key to allow the crew to interact further with the computer. (*For more information on operating the computer during flight please refer to the Lunar Module chapter.*)

A computer to take you to the Moon (Apollo 7 & 8)

Following a number of unmanned test flights of the GN&C system, Apollo 7 became the first manned Apollo mission to test it in space in October 1968. For almost 11 days the three astronauts orbited the Earth, using the sextant successfully to realign the inertial guidance system and the computer to home in on the spent upper stage of the Saturn. The computer eventually brought them home – dropping the Command Module into the ocean within a mile of its target point. It was time to test the Apollo GN&C system even further from home, on a voyage to the Moon.

Within a few weeks of Apollo 7's successful mission in Earth orbit, NASA decided, after consulting Charles Draper amongst others, to send Apollo 8, without its LM, all the way to the Moon.

The mission launched from Pad 39A on 21st December 1968 with the aim of making ten orbits of the Moon before returning to Earth. Once it was safely in Earth orbit and with the systems checked, Houston sent the commands to instruct the Saturn's computer to reignite the third-stage engine to send them away from the Earth and the rocket came alive – propelling the first humans to leave their home planet onwards to a new world.

Jim Lovell's job as Command Module Pilot was to test the celestial sextant, accessed in the lower equipment bay. To his surprise, when he first attempted this, shortly after heading for the Moon, Lovell found that a blizzard of ice particles vented from the final stage of the Saturn V was still following them to the Moon and at first all he could see was this debris, sparkling in the light and distracting him from the real stars.

But the guidance was so accurate that only three of the planned seven mid-course corrections were needed (two outbound and one on the way back) and these were all minor. Less than a day later, as the spacecraft prepared to go behind the Moon, losing contact with the Earth completely, the flight director took a poll around the system experts to check they are all go. MIT gave its final go on the guidance system which would now carry out the crucial rocket burn to place the spacecraft into orbit around the Moon. The entire mission hung on the success of this burn on the far side of the Moon, out of contact from Earth.

It was Christmas Eve 1968 and as Apollo 8 slipped behind the Moon and into silence you could feel the tension at Mission Control. It was the same in the Instrumentation Lab in Cambridge, where the guidance and navigation team listened to the radio static on the squawk box and counted down the minutes before Apollo 8 would reappear.

To everyone's relief, and right on cue, Apollo 8 re-emerged and the astronauts read out their orbital parameters from the computer. When ground radar confirmed the numbers in Houston, several minutes later, they agreed with the computer's readings perfectly. Throughout the development of the Apollo GN&C system the naysayers had been sure it would never work, but here was proof that MIT's tiny computer 250,000 miles away was in agreement with NASA's huge navigation computers here on Earth. It was an emotional moment for the team at MIT.

The GN&C system would control one further historic and critical burn, achieving the precision needed to send the mission back home. That Christmas morning manoeuvre was so accurate that it required only one minor mid-course correction, changing the speed by just 4.5 feet per second, to enter the Earth's atmosphere precisely on target three days later and splash down within sight of their rescue ship. Lovell had made over 300 successful sextant sightings on the way to the Moon and back, keying them in to the Colossus software on the Command Module's guidance computer. He had proved that the entire flight could have been accomplished without any navigational assistance from Earth. MIT's new silicon chip computer had triumphed at its latest test. But there was one last task to accomplish – guiding a lunar lander to a precise point on the surface of the Moon.

LEFT **Earth rise seen from the LM on the Moon's surface** (NASA)

LEFT **The Apollo 8 Command Module caught on film as it re-enters the Earth's atmosphere right on target, after mankind's first flight away from the Earth in December 1968.** (NASA)

A Computer to Land on the Moon

Descent and landing on the moon involved the most complex series of continuous spacecraft operations of the entire journey, and a bespoke suit of software called Luminary was written to control the Lunar Module during this period of the flight. The LM's guidance computer which ran this software was identical to that in the Command Module, with a DSKY in the centre of the cabin for both crewmen to interact with. But, unlike the Command Module, the LM had two separate guidance systems to manage the complex landing manoeuvres.

The Primary Navigation and Guidance System – PNGS, pronounced 'pings' – carried another inertial platform (IMU) to monitor the LM's movements, and a landing radar which switched

BELOW **The Lunar Module Guidance and Navigation Control System units.** (The Charles Stark Draper Laboratory, Inc)

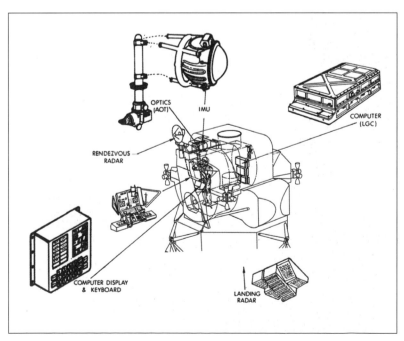

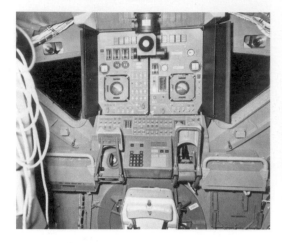

RIGHT The sextant mounting inside the LM crew compartment. *(The Charles Stark Draper Laboratory, Inc)*

FAR RIGHT Ergonomics testing with a subject dressed in a pressure suit to see if the sextant can be operated with gloves and a helmet visor. *(The Charles Stark Draper Laboratory, Inc)*

on at 40,000 feet above the surface to record the spacecraft's altitude and rate of descent. During ascent from the surface, a separate rendezvous radar would help the LM computer to home in on the Command Module from up to 350 miles away. The LM had an Alignment Optical Telescope that provided a similar function

to the CM sextant to align its IMU.

The LM's second guidance system, used as a backup, was known as the Abort Guidance System. The AGS system had its own less-sophisticated inertial measurement unit and also took a feed from the landing or rendezvous radar to keep watch over the performance of the PNGS. The crew interacted with it through its own Data Entry and Display Assembly (DEDA) which was similar to the DSKY. If the PNGS failed then the landing would be aborted and the AGS would get the ascent stage back to the Command Module (see Chapter 4 for more details).

Apollo 11 – landings and alarms

On 20th July 1969, as Neil Armstrong and Buzz Aldrin dropped towards the Sea of Tranquillity, a programme alarm went off in the LM computer. Aldrin immediately keyed in 'Verb 09' followed by 'Noun 05' to find out what the alarm was about. The green figures displayed on the DSKY noted it as a '1202' alarm. Unsure what this number actually referred to or if it was a serious enough problem to abort, Armstrong quickly radioed back to Houston for advice. No one in the main Mission Operations Control Room (MOCR) knew what the alarm meant either, but one of the guidance and navigation engineers

LEFT Jack Garman's scribbled notes, recording the meaning of various programme alarms which might occur during the LM's descent to the surface. *(Jack Garman)*

sitting listening in a support room beyond knew. Jack Garman or 'Garflash' as the MIT team called him, (because of his fast reactions), had even got the number scribbled on a crib sheet, fixed to a piece of cardboard and shoved under the Perspex on his desk. Next to '1202' it read 'Exec. O.F.' standing for an 'Executive Overflow'.

This was a problem which had arisen during simulations in the weeks running up to launch and it meant that the LM's guidance computer was being overloaded. The alarm simply told them that it was struggling to keep up with what it was being asked to do, and repeatedly failing to get to the end of its pre-prioritised task list. Distracting as this was for the crew, Jack Garman knew it meant the computer was coping and still keeping up with the most important jobs. He swiftly passed on the message to Steve Bales in MOCR that he was confident it was OK to continue as long as it did not recur. Bales relayed this to Capcom Charlie Duke who in turn passed on the good news to the crew.

The landing continued, and overload alarms occurred five more times as the computer continued to be distracted by more jobs entering the queue. Garman cleared them each time as the same type as before and the descent continued. Despite the repeated overloads the computer was continuing to operate, prioritising the essential tasks needed to keep the LM flying. Rather than being too slow for the jobs coming in, it was displaying an ability to recover from unexpected overloads, to keep the LM in flight, as Laning had designed it to do.

In landing on the Moon the digital computer had come of age.

The computer overload

Running at full speed, the Apollo Guidance Computer could cope adequately with the programmes that would be needed during a descent but during some simulations it would appear to run more slowly when the LM's rendezvous radar was switched on in its 'slew' or 'auto track' positions. Nothing had been done about the problem as no one at MIT expected the rendezvous radar ever to be switched on at all during a descent. And in fact the reason that no one from MIT had spotted this problem during training sessions at Grumman was that in the simulator the rendezvous radar switch had never been connected to the real computer.

Shortly after the *Eagle* had landed the team at MIT checked on the telemetry data and found to their surprise that the rendezvous radar had indeed been left on in its slew position during the descent. Unbeknownst to the crew, in this mode it had been constantly interrupting the computer with external signals as it searched fruitlessly for the Command Module.

In response the computer had not only prioritised the most vital jobs, but it had also entered a Bailout subroutine in which it repeatedly restarted itself to flush out the lower priority jobs, picking up the vital ones seamlessly where it had left off.

A check in the astronaut procedures book revealed that the rendezvous radar was indeed supposed to be on during descent, just in case they had to make a sudden abort back to orbit. The fact that it had been overlooked was as much of a mistake of crew checklist and communication as it was of engineering design. And far from being a computer error which had caused the problem it was robust computer design which had saved the day.

BELOW Dr Charles Draper toasts his team at the Instrumentation Lab following the successful return of Apollo 17 in December 1972. *(The Charles Stark Draper Laboratory, Inc)*

Chapter 4

The Lunar Module

It is 22nd May 1969. Dressed in pressure suits, Tom Stafford and Gene Cernan stand shoulder to shoulder in a boxy angular spacecraft, their feet 'Velcroed' to the floor for stability. The tiny spacecraft they fly soars across the dramatic lunar mountains beneath. Its paper-thin walls, buckled by the force of a Saturn V launch a few days before, are all that is between them and the vacuum of space. Two triangular, meniscus-thin windows bulge outwards, strained by the cabin air pressure. The men charged with flying this craft's maiden mission to lunar orbit are confident that it will keep them safe. Despite its looks it is the finest flying machine Stafford has ever piloted.

Its designers, the Grumman Corporation in Bothpage, are more used to building big heavy aircraft, but the first craft built to fly exclusively in space has required a different approach. To get all the way to the Moon on a limited propellant budget they have made it so light that it is too flimsy to fly in the air and is only released from its protective shroud, inside the Saturn V, once it has reached the vacuum of space.

Now in lunar orbit, coasting along the trajectory it was made for, the stripped-down spacecraft 'buzzes' the lunar mountain tops like a nimble, responsive jet fighter. Its unique, throttleable descent engine, the first in spaceflight history, gives the pilots unprecedented control over their wingless, airless flight. And with sixteen smaller engines to orientate themselves precisely in any direction the LM is proving to be as agile as any flying machine ever built. Two small onboard computers help the astronauts to fly. They are the forerunners of the micro-computers which run our lives today.

"We is down among them Charlie", soars Gene Cernan's voice back to Houston, as the first LM to be unleashed near the Moon tips over and drops to its lowest, fastest point in lunar orbit. The fourth Lunar Module Grumman has built is now cruising the Moon's mountain tops at over 3,500mph – more than twice as fast as a Concorde's top speed. Stafford and Cernan's mission is to descend to within eight miles of the lunar surface and then return to rendezvous with John Young in the Command Module above. Success will pave the way for Neil Armstrong and Buzz Aldrin to attempt the first lunar landing in two months' time on Apollo 11. Back on Earth the Grumman engineers hold their breath.

LEFT Apollo 16 Lunar Module 'Orion' above the Moon's surface after undocking and separation. Photographed from the Command Module 'Casper' by Ken Mattingly. *(NASA)*

'We are banking our whole program on a fellow not making a mistake on his first landing.'

Pete Conrad
Commander Apollo 12

by NASA's indecision over how to reach the Moon. When Lunar Orbit Rendezvous was finally approved as the way to go the hunt was on for a company to build a dedicated Lunar Lander spacecraft to compliment the Command Module mother ship which was already being built by North American Aviation.

The favourite company to build the new spacecraft was Martin Marietta. But among the half dozen or so competitors in the autumn of 1962 was also a small aircraft company on Long Island called Grumman. It had already spent almost two years studying the idea of a dedicated lightweight lunar landing craft. No one had ever really considered the practicalities of designing such a thing and not everyone at the Grumman Corporation thought that the company should attempt something it had no experience of building. Grumman was best known for its heavy, well-built WWII fighter planes, designed to land on aircraft carriers. But a lot of Grumman's managers were excited about the chance of playing a part in Apollo so they applied what they had learnt over the last two years to a bid for the contract.

Grumman decided LOR meant that the landing craft would need two stages, each with its own engine. A lower descent stage incorporating the landing gear would carry the vehicle down to the Moon's surface, and then a smaller upper ascent stage would lift off, leaving the bulky descent stage behind, to carry the cabin and the crew back to lunar orbit and a

ABOVE The Apollo 14 Lunar Module photographed against a sun glare. A trail left by the two-wheeled Modularized Equipment Transporter (MET) leads from the LM. *(NASA)*

BELOW A scale model of an early prototype Lunar Lander is tested for stability during a simulated landing on soft material. *(NASA)*

In the beginning

Everyone who lived with, worked with or flew the Lunar Modules fell in love with them. The astronauts saw them as a safe refuge in an otherwise hostile lunar landscape. Just ten of them were eventually built to fly in space and today seven of them rest on the surface of the Moon – extra-terrestrial monuments to the ingenuity of those who built the only true spaceships ever to carry humans to another world.

Progress on the Lunar Module, following Kennedy's challenge, was initially held up

rendezvous with the Command Module, This weight-saving idea would prove a crucial factor in winning the contract.

Grumman's winning design had five legs – giving more stability than four and greater safety than three. The cabin boasted two docking hatches, swivelling barstool-type seating in front of the controls and a glass cockpit which looked more like a helicopter than a spacecraft. Once on the lunar surface, the astronauts would climb out of a side hatch and down a knotted rope to go exploring.

The Lunar Module contract was not signed until January 1963, two years after work on the Command Module had begun. It was going to

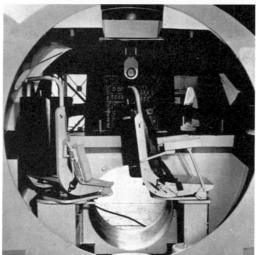

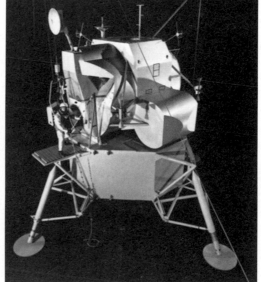

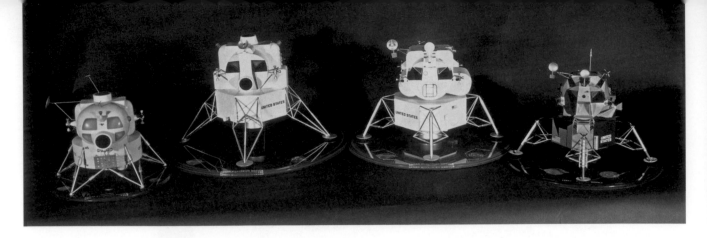

ABOVE Evolution of the shape of the Grumman Lunar Module – from a five-legged design with a round hatch and large windows, to a four-legged design with smaller windows and a square hatch. *(Grumman/NASA)*

BELOW Scale model of the final Grumman LM configuration descent and ascent stages. *(Grumman/NASA)*

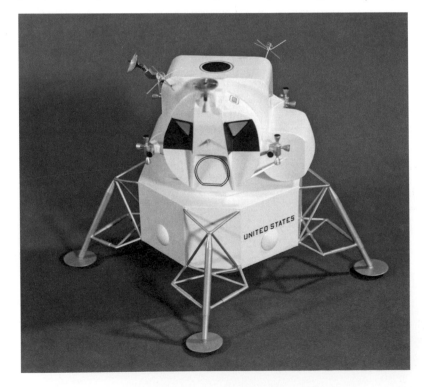

take a lot of catching up if Grumman was to deliver the new craft in time for the first Apollo flights set for 1967.

Back to the drawing board

Grumman soon began to realise that its winning design was still far from being suitable for the job of landing on the Moon. Winning the contract had merely been an entrance exam it had passed to take part in the business of defining the actual requirements of a lunar lander.

For the first few months of 1963 Grumman led a study with NASA, North American Aviation (builders of the Command Module) and the Massachusetts Institute of Technology (which was working on the Apollo navigation system)

to come up with a concept for a real moon landing flight set for May 1968. The 'reference mission' they came up with would involve landing two men on the lunar surface, carrying 250 pounds of equipment, keeping them alive for 48 hours, and returning them to the CSM in orbit with 100 pounds of rock samples.

Every detail they could imagine, from trajectories to propellant budgets, was calculated and published in a bulky three-volume document which specified the exact requirements for the Apollo lander. To reach the surface, in a controlled descent, the LM would need a new kind of throttle-controlled rocket engine. And the life-support systems would need to be as reliable and efficient as those of the Command Module, but at a fraction of the weight.

Unlike every other flying machine Grumman had created, this one would never be test-flown on Earth before being sent on a mission. The engineering would have to be so perfect that flight testing would not be necessary. Such unique and stringent demands would prove to be a huge burden on those who tried to build the LM, but it would ultimately also make them better aircraft builders.

Weight watching

As with every piece of Apollo hardware, keeping weight down was crucial as ever and from the very start Grumman was under instructions to lose anything that was superfluous. The first casualty of this weight cull was one of the five legs. The circular chassis configuration was swapped for a square stronger cross structure with one leg at each corner. The knock-on effect of these structural changes was that six propellant tanks from the original design now became four, with an engine in the middle. This also reduced the piping needed, which brought the weight down further.

Space inside the prototype LM cabin was also being rethought. Grumman quickly began to realise that there was simply not enough room in the original design for the crew's pressure suits, their bulky life-support backpacks, helmets, boots, gloves, and somewhere to stow the rock samples the astronauts would collect. The designers could not make the cabin any bigger because of the weight limits, so more space was created by losing the seating. The astronauts would stand up for the 15-minute landing, anchored to the floor with waist harnesses and foot holds. Their legs would act as shock absorbers on landing and lift-off. Fold-down armrests would also be added so they could steady themselves at the controls during flight. This redesign also allowed for smaller, triangular downward-tilted windows placed at head height. A third, small, rectangular window was built into the roof of the LM to give the commander a view of the Command Module during approach and docking.

Early studies on the knotted rope access idea to enter and exit the LM on the Moon quickly revealed how impractical it was. Even with a winch system an astronaut in a pressure

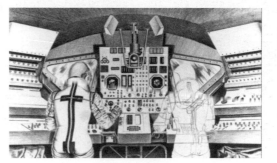

LEFT Artist's concept of the LM interior layout with the two astronauts standing at the main control panel and looking out of the triangular windows at head height.
(Grumman/NASA)

suit and life-support backpack struggled to haul himself back up to the hatch and so a ladder was added to one of the legs instead. A small flat 'porch' was also added just outside the hatch to bridge the gap to the ladder.

By the beginning of 1964, three years after Kennedy's challenge was announced, Grumman was still changing the design of the lunar lander to accommodate new ideas. These constant changes begin to push back the spacecraft's construction schedule and NASA set a deadline in late 1965, after which no more changes would be allowed.

The final design which emerged was not the prettiest machine in the world, resembling a giant other-worldly insect. But, shaped by the environment it would dwell in, Grumman's lunar module was perfectly tuned to the mission it would be called upon to perform.

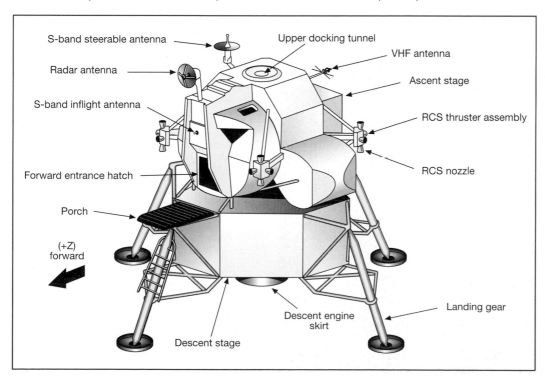

S-band steerable antenna
Radar antenna
S-band inflight antenna
Forward entrance hatch
Porch
(+Z) forward
Upper docking tunnel
VHF antenna
Ascent stage
RCS thruster assembly
RCS nozzle
Descent engine skirt
Descent stage
Landing gear

LEFT The final Grumman LM configuration descent and ascent stages.
(Matthew Marke)

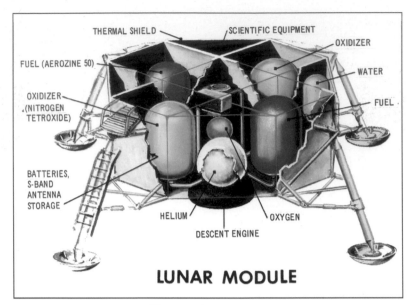

THERMAL SHIELD   SCIENTIFIC EQUIPMENT

OXIDIZER

FUEL (AEROZINE 50)

WATER

OXIDIZER
.(NITROGEN
TETROXIDE)

FUEL

BATTERIES,
S-BAND
ANTENNA
STORAGE

HELIUM   OXYGEN

DESCENT ENGINE

LUNAR MODULE

ABOVE The Lunar
Module's descent
stage, showing the
chasis configuration
and arrangement
of propellant tanks
and instrument bay.
(Grumman/NASA)

The descent stage

The LM's lower stage was dominated
by the landing gear and the big gold
aluminised Kapton and Mylar-foil-covered frame
the legs were attached to and which housed

four propellant tanks and the descent engine.
Although it appeared to be square with a leg at
each corner, the main chassis was in fact more
of an octagon, with a 'diameter' of 14ft 1in. The
fully unfurled legs roughly doubled this span to
31 feet.

In the centre of the lower stage was the
descent engine. Like the other Apollo engines
it gimballed to compensate for the changing
centre of gravity on the LM as it used up its
propellant. More importantly the descent engine
also needed to provide variable thrust. It would
need powering up to its maximum force initially
to slow down from orbital speed and drop
towards the Moon's surface. Once on its final
approach, as it tipped over and attempted
to land almost vertically, it would need to be
throttled slowly back to alight the spacecraft
gently on the surface.

It would be the first variable-thrust engine
ever developed for space flight. To improve the
chances of success in the short time available,
Grumman simultaneously commissioned
two different companies to invent a suitable

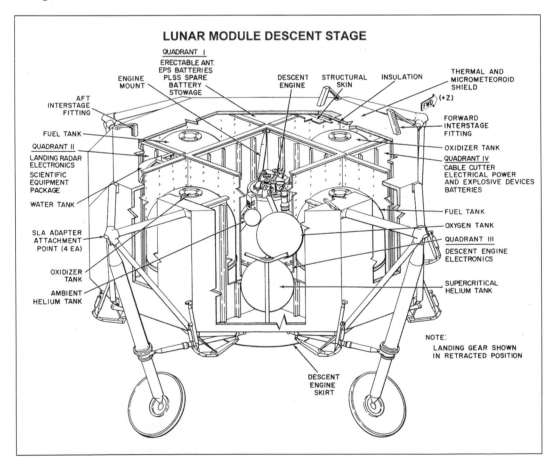

LUNAR MODULE DESCENT STAGE

QUADRANT I
ERECTABLE ANT.
EPS BATTERIES
PLSS SPARE
BATTERY
STOWAGE

ENGINE
MOUNT

DESCENT
ENGINE

STRUCTURAL
SKIN

INSULATION

THERMAL AND
MICROMETEOROID
SHIELD

AFT
INTERSTAGE
FITTING

FWD. (+Z)

FORWARD
INTERSTAGE
FITTING

FUEL TANK

OXIDIZER TANK

QUADRANT II

QUADRANT IV

LANDING RADAR
ELECTRONICS

CABLE CUTTER
ELECTRICAL POWER
AND EXPLOSIVE DEVICES
BATTERIES

SCIENTIFIC
EQUIPMENT
PACKAGE

FUEL TANK

WATER TANK

OXYGEN TANK

QUADRANT III

SLA ADAPTER
ATTACHMENT
POINT (4 EA)

DESCENT ENGINE
ELECTRONICS

OXIDIZER
TANK

SUPERCRITICAL
HELIUM TANK

AMBIENT
HELIUM TANK

NOTE:
LANDING GEAR SHOWN
IN RETRACTED POSITION

DESCENT
ENGINE
SKIRT

RIGHT The Lunar
Module descent stage
with the legs in their
stowed position.
(NASA)

engine. The Rocketdyne Company built one prototype, changing the engine's thrust by adding varying amounts of the inert gas helium to the propellant. The second company, Space Technology Laboratories (STL), accomplished the variable thrust with a mechanical throttle which simply controlled the amount of propellant reaching the combustion chamber, in the way a car's throttle works.

In January 1965 the STL engine was picked. At full power it could lift almost 5 tons of weight but could be throttled back to produce less force than the weight of a new baby.

The hypergolic propellant was stored in four eggshell-thin tanks placed around the central engine. Rumour had it that they were so thin and precisely tuned to their task in space that on Earth they stretched under the weight of the propellant as it was pumped in. These chemicals were so corrosive that they could not be tested in the rocket motors without doing damage to the components. An engine only had a 40-day life once it had been exposed to the propellants so each new engine could not be tested until it was called upon to work for the first time on a flight. As graduates of the aircraft business, the engineers found it almost inconceivable that their new engines would not be tested until they were 240,000 miles from home.

To protect the seams, joints and the propellant tanks on the lower stage from the temperature extremes of space (–150 to +130°C) 16 layers of distinctive, golden Mylar aluminised foil covered its frame. The multiple layers of this novel material, invented by DuPont, provided excellent thermal and micro-meteorite protection without adding much weight.

Within the descent stage, between the leg attachment points, were bays for the Modularised Equipment Stowage Assembly (MESA) and room for the Apollo Lunar Surface Experiment Package (ASLEP). These could be accessed on the surface, to extract scientific experiments, a surface TV camera and tools once the astronauts were outside exploring. The collapsible Lunar Roving Vehicle, carried to the Moon on Apollos 15–17 would also eventually occupy one of these compartments.

Protruding from this golden skirt were the LM's four legs, positioned 90 degrees apart. Their struts were filled with a honeycomb material that crushed on contact with the lunar surface, to help absorb the impact. There was no need for the legs to rebound with a complex hydraulic mechanism, as each LM was only ever going to make one landing. At the end of each leg was a giant footpad designed to land

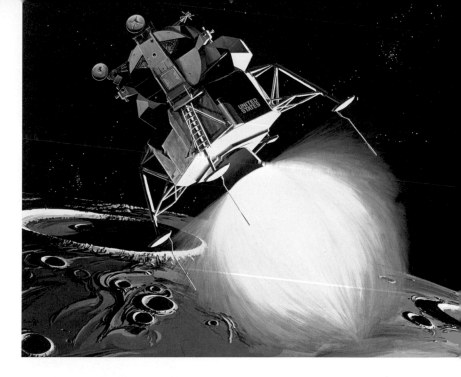

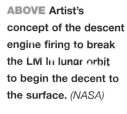

ABOVE Artist's concept of the descent engine firing to break the LM in lunar orbit to begin the decent to the surface. (NASA)

LEFT LM4 is moved from its clean room for stowage in the launch shroud on the top of the Saturn V for the LM's maiden flight to the Moon on Apollo 10. (NASA)

Working with toxic propellant

The hypergolic propellants used for the LM engines (aerozine 50 fuel and a nitrogen tetroxide oxidiser) were too toxic to be tested near human habitation, so Grumman built a new test facility out at a remote site in White Sands, New Mexico. The oxidiser was so lethal that if you inhaled more than five parts per million it would start to eat away at your lungs. In the event of a leak, when a menacing red cloud would form, the police were quickly called to evacuate everyone nearby until it had dissipated.

Rocket propellant comes as two chemical components, a fuel and an oxidiser, and to burn properly they have to be mixed. One issue that dogged all the Apollo engine systems was how to ensure their propellants travelled reliably from their tanks to the engines in zero-gravity conditions. The solution had apparently come to a Grumman engineer as he contemplated the froth bubbling out of his bottle of beer. By introducing a high-pressure inert gas into the tanks, the two propellants would be forced out evenly and together without the need for unreliable pumps. The elegant solution, however, came with a drawback. The inert chemical that worked best was helium and it would need storing at around 1,500 psi and –232°C. Developing such a high-presure cryogenic system would be constantly plagued by leakage problems.

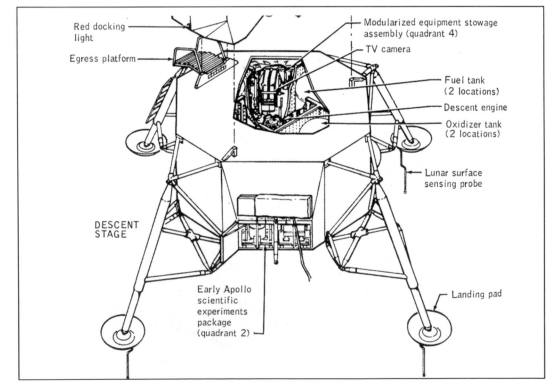

Red docking light

Egress platform

Modularized equipment stowage assembly (quadrant 4)

TV camera

Fuel tank (2 locations)

Descent engine

Oxidizer tank (2 locations)

Lunar surface sensing probe

DESCENT STAGE

Early Apollo scientific experiments package (quadrant 2)

Landing pad

RIGHT The LM decent stage showing the location of the early scientific experiments package and the TV camera which would deploy from the side to cover the first steps on the Moon's surface. *(Grumman/NASA)*

in potentially deep dust. Beneath three of these pads protruded 68-inch long probes which triggered a blue 'contact' light inside the cabin when they touched the surface, signalling the crew to cut the main engine and drop the few feet to the ground.

The landing gear was so finely balanced that it could not support the weight of the spacecraft on Earth. But, once on the Moon's surface, the descent stage would be strong enough to function as a launch pad for the upper or ascent stage of the LM.

The ascent stage

Like the Service Module's main engine, there was no back-up or secondary system for the Lunar Module's ascent engine. If it failed the crew would be stranded on the lunar surface with no hope of a rescue – it was one of those worrying weak links in the Apollo daisy chain. Grumman selected the Bell Aerosystems company to deliver an engine it could depend on.

The Bell engineers' approach was to try and eliminate anything which could go wrong with the engine. They started by doing away with

the ignition system, instead using hypergolic propellants which would ignite spontaneously when exposed to the vacuum of space. Propellant pumps were discarded by forcing the hypergolic reactants into the engine bell

ABOVE The LM 'Eagle' starboard footpad and contact probe on the Sea of Tranquillity at mankind's first lunar landing site. (NASA)

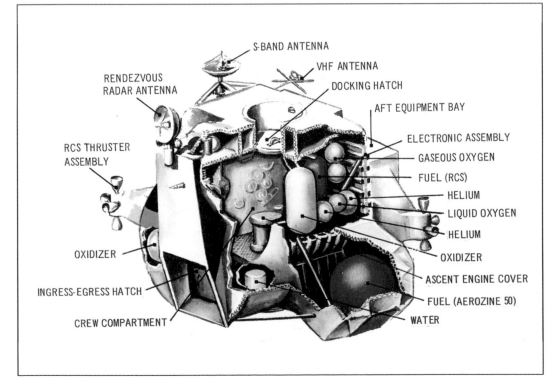

- S-BAND ANTENNA
- VHF ANTENNA
- RENDEZVOUS RADAR ANTENNA
- DOCKING HATCH
- AFT EQUIPMENT BAY
- RCS THRUSTER ASSEMBLY
- ELECTRONIC ASSEMBLY
- GASEOUS OXYGEN
- FUEL (RCS)
- HELIUM
- LIQUID OXYGEN
- HELIUM
- OXIDIZER
- OXIDIZER
- ASCENT ENGINE COVER
- INGRESS-EGRESS HATCH
- FUEL (AEROZINE 50)
- CREW COMPARTMENT
- WATER

LEFT The LM's ascent stage, showing the location of the propellant tanks and other systems packed around the crew's pressurised compartment. (NASA)

RIGHT Lowering the
LM ascent stage onto
a testing rig at White
Sands for ascent
engine test firings.
*(White Sands Test
Facility)*

using a pressurised helium system. And even
the mechanics of the engine bell itself were
simplified by replacing a conventional piped
cooling system with an ablative coating which
protected it from the heat by slowly charring
and burning off. This last approach would
slightly alter the thrust characteristics of the
engine during firing, making the LM more
challenging to fly, but the trade-off for greater
reliability was considered worth it.

Despite these innovations, which left
only four moving parts to go wrong in the
entire ascent engine, NASA worried about
combustion instability – the problem which
had plagued the Saturn's F-1 engines. So, in
mid-1964, Grumman started setting off small
explosive charges inside the ascent engines
during test firings. The Bell engineers expected
the resulting instability to dampen down quickly
but to their surprise, under certain conditions, it
failed to disappear and instead risked damaging
the engine. For the next two years Bell tried
everything it or NASA could think of to fix the
instability, but nothing would work.

In 1967, with just months to go before the
LM's first space flight, NASA decided to call in
Rocketdyne to develop an alternative engine.
Rocketdyne came up with an improved injector
system which seemed to fix the problem, but
other aspects of the new engine were not as
good as Bell's. So NASA opted for a hybrid
system, using Rocketdyne's injector fitted in
Bell's original engine. This combination seemed
to work well and in June 1968 it passed 53
bomb tests, damping down the explosion-

induced instability oscillations within 400
milliseconds.

This bold last-minute fix had worked. Every
question had been answered, every failure
had been understood, every problem had
been solved. And thanks to endless 'what if'
experiments, no astronauts on the Moon were
ever put at risk by the LM's 100 per cent reliable
ascent engine.

The crew compartment

Built around and on top of the ascent engine
was the crew cabin. Its pressurised hull
was shaped like a horizontally mounted tube
92 inches in diameter and 42 inches long. This
gave a habitable space of 160 cubic feet, and
was just large enough for the two astronauts
wearing their pressure suits to stand side
by side.

Around them, to the front and sides, were
the main controls whilst behind them was the
ascent engine and a rear equipment bay, which
housed the major electronics of the life-support
system and communication equipment. This
bay balanced the weight of the crew in the
front. These electronic systems were fitted
with heat sinks through which water and glycol
were circulated to external sublimators for heat
regulation. Storage space for the pressure suits,
life-support backpacks, helmets, food and other
equipment was provided in this rear section too.

Outside the cabin, on either side, were two
spherical propellant tanks for the ascent engine.
Sticking out on either side of the boxy cabin
they gave the LM its 'cheeks' when viewed
face-on from the front. Because a full tank of
oxidiser was heavier than a tank of fuel, the fuel
tank was mounted further out from the engine,
giving the 'face' a lop-sided look.

The crew would enter the LM cabin, from
the CM, through the docking hatch on its
ceiling. The second hatch, used to exit and
enter the spacecraft after landing on the Moon,
gave the LM 'face' its square 'mouth'. Inside
it led to a space at foot level, in the middle of
the control panel between the crew stations.
From the inside, it was hinged on the right,
opening inwards, and making it necessary for
the Commander standing on the left to exit first

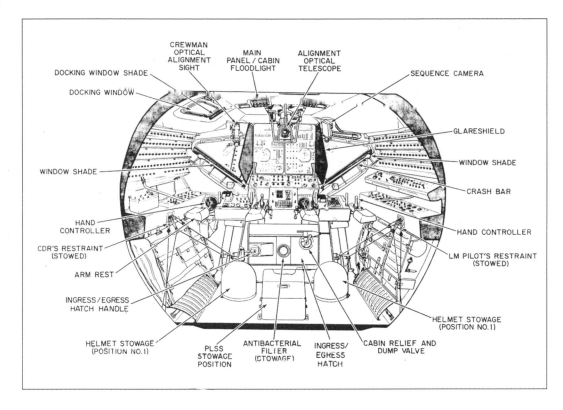

CREWMAN OPTICAL ALIGNMENT SIGHT

MAIN PANEL / CABIN FLOODLIGHT

ALIGNMENT OPTICAL TELESCOPE

DOCKING WINDOW SHADE

DOCKING WINDOW

SEQUENCE CAMERA

GLARESHIELD

WINDOW SHADE

WINDOW SHADE

CRASH BAR

HAND CONTROLLER

HAND CONTROLLER

CDR'S RESTRAINT (STOWED)

LM PILOT'S RESTRAINT (STOWED)

ARM REST

INGRESS / EGRESS HATCH HANDLE

HELMET STOWAGE (POSITION NO.1)

HELMET STOWAGE (POSITION NO.1)

PLSS STOWAGE POSITION

ANTIBACTERIAL FILTER (STOWAGE)

INGRESS/ EGRESS HATCH

CABIN RELIEF AND DUMP VALVE

before the Lunar Module Pilot, standing on the right. Both astronauts would need to get on all fours to back out of the hatch onto the porch and then down the nine rungs of the ladder to the surface.

Although it was pressurised, there was little separating the astronauts inside the cabin from the vacuum of space. The skin of the cabin was just 0.012 inches thick, about the same as three layers of kitchen foil. When pressurised it would bow outwards like some big aluminium balloon rather than a tough, rigid, protective shelter. But this was considered enough to protect the two astronauts and contain their

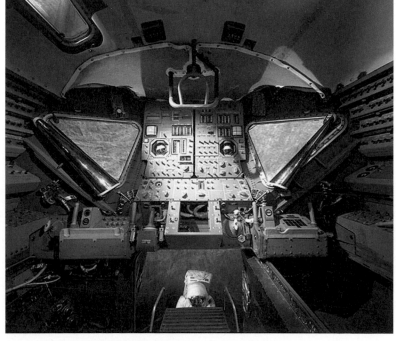

RIGHT Lunar Module ascent stage interior – looking aft. *(NASA/ Frank O'Brien)*

BELOW Aft view of the crew compartment looking towards the left, showing the controls of the LM's Environmental Control System. *(NASA/ Frank O'Brien)*

BELOW RIGHT Aft view of the crew compartment looking towards the right, showing the controls and the stowage locations for the PLSS backpacks and other expedition equipment. *(Ken Thomas/Hamilton Standard/Frank O'Brien)*

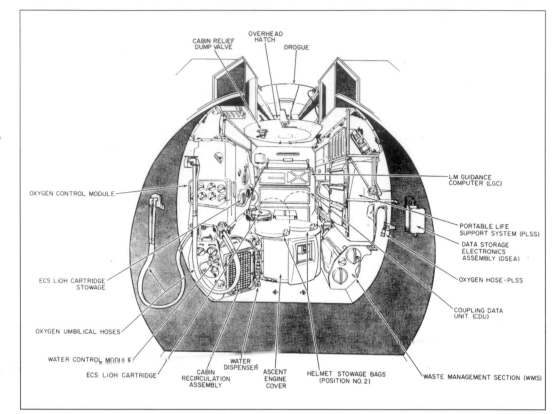

CABIN RELIEF DUMP VALVE
OVERHEAD HATCH
DROGUE
LM GUIDANCE COMPUTER (LGC)
OXYGEN CONTROL MODULE
PORTABLE LIFE SUPPORT SYSTEM (PLSS)
DATA STORAGE ELECTRONICS ASSEMBLY (DSEA)
OXYGEN HOSE-PLSS
ECS LiOH CARTRIDGE STOWAGE
COUPLING DATA UNIT (CDU)
OXYGEN UMBILICAL HOSES
WATER CONTROL MODULE
ECS LiOH CARTRIDGE
CABIN RECIRCULATION ASSEMBLY
WATER DISPENSER
ASCENT ENGINE COVER
HELMET STOWAGE BAGS (POSITION NO. 2)
WASTE MANAGEMENT SECTION (WMS)

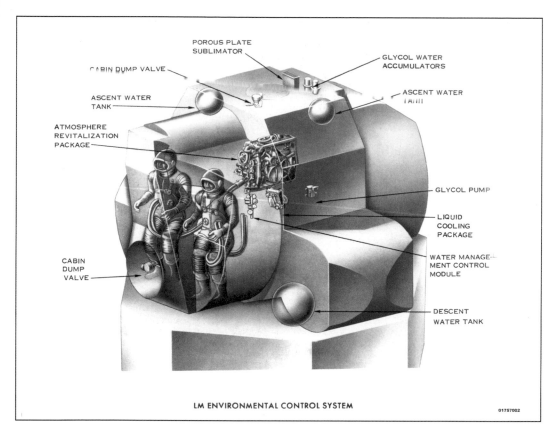

POROUS PLATE
SUBLIMATOR

CABIN DUMP VALVE

GLYCOL WATER
ACCUMULATORS

ASCENT WATER
TANK

ASCENT WATER
TANK

ATMOSPHERE
REVITALIZATION
PACKAGE

GLYCOL PUMP

LIQUID
COOLING
PACKAGE

CABIN
DUMP
VALVE

WATER MANAGE-
MENT CONTROL
MODULE

DESCENT
WATER TANK

LM ENVIRONMENTAL CONTROL SYSTEM

01757002

LEFT Location of the Environmental Control System inside the LM in relation to the crew positions for descent and lift off. *(NASA/Hamilton Standard)*

BELOW LM Environmental Control System with the cover removed, showing the atmospheric revitalisation section. *(Ken Thomas/Hamilton Standard)*

life-giving atmosphere. Like the CM, the LM air supply was maintained by a life-support system built by the Hamilton Standard Company. The Apollo 11 crew would only spend a few hours inside the LM but future crews would live in the lander for days at a time, gulping in life-giving gas and exhaling poisonous breath. Like a plumber's dream, engineers from Hamilton Standard had managed to squeeze the LM's environmental-control system into a discreet corner of the ascent stage. Its hoses provided pure oxygen to two astronauts at a pressure one-third that of normal atmosphere, and at a comfortable temperature. The unit recirculated the gas, scrubbed out the CO_2 and replenished the oxygen which was used up.

When the crew were inside, wearing their pressure suits during a landing and launch, they plumbed themselves into this machine to supply oxygen and cooling water. On later missions the personal life-support backpacks could also be topped up with power, water and air from this system.

Whilst on the lunar surface during Apollo 11 the crew slept on the floor in the front section of the crew cabin – the lunar module pilot

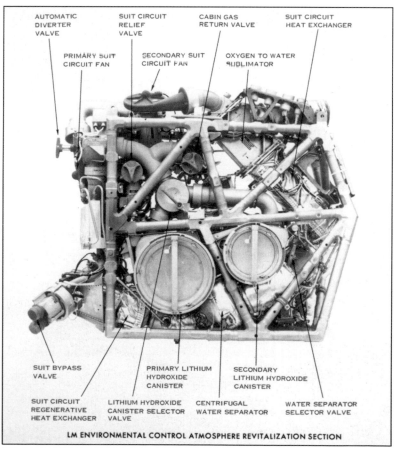

AUTOMATIC
DIVERTER
VALVE

SUIT CIRCUIT
RELIEF
VALVE

CABIN GAS
RETURN VALVE

SUIT CIRCUIT
HEAT EXCHANGER

PRIMARY SUIT
CIRCUIT FAN

SECONDARY SUIT
CIRCUIT FAN

OXYGEN TO WATER
SUBLIMATOR

SUIT BYPASS
VALVE

PRIMARY LITHIUM
HYDROXIDE
CANISTER

SECONDARY
LITHIUM HYDROXIDE
CANISTER

SUIT CIRCUIT
REGENERATIVE
HEAT EXCHANGER

LITHIUM HYDROXIDE
CANISTER SELECTOR
VALVE

CENTRIFUGAL
WATER SEPARATOR

WATER SEPARATOR
SELECTOR VALVE

LM ENVIRONMENTAL CONTROL ATMOSPHERE REVITALIZATION SECTION

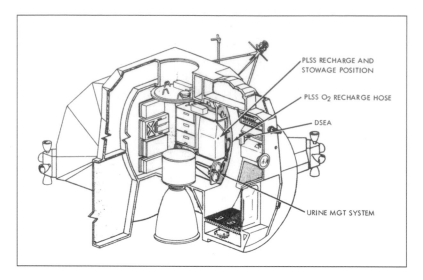

PLSS RECHARGE AND
STOWAGE POSITION

PLSS O₂ RECHARGE HOSE

DSEA

URINE MGT SYSTEM

ABOVE LM cabin interior – right half. *(NASA)*

trying to grab a few hours of rest on top of the ascent engine, apparently an uncomfortable and cold place to rest. From Apollo 12 onwards hammocks were strung up in the front section of the cabin one above the other, to make the rest periods more relaxing. Astronauts reported that in the one-sixth gravity these hammocks were very comfortable.

BELOW Original sleep stations used for the crew on Apollo 11. Later missions utilised hammocks strung up during sleep periods for the crew to get more rest. *(Matthew Marke)*

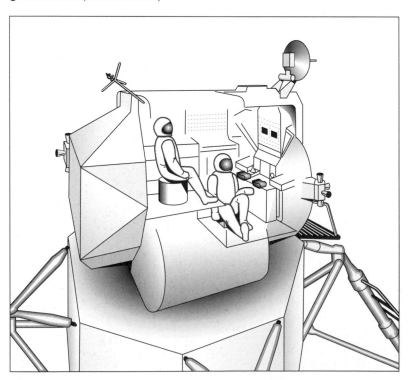

Overweight

As the LM concept progressed, its original target weight of 22,000 pounds was quickly abandoned. NASA's contract with Grumman had stated a new limit of 25,000 pounds, but a year later, in January 1964, with multiple changes and additions now adopted, this limit had been increased again to 29,500 pounds, and then once again in November that year to 32,000 pounds.

Further difficulties with the new technologies being pioneered for the LM soon started to push it over this latest weight limit. Problems with the reliability of the fuel-cell power system caused the designers to switch to silver–zinc batteries. Whilst this removed the need for extra oxygen and hydrogen propellant tanks and the associated piping, the new batteries were much heavier and initially just as unreliable. The dependability of the LM guidance system was also being called into question and a decision was made early on to add a second back-up guidance system called the AGS (Abort Guidance System) for use in the event of an abort back to orbit.

The extra weight this added had a further knock-on effect. Every extra pound the LM weighed would require three more pounds of propellant to fly it down to the Moon's surface and back up again into orbit. And each lost second of flying time could mean the difference between success or failure and even life and death. On top of this, a heavier LM would also require more lifting power from the Saturn V to boost it into space and on to the Moon. By the beginning of 1965 even the new 32,500-pound weight allowance was looking difficult to achieve and in July that year NASA decided to offer Grumman a financial incentive to bring the weight under control.

For every pound of weight Grumman shaved off the LM, NASA would pay them a $25,000 bonus. Unable to change the designs at this late stage, Grumman introduced both 'Operation Scrape' and a study it called SWIP (Super Weight Improvement Program). Scrape, as the name suggests, sought to sculpt cuts from anything that was not already at its minimum safe thickness. They even shaved metal from individual bolts. The SWIP team pored over drawings and plans looking for further ways to lighten the craft. Perhaps the most striking change to come from this work was to replace the rigid descent-stage thermal shields with the iconic gold-coloured aluminium–Mylar foil blankets.

Eventually, through a strategy of chemical milling – etching weight from the surface of components with acid, and forcing subcontractors to reduce the weights of the parts they were supplying – another 2,500 pounds was removed from the spacecraft. Even a layer of varnish-like material which protected the aluminium frame from the weather was discarded, and together with the other provisions this brought the spacecraft to just within its design limits.

Apollo 4

On 27th June 1967, after months of intense pressure, the reconfigured LM-1 was delivered to the Kennedy Space Center for its maiden flight on the unmanned Apollo 4 mission. This first 'all-up' test of the Saturn V launch would carry both the Command and Lunar modules into space for a complete test of the technology designed to take men to the Moon. This make-or-break mission was critical to get NASA back on track following the Apollo 1 fire, and the agency poured inspectors into the clean room to crawl all over the first LM. Much to Grumman's embarrassment hundreds of technical faults were discovered and the spacecraft was rejected.

The biggest problems were breaking wires and leaks in the pressurised propellant system. These leaks were often tiny, almost imperceptible affairs with less than the volume of a sugar cube leaking out in a day. But even the slightest leakage and mixing of these highly reactive hypergolic chemicals would prove disastrous to a mission. Until every one of them was plugged LM-1 was grounded and NASA decided to fly Apollo 4 without it. Grumman redoubled its efforts through the end of 1967, eventually solving the leakage problem by welding the troublesome joints and then inspecting them with X-rays to certify their integrity.

As 1968 dawned LM-1 was at last ready for its first space flight.

Apollo 5 – the LM's first flight

The first unmanned Lunar Module eventually lifted off Pad 37 aboard Apollo 5 on 22nd January 1968. It had taken Grumman five very full-time years to build this first LM and it would fly in space for just eight hours.

The S-IB booster, which had originally been on the pad for the doomed Apollo 1 flight, carried it aloft. LM-1 had no legs. It would not make a landing anywhere, burning up in the Earth's atmosphere after five orbits. However, it would still provide a chance to test the cabin integrity, attitude thrusters, throttling capabilities of the descent engine, stage separation and firing of the ascent engine. These tests did not go completely to plan. After igniting the descent engine remotely from mission control, it was shut down after just four seconds by the onboard computer, detecting that its full thrust had not been achieved fast enough.

The problem turned out to be a software error, and a workaround was sought before a re-test was tried one orbit later. There was just sufficient time to retry this and attempt the other tests before LM-1 ended its short life in a ball of fire, re-entering the atmosphere over the west coast of Panama. The next LM to fly in space would carry its first crew.

Flying the LM

In flight the LM could be manoeuvred very accurately for rendezvous and docking using four clusters of small rocket thrusters known together as the Reaction Control System (RCS). These tiny engines were mounted on struts at the four corners of the spacecraft,

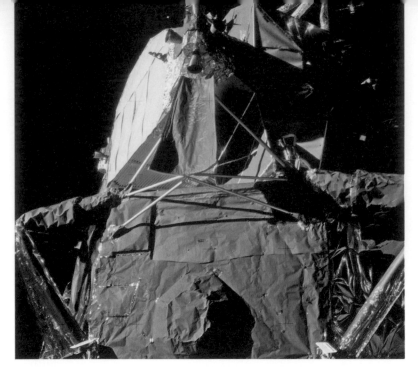

ABOVE The Reaction Control System (RCS) engines seen on the rear struts of the 'Eagle' lander following its Apollo 11 lunar landing. *(NASA)*

BELOW Positions of the RCS engines on the four corner struts of the spacecraft. *(NASA)*

arranged to keep the door and windows clear of obstruction. They were powered by the same hypergolic propellants as the LM's main engines, stored in spherical tanks mounted around the outside of the crew compartment.

The difficulty in controlling this unique vehicle was that the LM had a different feel depending on whether the ship was heavy with propellant and landing gear or ten times lighter with only the ascent stage remaining. So, whilst the firing of these RCS engines and the throttling of the main engines was handled by a crewman

using one of the control sticks, crucially it was managed by the flight computer. Software running in the LM's computer would respond to the craft's changing flight characteristics, sensed through the vehicle's inertial-guidance platform, and compensate for them in real time as it interpreted the astronaut's control-stick movements. Together this system was known as the Primary Navigation and Guidance System or PNGS, and it was the first major application of digital 'fly-by-wire' technology in history (*see Chapter 3*).

Along with the changing characteristics of the descent engine as the ablative coating burnt off, and the challenge of making a landing with such limited propellant, this fly-by-wire system was considered essential for flying the LM. Should the PNGS fail during descent, an abort was considered mandatory. In this event the back up Abort Guidance System would be selected to take over, with the single task of returning the spacecraft to a safe orbit around the Moon.

Apollo 8

Apollo 8 would be the first manned test flight of a LM in Earth orbit. Grumman had most of 1968 to get it right but in the middle of that year another setback with its designs threatened the programme again. During a routine pressure test in a vacuum chamber one of the triple-paned, triangular observation windows suddenly shattered. Such a fundamental failure at this late stage troubled everyone at NASA. Each tiny fragment of glass was located inside the vacuum chamber, to piece the pane back together again, to try and understand the failure. The team found that the glass had absorbed moisture during its manufacture which had then expanded as the pressure dropped in the vacuum chamber causing the window to shatter. The problem took months to solve, and LM-3 was only delivered to the Cape just in time for Apollo 8.

NASA began its usual quality-control tests and to Grumman's despair, over 200 defects were discovered, many of them wiring and propellant-leak problems. It was clear LM-3 would not be ready in time for its first manned flight and NASA was forced to change Apollo 8

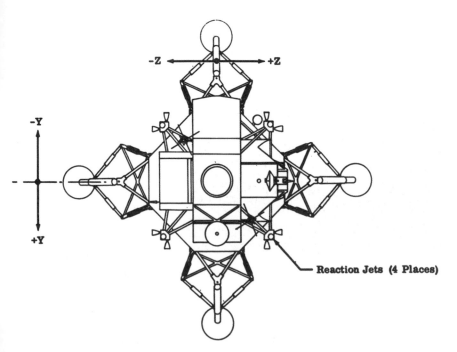

to a Command Module-only test flight, which it eventually sent around the Moon. This mission switch-around gave Grumman another three months to fix the problem before the Apollo 9 crew test-flew the craft in Earth orbit.

Apollo 9 – the LM's first manned flight

On 3rd March 1969 Jim McDivitt, Dave Scott and Rusty Schweickart embarked on the first manned test flight of the Lunar Module (LM-3). Once in space Dave Scott undocked the Command Module, which the crew had called *Gumdrop*, turned it around and delicately approached the Lunar Module they had called *Spider*. After docking with the top hatch he carefully backed away, extracting the LM from the top of the Saturn V. For the next four days the two docked spacecraft orbited the Earth together – using the Service Module's engine to push both craft into a higher orbit ready for the big test.

On day five, despite Rusty Schweickart suffering a bout of sickness, he and Jim McDivitt powered up the LM, extended the landing gear and, still docked with the Command Module, fired the descent engine to drop both craft back down to a lower orbit. Then, on 7th March, following a spacewalk to test the new Apollo EVA (Extra-Vehicular Activity) pressure suit, McDivitt and Schweickart boarded the LM once

more, leaving Scott in the CM and undocked – releasing LM-3 into free flight for the first time. After a false start when the docking latches got caught, a second attempt propelled the two craft away from each other.

After conducting a full test of the attitude thrusters, McDivitt throttled up the descent engine to 10 per cent thrust, propelling the LM to a higher, slower orbit which carried it 15 miles away from the CM. McDivitt and Schweickart eventually reached over 100 miles from the safety of *Gumdrop* before firing the LM's descent engines once more to slow down, dropping to a lower, faster orbit below the CM and allowing the two craft to catch up again.

The final test, which simulated lift-off from the lunar surface, separated the descent and ascent stages in a cloud of debris as the

ABOVE LEFT LM-3 'Spider' waiting to be extracted from the S-IVB stage of the launch vehicle. *(NASA)*

ABOVE Apollo 9 Command/Service Modules (CSM) nicknamed 'Gumdrop' and Lunar Module (LM), nicknamed 'Spider' are shown docked together as Command Module Pilot David R. Scott stands in the open hatch. The photograph was taken by Rusty Schweickart from his vantage point standing on the porch of the Lunar Module. *(NASA)*

LEFT View of the Apollo 9 Lunar Module 'Spider' in a lunar landing configuration on the fifth day of the Apollo 9 Earth-orbital mission. *(NASA)*

Apollo 10 – the LM's first flight to the Moon

Designed as a dress rehearsal for a landing mission, Apollo 10 would practise every step of a landing short of the final descent to the lunar surface. It would be the first time the Lunar Module was taken to the Moon. The crew, Tom Stafford, Gene Cernan and John Young, had christened LM-4 *Snoopy* to go with their Command Module *Charlie Brown*.

The mission lifted off on 18th May 1969, and despite severe pogo oscillations of the second stage of the Saturn V, they reached Earth orbit and continued on to arrive at the Moon by 21st May. The next day Stafford and Cernan boarded the LM and, after some concern over an undocking problem, the two spacecraft separated successfully on the far side of the Moon. At nearly 100 hours into the mission Stafford fired up the descent engine for a 30-second burn which would take them lower towards the surface.

At a point 300 miles east of the Sea of Tranquillity the crew fired the descent engine once more to place them in an elliptical orbit and on a trajectory which would swoop them down to an altitude of 47,400 feet above the rehearsal landing site on their next pass. Grumman's LM-4 was too heavy to make a full landing and lift off back from the surface and so there was never a thought of attempting a full landing.

As they came round for this final orbit the astronauts prepared to jettison the descent stage and return to *Charlie Brown*. Suddenly, without warning, the LM began to roll unexpectedly. The incident startled the crew and through a hot microphone Cernan exclaimed "Son of a bitch … what the hell happened?" Stafford quickly jettisoned the heavy descent stage and used his hand controllers to stabilise the tumble. It turned out that the problem was caused by human error. A switch for the Abort Guidance System had been left in the wrong 'automatic' position and the LM was searching for the Command Module above, as it had been instructed to do.

After a successful rendezvous and docking, using the LM's rendezvous radar for the first time in lunar orbit, the crew transferred back to

ABOVE The Lunar Module 'Spider' ascent stage is photographed from the Command/ Service Module on the fifth day of the Apollo 9 Earth-orbital mission. The Lunar Module's descent stage had already been jettisoned. *(NASA)*

explosive charges blew off fragments of foil from the lower stage. Using the ascent engine McDivitt spent the next two hours playing catch up as he manoeuvred the LM's ascent stage back towards Dave Scott in the CM.

The first LM to fly in space had proved it could keep two astronauts alive for up to six hours, manoeuvring them safely between orbits and ultimately to a safe and successful rendezvous with the Command Module. Back on Earth McDivitt wrote to the designers with a photograph of his *Spider* in space. The caption below read: "Many thanks for the funny-looking spacecraft. It sure flies better than it looks." The next Lunar Module to fly (LM-4) would carry its crew to within 8 miles of the Moon's rugged surface on Apollo 10.

RIGHT The ascent stage of the Apollo 10 Lunar Module (LM) is photographed from the Command Module prior to docking in lunar orbit. The LM is approaching the Command/Service Modules from below. The LM descent stage had already been jettisoned. *(NASA)*

the CM and jettisoned LM-4 – propelling it into a solar orbit. The Service Module engine was fired up on 23rd May and the crew headed home.

With the Apollo 10 dress rehearsal mission declared a triumph, Apollo 11, carrying LM-5, was already being rolled out towards Pad 39A in preparation for mankind's first attempt to land on the Moon.

How to land on the Moon

Any Apollo flight required hundreds of complicated procedures which had been planned and tested, modified, re-tested, and rehearsed until all those concerned could execute them in their sleep. But undisputedly at the top of this list was the 12-minute time line it took to go from travelling at the equivalent of Mach 5 in lunar orbit to standing still at a precise point on the Moon's surface. This task was divided up into three distinct phases each controlled by a separate computer programme: braking (P63), approach (P64) and terminal descent (P66).

Braking (P63)

The final descent to the lunar surface was always begun from the low point of an orbit which occurred 250 miles east of the designated landing site. Ten minutes prior to Powered Descent Initiation (PDI), the

BELOW A view looking forward towards the windows inside the LM, showing the locations of the various control and instrument panels ('Panel 1', 'Panel 2', etc). Refer to the illustration on pages 132–133 for further details of the panels. *(NASA/Frank O'Brien)*

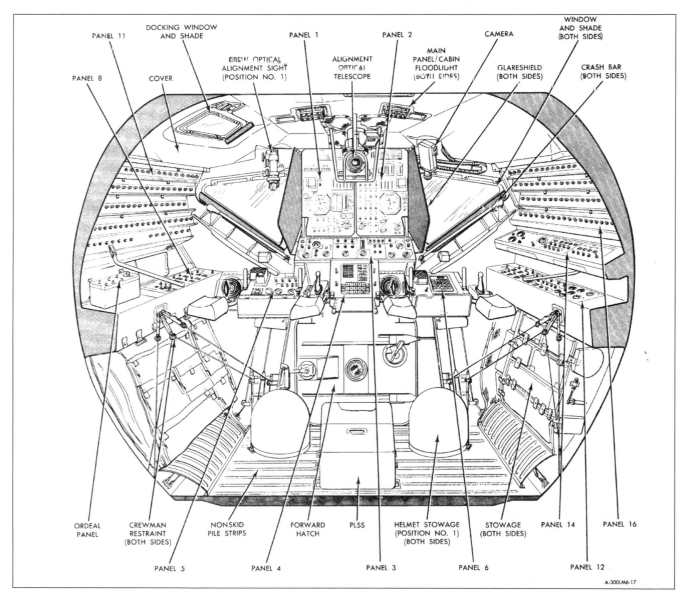

A-300LM6-17

The pilot's perspective – inside the LM

Standing on the left, the Mission Commander was in control of the Lunar Module, verifying the computer programmes and landing phases, re-evaluating the landing point the digital autopilot had picked and manually flying the final few hundred feet of the descent.

Technically the Lunar Module Pilot on the right was more of a co-pilot or systems engineer, who followed the checklists, entered commands into the computer, compared PGNS and AGS altitudes, and monitored the thrust of the descent engine and other parameters. In the final minutes of a landing he would also call out the altitude, velocity and propellant levels, so the Commander could concentrate on the actual landing, watching the ground through his window on the left.

The most important instruments in front of each astronaut were two 8-ball artificial horizon indicators which displayed the craft's orientation relative to a vertical line perpendicular to the Moon or Earth's horizon. A velocity indicator just above the 8-ball displayed the craft's forward and lateral speed using a cross pointer. On the Commander's side, to the right of the 8-ball was an instrument displaying the altitude and descent rate, as calculated by the autopilot from the radar data.

The LM was steered through two hand-controller sticks; one for the right hand (called the ACA – Attitude Control Assembly) which controlled rotation or attitude and one for the left hand (called the TTCA – Thrust/Translation Controller Assembly) which through two modes controlled the craft's translation (horizontal location) and its vertical velocity. Under normal flight conditions these controllers communicated with the

engines through the digital autopilot, but the crew could vary the modes which the autopilot operated in – a bit like adjusting the responsiveness of a suspension and engine management system in a modern car from a smooth to a sporty ride.

For example in its 'impulse mode', designed for making precision manoeuvres during rendezvous and docking, the engines would fire in short bursts in response to movements of the control stick. At the other extreme was 'hard over mode' – designed for emergencies, and accessed by pushing the stick as far as it would go. This bypassed the autopilot controller completely, enabling the astronaut, in the event

of a computer failure or other emergency, to operate the RCS thrusters directly.

Other digital autopilot modes included 'rate command/attitude hold' which was akin to a cruise control in a car. This mode was accessed by flipping a switch from PNGS AUTO to ATT HOLD, or by keying in Verb 77 through the DSKY keypad and display. When this was done the autopilot would automatically fire the RCS engines to hold the LM's attitude, as soon as the stick was released. In this mode, by entering Verb 48 into the DSKY further fine adjustments to a rate of change of the LM's attitude could be dialled in.

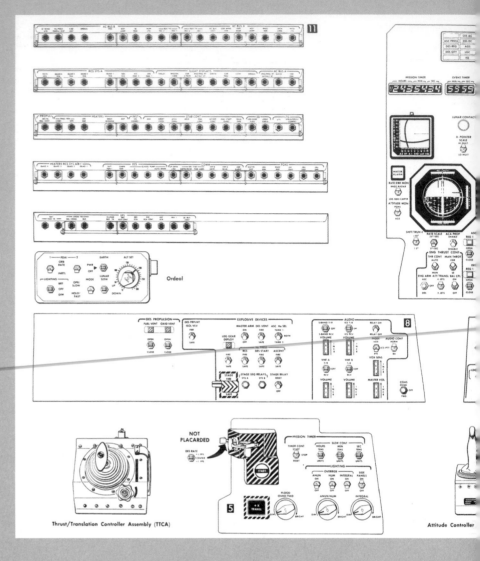

Ordeal

Thrust/Translation Controller Assembly (TTCA)

NOT PLACARDED

Attitude Controller

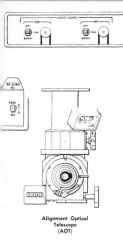

Alignment Optical
Telescope
(AOT)

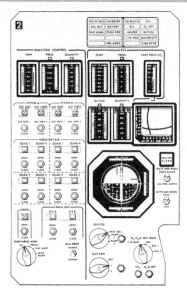

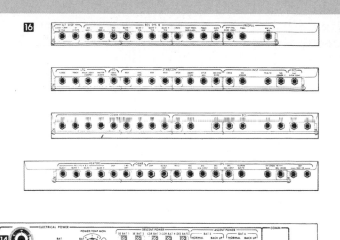

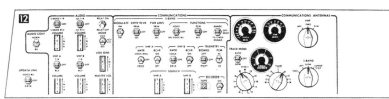

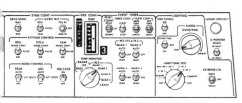

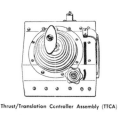

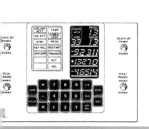

Thrust/Translation Controller Assembly (TTCA)

Attitude Controller Assembly (ACA)

G-300LMS-1

(NASA)

Panel 1: The Commander's primary instrument panel. Contains the primary flight instruments, including the attitude indicator (8-ball), altitude and altitude rate tapemeters, engine and guidance system controls and displays, and horizontal velocity display. Note the Abort and Abort Stage push-buttons in the centre right. Warning lights are at very top of picture.

Panel 2: The Lunar Module Pilot's primary instrument panel. Attitude indicator, Reaction Control System thruster controls, environmental system controls. Warning lights again are at the top of the panel.

Panel 3: Engine and guidance system controls, radars, system temperature monitors, and lighting.

Panel 4: The guidance computer Display and Keyboard (DSKY)

Panel 5: The Commander's timer and lighting panel, with engine start and stop buttons, and the 'ullage' ('+X TRANSL') button.

Panel 6: Abort Guidance System computer keyboard and display (Data Entry and Display Assembly – DEDA).

Panel 7: The ORDEAL: Orbital Rate Display – Earth and Lunar. This was a panel and device that adjusted the attitude indicators to have them track the attitude of the spacecraft relative to the surface below them (think of it showing the horizon in an aircraft). This is in contrast to showing the attitude relative to the stars.

Panel 8: Pyrotechnics (explosive devices) and Commander's intercom.

Panel 11: The Commander's circuit breaker panel. Conceptually the same as housefholdcircuit breaker unit, the breakers on this panel apply or remove power to many of the systems in the spacecraft.

Panel 12: LMP's intercom and radio communications panels.

Panel 14: Battery and electrical power controls.

Panel 16: The LM Pilot's circuit breaker panel. Similar to the Commander's Panel 11. Handles the systems in the LM that are not on the Commander's panel.

Commander started the braking programme, P63, by keying in 'V37' (standing for Verb 37), followed by the number 63, (to initiate Program 63). Knowing the LM's orbit above the Moon, and the location of the landing site, Program 63 worked out how to burn the descent engine to slow the LM in the most efficient way possible.

Interaction with the LM's computer was done through a DSKY keypad interface in the same way as it was done for the CM computer (*see Chapter 3*). Good situational awareness demanded that the astronauts approved each step in the computer's process, so the DSKY would display the information about the upcoming burn for the crew to review and accept, pressing the PRO (for proceed) button on the keypad. So the computer would then display the manoeuvre it was about to make to position the LM to the right attitude (pointing backwards) to fire the descent engine. Once the crew had approved this and the spacecraft had slewed around, the DSKY display would go blank, giving the astronauts time to confirm that they wanted to initiate the powered descent. Five seconds before the burn time, the display would reappear, flashing the Verb 99 and giving the crew one last chance to hit PROceed to approve the engine burn. If after ten seconds no key had been pressed they would have to wait two hours, to try again on the next orbit.

To force any free-floating propellant into the bottom of the tanks, the main engine burn would be preceded by a short burst of thrust from the RCS engines. After a few seconds the main engine would ignite – initially throttling up to an almost imperceptible 10 per cent of its full thrust capacity, whilst it gimballed into position ensuring that it was firing through the LM's centre of gravity. After 26 seconds thrust would then rise to 92.5 per cent of its rated power. The idea of this was to avoid operating the engine between 60 and 92.5 per cent of its full thrust – a range which could cause it the most damage.

This first major engine burn would last about 7½ minutes, slowing the vehicle from 3,750mph down to 410mph, and dropping its altitude to just 10,000 feet. In this time the LM had covered almost 250 miles of ground distance. During this automated braking burn the LMP's job was just to monitor the PNGS and AGS guidance systems, comparing them, with the help of Mission Control, to data from tracking systems on Earth. It was important that these three systems agreed. A discrepancy between any of them could indicate a problem.

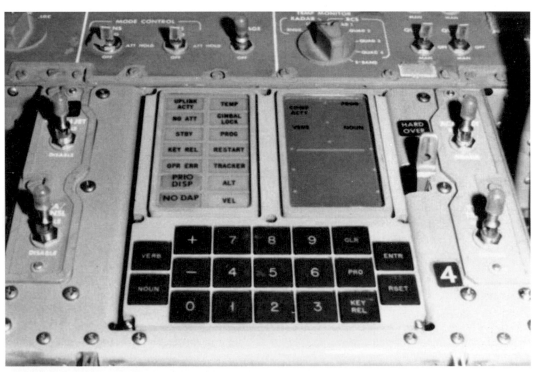

RIGHT The DSKY computer interface inside the Lunar Module. *(NASA/Apollo Flight Journal)*

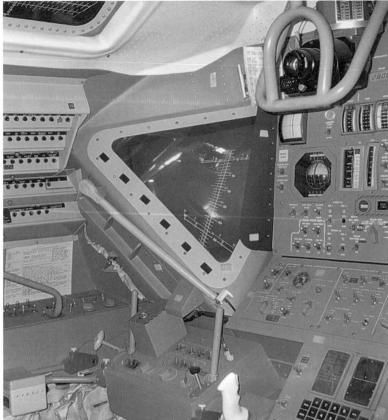

On Apollo 11, the PDI engine burn was started with the astronauts facing the Moon's surface, so they could monitor the timing of landmarks passing below them. But at 40,000 feet altitude the LM rolled over so that the crew were now lying with their backs to the Moon, looking out into space. This manoeuvre was done to give the landing radar mounted in the rear a clear view of the lunar surface.

Up until this point the autopilot relied on the inertial platform to know the LM's position. But in order to get real ground data, the radar now bounced four beams of radio waves off the lunar surface. It measured the Doppler shift of three of the beams to calculate the spacecraft's velocity and the two-way travel time of the fourth beam to work out the spacecraft's altitude. Entering 'Verb 16' and 'Noun 63' into the DSKY would then prompt the computer to display the difference between the inertial guidance data and the new radar results. If the data generally agreed and the computer could still aim for the planned landing site then all was well. But if there was too much of a difference, mission rules called for an abort back to orbit.

Approach (P64)

The landing spots had been picked from maps, robotic orbiter images and ground-based telescopes, none of which had sufficient resolution to confirm that the terrain was smooth and safe enough to land a LM on. So in the final approach, 4.3 miles out and between 9,000 and 8,000 feet up, guidance was handed over to the Commander to eyeball the ground.

To achieve this, the computer, running P64, would tilt the LM into a more upright attitude so that the Commander could see where they were being taken. In this phase of the flight, he had his first opportunity to actually pilot the spacecraft. The Commander's window was etched with graduation markings on the outer and inner panes, called the Landing Point Designator or LPD. By aligning the two sets of markings, he knew he was in the right place for the LPD to work. Then, using the numbers the LMP was calling out, he could identify the position on the ground that the computer was heading for and choose whether or not to let it land there.

With a mere nudge of a control stick, the landing site could be re-designated. The

ABOVE LEFT AND ABOVE LPD markings on the left-hand LM window viewed from inside, on a LM training vehicle housed today at Grumman's Cradle of Aviation on Long Island. *(Frank O'Brien)*

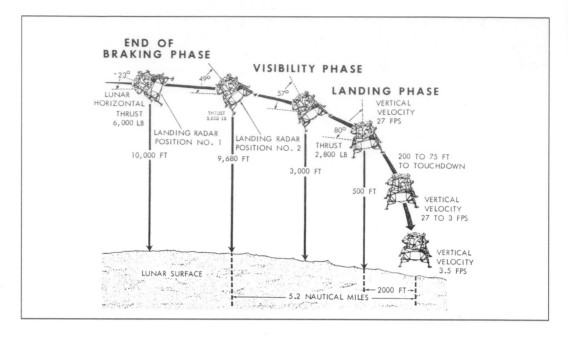

BELOW Neil Armstrong in a Lunar Module simulator. *(NASA)*

computer would then simply update itself with new positional data it had computed. Using this feedback between the human and the computer guidance systems in this way a new, safer landing site could be selected manually by the Commander whilst control of flying the trajectory remained with the autopilot.

At 500 feet above the surface the computer would refuse to accept further changes of landing site, homing in on the latest point the Commander had chosen. P64 was designed to take the craft to a point 500 feet above the final landing site from where the final phase of landing would be conducted.

Terminal descent (P66)

Terminal descent was designed to begin at this point 500 feet above the landing spot, from where the LM's rate of descent could be fixed using a computer programme called P66. In this mode fine adjustments in single feet per second could be trimmed from or added to the descent with another switch on the left-hand controller (the TTCA) and the LM's horizontal position could still be controlled manually with the right-hand controller as in a helicopter. This was a popular feature of LM control with the astronauts, and all six Commanders who landed on the Moon chose to use this mode before the 100-foot point in the descent.

Below 100 feet any lateral motion of the LM needed to be stopped before touchdown to avoid collision with any rough terrain. Although this could easily be achieved by the autopilot, the Commanders were also able to steady the LM manually using the right-hand stick to fire

the RCS thrusters and keeping one eye on the velocity instrument and the other on the surface, listening to velocity call-outs from the LMP. Using the left-hand controller the rate of descent would then be slowed to just a few feet per second. At this point the autopilot would still be maintaining the descent rate and holding the spacecraft attitude that the Commander was setting.

As a further aid to judging distance in this final phase of the landing, approaches were always executed with the Sun behind, to illuminate the terrain ahead and cast the LM's shadow into view as an extra indicator of altitude. The contact light illuminated by the probes extending from the footpads would signal when they were just above the surface and that it was time to shut down the descent engine, letting the LM drop the final 3–4 feet to the surface.

In case the LM had landed at a tilt, the Commander would then take the ACA (attitude control assembly stick) in his right hand out of its 'detent' position momentarily, fooling the autopilot into thinking that the craft was at its desired attitude and stopping the jets from firing to try and keep the spacecraft horizontal.

This hybrid system – perfectly fusing the aeronautical strengths of both the human and the computer in a collaborative touch-down on another world – epitomised the engineering ingenuity which was at the heart of the Apollo programme's triumph.

Apollo 11 – the LM's first landing

As Apollo 10 had proved, even the tiniest mistake in a check list could jeopardise the complicated descent procedure. And so, on 20th July 1969, Neil Armstrong and Buzz Aldrin orbited silently inside LM-5, which they had called *Eagle*, station-keeping not far from Michael Collins, now alone in the Command Module they had called *Columbia*. Two hundred and forty thousand miles away, Flight Director Gene Kranz made his final checks with his team and gave the 'Go'. CAPCOM Charlie Duke, the only point of contact with the astronauts, and struggling to hear them, passed on the message: "*Eagle*, Houston. If you read, you're Go for powered descent."

After a decade of dedicated effort, the pride of a nation and the hopes of 400,000 engineers and 3 billion other people watching from Earth hung on the next 12 minutes.

The braking phase began, dropping LM-5 rapidly towards the Moon. Then, at 33,500 feet above the surface, a computer programme alarm sounded. Armstrong immediately radioed back for advice, his voice tinged with urgency, "Give us a reading on the 1202 Program Alarm." (*For a full analysis of the problem see Chapter 3.*) After consulting back room staff in Houston the alarm

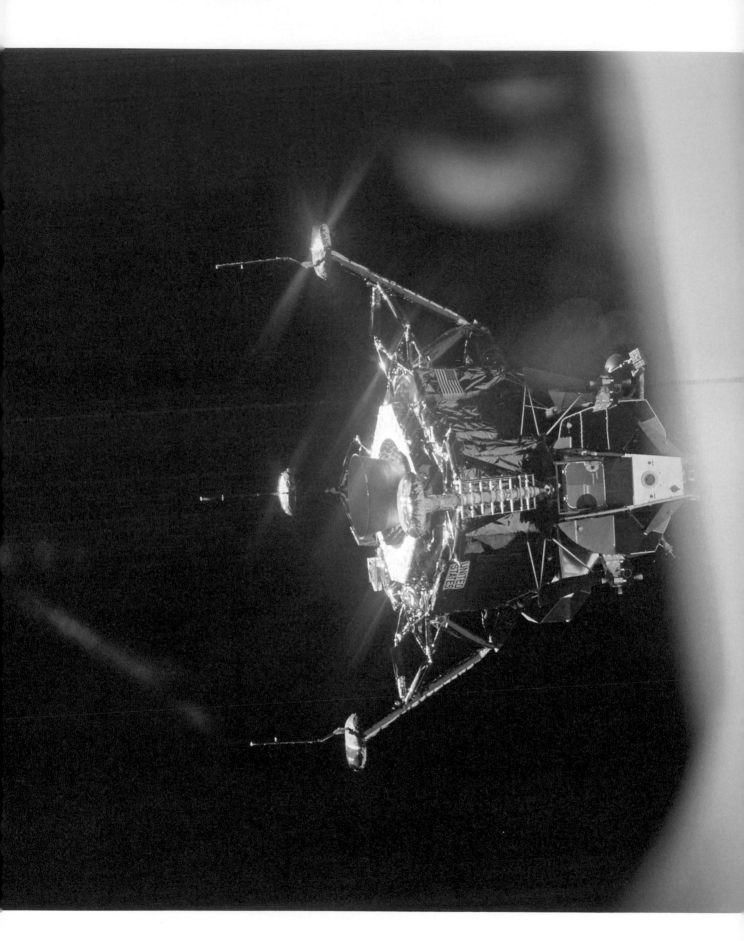

was cleared and the mission was given the green light to continue. Similar alarms recurred five times during the descent but the LM continued to fly as it was designed to do.

At 0,000 foot, as planned, the *Eagle* pitched over, giving the astronauts their first close-up view of the Sea of Tranquillity. Armstrong had studied maps of this terrain fastidiously since his assignment to the mission and knew this area on the Moon better than his own neighbourhood back on Earth. He quickly realised that the LM was not where he was expecting it to be. They were passing landmarks too early and were too far downrange to make the designated landing point.

Despite the earlier alarms Armstrong decided to continue to use the computer to re-target the landing site as he moved it further downrange. Extra propellant had been included in the LM's design to give the Commander a minute of hover time to select a safe landing site more carefully in this way.

But, as they approached the new site, Armstrong realised it was littered with boulders and dominated by a big crater. Holding the

LM's altitude, to slow its rate of descent, he tilted the craft forward to fly further downrange – forcing a new landing point away from the boulders. He did the same again a few moments later, when finding a crater in the new spot. The LM's lateral motion was quite fast – greater than 20 feet per second – causing the velocity cross pointer read-out to hit its limiter. All this extra hover time burnt up more propellant than anticipated and 'fuel' warnings were called out with 60 seconds and 30 seconds left. These time checks were countdowns to the point where mission rules demanded an abort. Later analysis revealed that the lack of baffles in the propellant tank to reduce sloshing were to blame for these fuel call-outs, and in fact significantly more propellant was left when the LM touched down. Anti-slosh baffles was introduced for Apollo 12.

Nine more nail-biting seconds passed as Armstrong cautiously selected his final landing point, tilted the LM back to slow its forward velocity and then throttled down the thrust until the probes on the end of the landing

OPPOSITE The Apollo 11 Lunar Module (LM) 'Eagle', in a landing configuration, photographed in lunar orbit from the Command/Service Modules (CSM) 'Columbia'. *(Michael Collins/NASA)*

LEFT Buzz Aldrin took this photo of the area under the descent stage to document the effects of the engine plume. *(NASA)*

ABOVE Neil Armstrong
photographs the
LM from a distance.
(NASA)

gear pushed into the lunar dirt. "Contact
Light" reported Aldrin. "Shut-down" confirmed
Armstrong, who had planned to shut the engine
down as soon as the contact light came on.
In the event he did not manage to do this,
doubting his recollection of the procedure for
engine shut-down before the footpads made
contact. The descent engine thus remained
running right up to touch-down making the
landing almost imperceptible.

A few lines of technical poetry followed,
confirming engine shut-down, resetting the
autopilot back to automatic, and telling the AGS
that it had landed on the Moon! In response
Charlie Duke radioed back "We copy you down,
Eagle", and Armstrong replied "Houston,
Tranquillity Base here. The *Eagle* has landed."
In this single change of a call sign from '*Eagle*'
to 'Tranquillity Base' the dreams of generations
had been realised.

Preparing for lift-off

In later debriefs Armstrong would admit that
on a scale of one to ten, landing on the
Moon was a thirteen, whilst the climb down the
ladder and the short walk which would follow
was more like a three! But for the Grumman
engineers, and particularly those at the
subcontractors Rocketdyne and Bell who had
designed and built the ascent engine, the most
nail-biting part of the mission was yet to come.

For the primary and back-up (abort)
computers to be able to fire an engine, there
was a manual switching system or circuit
breaker which needed to be turned on. The
breaker had three positions on the LM: 'off'
when no engine could be fired, 'ascent' when
the ascent engine was armed and 'descent'
when the descent engine was armed. During
Apollo 11's time on the surface this circuit-

breaker switch was broken at some point in the process of the astronauts putting on their life-support backpacks and other extra suit protection and then taking it all off again later. There was a solution which involved pressing the abort button and bypassing the broken switch – providing the engine-arming signal through a different route. But instead the crew chose to reactivate the switch by pushing it with a pen. Circuit-breaker guards were fitted to protect these switches for Apollo 12 onwards.

For a successful lift-off several things had to happen simultaneously. Commanding the computer to launch them using Program 12 would ignite explosive bolts holding the upper ascent stage of the LM to the descent stage. It would also trigger a guillotine severing the power cables between stages. And finally it would fire up, for the first time, the 'untested' ascent engine. Everything had to happen perfectly. There was no back-up this time.

For the first time in human spaceflight history the crew would also run their own countdown to the moment of lift-off, independent of Mission Control. Their launch window was defined by Michael Collins in the Command Module passing above them.

At the chosen time Buzz Aldrin began to read out the computer countdown from nine to five, before he resumed his running commentary

"Abort Stage, Engine Arm, Ascent, Proceed," as he pressed PROceed on the DSKY. Flawlessly the two stages separated in a cloud of aluminised Kapton and Mylar debris and the upper stage rose into the black sky. Three hours and forty one minutes of catch-up later and the LM upper stage re-docked with the CM to reunite the crew. After transferring across the first precious rock samples to be collected from the Moon, LM-5's upper stage was jettisoned into lunar orbit. It later crashed back onto the Moon's surface and rests today in an uncertain location, a suitably anonymous monument to the tens of thousands of unnamed engineers who created the first spacecraft to have carried mankind to the surface of another world.

ABOVE Armstrong allows himself a smile of satisfaction once back inside the LM after his historic Moonwalk. *(NASA)*

LEFT The Apollo 11 Lunar Module ascent stage, with Astronauts Neil Armstrong and Buzz Aldrin aboard, is photographed from the Command Module by Michael Collins during rendezvous in lunar orbit. The large, dark-colored area in the background is Smyth's Sea, on the lunar surface (nearside). The Earth is rising above the lunar horizon. *(NASA)*

'This is the goal: to make available for life every place where life is possible. To make inhabitable all worlds as yet uninhabitable and all life purposeful.'

Hermann Oberth
Man into Space, 1957

Chapter 5
The space suits

It is 1966 and Apollo spacesuit engineer Jim Leblanc is standing upright inside a small vacuum chamber at NASA's Johnson Space Center. His colleague Cliff Hess, the supervising engineer running the test, begins to pump the air out of the chamber. The hiss and whirr of pumps and valves signals the danger he is placing Leblanc in as the life-sustaining air pressure which keeps his lungs inflated and his blood from boiling is sucked away. After a few minutes all that is now keeping Leblanc alive is the new Apollo pressure suit he is wearing. Air passes into it through the pair of life-support hoses connected at the front.

Suddenly, without warning, the pressure inside the suit begins to drop rapidly. Over the headset Hess can hear that his friend is in trouble. One of the pipes supplying the suit with air has become disconnected. Leblanc is abruptly exposed to a rapid drop in pressure and his bodily fluids are in danger of boiling. The last thing he remembers is the saliva on his tongue beginning to bubble. Within a few seconds he loses consciousness and topples backwards over a railing breaking the neck ring around the helmet. The fall forces the last bit of air from his suit and his lungs.

At the normal rate of repressurisation it will take 30 minutes to make the chamber safe again, but these are not normal circumstances and Hess now frantically opens all the valves he can to restore the pressure in the chamber as rapidly as possible. This in itself is highly dangerous and risks bursting Leblanc's ear drums. It is another 25 seconds before a colleague from a partially pressurized antechamber can dash in, wearing an oxygen mask, to assist Leblanc. It is another 35 seconds before a doctor can get into the chamber to try further resuscitation. Miraculously, now at the air pressure equivalent of about 12,000 feet of altitude, Leblanc starts to regain consciousness and once the chamber returns to 'sea level' he is even able to get up and walk out. His eyes are a little red and all that hurts are his ears! He is back at work the next day.

LEFT Alan Bean, Apollo 12, carries the ALSEP package away from the LM. The unit's mass is nearly the same as his own, including the suit and backpack, and requires flat-foot walking rather than a more playful loping stride or kangaroo hop. Note the flag and the S-Band antenna to the left of the LM. *(NASA)*

ABOVE An artist's impression of what an Apollo space suit might look like. *(NASA)*

key area of expertise it knew nothing about: space suits. NASA was used to dealing with hard materials and the blueprints and drawings which went with them, but when it came to soft fabrics and cloth stitching patterns it was stumped. The truth was that at the time nobody really knew for sure how to build a space suit which would enable a human to survive and function in the lethal lunar environment.

A company called B. F. Goodrich had been making the suits for the Mercury astronauts but these first iconic silver spacesuits were little more than high-altitude garments – not dissimilar to the suits that US fighter pilots had been wearing since the 1950s. They were coloured silver as much for PR reasons as thermal control and were made to be worn inside a pressurised spacecraft (intra-vehicular activity or IVA). Only in the event of an emergency, if the capsule started to leak, would they fill with air and even then the astronaut would not be required to move very much.

An Apollo suit would need to be very different, allowing the astronaut to move with ease whilst pressurised as he walked around exploring the lunar surface. A pressurised space suit is not unlike a fully inflated dingy which becomes rigid and does not lend itself

Leblanc is one of the few human beings to have lived through exposure to a vacuum. The astronauts who will wear this suit further from home will not be as lucky if theirs develop a leak on the surface of the Moon.

A wearable spacecraft

In the early 1960s, when NASA began training astronauts, it was realised there was one

---

First pressure suits

The world's first high-altitude pressure suit for aviators was patented by Fred Sample in 1917. Three years later, in 1920, British medic John Scott Haldane published a concept for flexible fabric high-altitude pressure suits. It was not until the 1930s that such concepts became a reality. In 1931 a Russian engineer called E. E. Chertovsky took the next step and produced the world's first pressure suit to help aviators with balloon altitude records. But this first effort so severely restricted an aviator's mobility that it never saw service in flight. The same year American pioneer Mark Ridge chamber-tested

a Haldane pressure suit for a balloon altitude record attempt.

US aviator Wiley Post is credited with the first use of pressure suits for high-altitude flight. Post was famous for his record breaking round-the-world flight in 7 days and 19 hours. In 1934 Post came up with an idea for a suit (pictured right) which was both warmed and pressurised from the aircraft engine's supercharger. He persuaded the B. F. Goodrich company to make it for him and in 1934 his third prototype suit successfully supported him in a flight to 40,000 feet above Chicago. Post died in a flying accident in August 1935.

(Smithsonian Institution)

LEFT The Mercury Seven dressed in their trademark silver pressure suits. Note that Deke Slayton's and John Glenn's boots (centre) are not regulation pressure-suit boots – but silver painted work boots, hastily found for the photo shoot! *(NASA)*

BELOW Six X-15 pilots fool around for the cameras – donning their helmets backwards. Their pressure suits are similar to the early space suits above. *(NASA)*

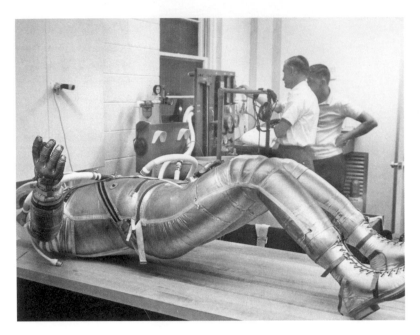

of temperature, radiation, micro-meteorites, potentially sharp and abrasive rocks and lunar dust. In many respects it was required to function like another spacecraft, albeit a soft one that could be worn. While the magnitudes of the challenges ahead were still unknown, NASA realised that an entirely new suit system would need to be developed. And so, in March 1962, it invited tenders from US industry for the first Apollo space suits.

At least eight corporate teams or organisations submitted proposals. These included some well-established aerospace firms like the David Clark Company, which was already making the pressure suits used by NASA's high altitude X-15 rocket plane programme, and B. F. Goodrich, which had been making the Mercury astronaut pressure suits. But there was one company which was better known for bras and girdles than pressure suits. The International Latex Corporation (ILC) had started as a division of Playtex in the late 1940s, and understood the requirements of comfortable garments which supported the human body. It had built its first prototype flexible pressure suit called the XMC-2-ILC for the US Air Force in 1957.

This early suit had no gloves and seemed to be a long way from the requirements of Apollo. But NASA had been impressed with the simplicity of its bellows-like moulded rubber joints which ILC had refined from an early B. F. Goodrich design nicknamed 'tomato worm' after the garden bug which had inspired its convoluted form. Crucially this structure did not change its internal volume when it was flexed – a vital feature for any pressure suit.

In 1962 ILC submitted its latest experimental design (the AX-1L) for the Apollo suit competition and suggested NASA use Westinghouse to provide the life-support backpack. A larger, more established aerospace company called Hamilton Standard had submitted a competing proposal, naming the David Clark Company as its suit provider.

NASA liked the ILC suit best but preferred the Hamilton backpack design. Picking and mixing the competition entries in this way NASA awarded the contract to Hamilton Standard, which would develop the life-support system backpack and oversee ILC's work on the suit,

ABOVE An early pressure-suit test. The suit has been inflated on a test bench, greatly restricting the subject's mobility. *(Smithsonian Institution)*

to flexibility. Complete human mobility would require an elaborate set of pressurised joints in the knee, wrist, shoulder, elbow, ankle and thigh.

In addition to mobility the new Apollo space suit would also have to supply the astronaut with air to breathe, water to drink and even snacks to keep his energy up. It would have to deal with bodily waste and protect him from the harsh vacuum of space, extremes

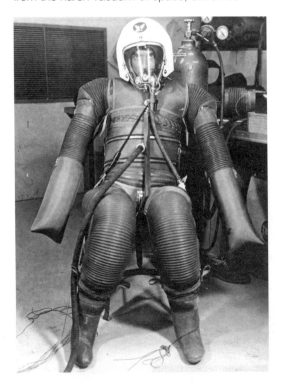

RIGHT An early ILC suit from circa 1955 – demonstrating the rubber convolutes around the elbows, shoulders and legs. A design for a pressure suit glove was still a long way off. *(ILC)*

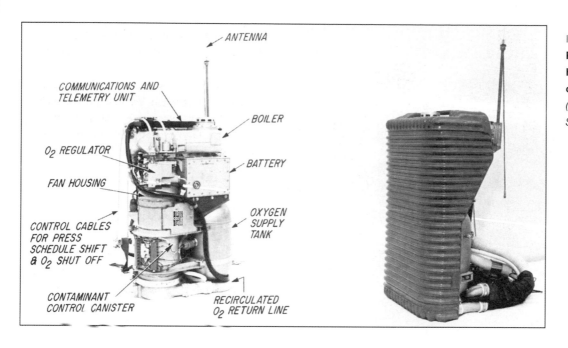

ANTENNA

COMMUNICATIONS AND
TELEMETRY UNIT

BOILER

O_2 REGULATOR

FAN HOUSING

BATTERY

CONTROL CABLES
FOR PRESS
SCHEDULE SHIFT
& O_2 SHUT OFF

OXYGEN
SUPPLY
TANK

CONTAMINANT
CONTROL CANISTER

RECIRCULATED
O_2 RETURN LINE

LEFT The first Apollo PLSS produced by Hamilton Standard, circa 1963. *(Ken Thomas/Hamilton Standard)*

marrying together these two key elements of the Apollo programme.

The seamstresses in the factory at ILC were more used to working on baby clothes and bras so when they were suddenly asked to work on something as prestigious as the Apollo space suits it came as a great surprise. Their new job demanded greater care and attention than any of them had experienced before. It was critical that the seams were consistently sown to within 1/32 inch, which was smaller than the width of a pin. Everything was inspected as it was finished – with the stitches being counted to ensure there was just the right number in each inch of fabric.

ILC and Hamilton were not natural collaborators and it quickly became apparent that their different approaches to engineering clashed rather than complimented each other. With both partners trying to lead the

BELOW LEFT A PLSS interface test at ILC in 1962. *(Ken Thomas/ Hamilton Standard/ILC)*

BELOW Fabricating the A7L Apollo suit in the ILC factory. *(ILC)*

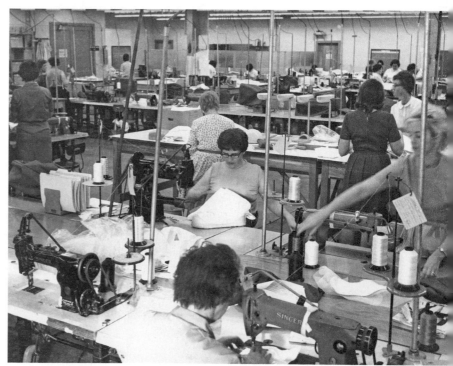

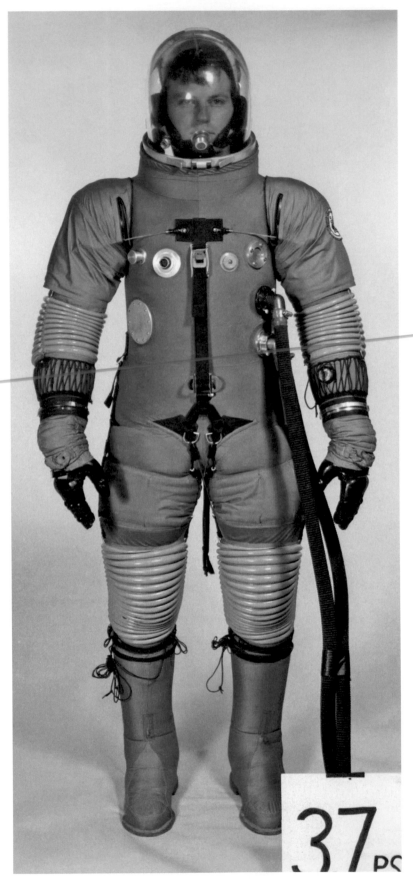

project relations soon started to break down. Complicating this further, the suits that ILC was producing also started to fall woefully short of NASA's quality and technical expectations. In the autumn of 1964, fearing that the Apollo spacesuit would never meet its needs, NASA took the bold step of cancelling the Hamilton contract. Gemini pressure suits looked like they would prove adequate for the first Apollo flights without spacewalks, and so NASA temporarily issued the David Clark Company a suit contract for the first Apollo missions, whilst it set about looking for a longer-term solution.

Once again NASA announced that there would be a competition to find a new design the following year. In July 1965, Hamilton Standard, supported by B. F. Goodrich, submitted a design to compete against a David Clark suit. ILC put in its best effort too. Working day and night and drawing heavily on past experience and research, ILC's design for the AX-5L suit was put together in just six weeks. Unencumbered by the constraints of the earlier contractual partnership, the new ILC design was a great improvement on the 1964 suit, with even greater mobility, a closer fit and narrower shoulders.

ILC's hard work paid off and once more NASA awarded it the suit contract. Hamilton was asked to supply the life-support backpack and this time, to keep the peace, the two companies would work directly to NASA rather than to each other. There was only one year left before their suits would be needed for the first Apollo test flights.

By 1966 the new Apollo suit (now known as the A6L) consisted of three separate garments: a water-cooled layer, a pressurised inner suit with flexible joints, and a white outer garment, made up from a separate slip-on jacket and trousers and finished in a toughened nylon fabric, which provided protection from the extremes of temperature and micro-meteoroids. In addition to these main components there was a lunar boot with a large flat heat-resistant sole to prevent the astronauts from sinking into the soft lunar surface, and a helmet with a series of sun visors to protect the astronauts from the raw glare of the sun. Following the

LEFT The AX5L ILC pressure suit 1965. *(Ken Thomas/ILC)*

Apollo 1 fire in January 1967, ILC redesigned the white outer layer as a single integrated garment. This new Apollo suit which would protect the first men to walk on the Moon was called the A7-L.

Water-cooled garment

In 1963, when NASA had put the space suit through its paces, it had discovered an unforeseen problem. Everyone had assumed that cool air, pumped through the suit from the backpack, would be enough to regulate the temperature. But under test conditions in the lab, suit subjects were becoming dangerously overheated and potentially dehydrated. The problem was so serious that an astronaut risked dying from his own body heat and in October NASA gave Hamilton just two weeks to find a better way of cooling the suits.

Aware of work done on liquid-cooled garments by the Royal Aircraft Establishment in the UK, Hamilton created its own design. It consisted of a loose woven tunic of a spandex fabric to be worn close to the skin. It was criss-crossed with a network of hundreds of feet of tubing through which cool water would flow. From the astronaut's body, the warmed

Water-cooled suits

A design for a cooling suit, which sent cold water around a network of pipes worn close to the body, had first been considered by researchers at the British Royal Aircraft Establishment at Farnborough, to help Spitfire pilots to keep cool when they were sitting in their cockpits in the sun waiting to be scrambled during WWII. By the early 1950s the RAE concept had evolved into a liquid-cooled vest using tubes to take body heat away from the torsos of fighter pilots. Published results of this work found their way to the United States and within a decade teams at both NASA's Manned Spacecraft Center in Houston, and at Hamilton Standard had independently started to use the concept in their own pressure-suit research.

Evaluation testing at Hamilton involved winding polyvinyl tubing around a test subject walking on a treadmill. To make sure he did not lose any heat by sweating he was covered in plastic from head to toe. When the PVC tubes were hooked up to a bucket of iced water it was so effective at sucking heat away from the subject's body that it apparently felt "like jumping into one of the Great Lakes during the winter!" But once he started walking on the treadmill the cooling effect became very comfortable – with no hot or cold spots.

Further refinements of the concept eventually yielded a winning design and Hamilton's new patented liquid-cooled garment became instrumental in the company securing its new 1965 contract to help build the Personal Life Support System backpack for the Apollo spacesuit.

FAR RIGHT AND RIGHT Early evaluation testing of the water-cooled garment concept at Hamilton Standard. *(Hamilton Standard)*

ABOVE AND ABOVE
LEFT **Gene Cernan
has a suit fitting –
trying out the mobility
of his pressure
suit, normally worn
underneath the ITMG.
Note the pulleys
and wires used for
controlling the rubber
convolutes.** *(NASA)*

water would flow into the backpack were it was cooled with a similar sublimator system to the one on the spacecraft – shedding heat by constantly boiling another supply of water off into the vacuum of space from a wet plate that the tubing passed through. Thorough testing showed that this was the ideal system for keeping the astronauts safe from their own body heat, and helped to reassure NASA that the problem could be solved.

The pressurised inner suit

Torso and Limb Suit Assembly – TLSA. ILC's perfected rubber 'convolute' joints could not be beaten when it came to creating an air-filled suit which could still be easily flexed. The tiny ridges allowed the air to compress on either side as the arm- or leg-shaped cylinders flexed at the knee, elbow or ankle joints. To stop them extending, as the convolutes expanded under the air pressure inside, metal cables attached on either side held them under compression without inhibiting movement.

Less movable joints in the neck and waist were also built using the convolute design. Cuff and neck rings attached the pressure suit to the helmet and gloves. By the time they had perfected this crucial pressurised part of the suit, it was flexible enough for a test subject to wear whilst playing American football. It was a

long way from the original rigid pressure suits of just a few years before.

Outer protective suit (Integrated Thermal Micro-meteoroid Garment – ITMG)

To wear above this pressurised suit DuPont came up with a combination of 21 layers of its most cutting-edge hybrid nylon and polyester fibre materials. Some of these layers had tough 'bullet-proof jacket' properties to protect against possible micro-meteoroid strikes and some were made of much thinner reflective Mylar foil for thermal protection, like the skirt on the descent stage of the Lunar Module.

Above these layers, to reflect as much of the Sun's energy as possible, the outside of the Apollo suit was covered in a glassfibre 'Beta cloth' which could withstand temperatures of up to 1,500 degrees. Learning how to work with the Beta cloth was not easy. The first batch was found to be too fragile and the manufacturers had to painstakingly coat each fibre in Teflon to strengthen it. Then ILC found that it could not simply stitch these thermal layers together as that resulted in heat seeping through the holes of the stitching. Instead, they had to be bonded together with specially developed adhesives.

The outermost layer of the suit was a white fire-proof Teflon cloth which also helped to protect against abrasion from rocks and tools.

The entire inner and outer suit would be donned through pressure-sealing zippers which extend from the left side of the waist around the back to the right side of the waist, and diagonally up to the right chest area of the suit. They were difficult for an astronaut to fasten on his own and ideally required a fellow crewmember to zip them up.

Helmet and visor assembly

Perhaps as iconic as the Saturn V rocket, was the futuristic-looking gold Apollo helmet visor; known as the Lunar Extravehicular Visor Assembly (LEVA). This costly gold-plated screen was a crucial component to protect an astronaut's face from the infra-red radiation (heat) and light of the Sun. Looking through the thin veneer of gold gave everything a slightly yellow hue and the lunar landscape a sort of jaundiced appearance. Along with a clear visor and adjustable eye shades at the top and to the sides, the visor assembly was really just a shield for the real helmet which it covered.

The clear domed pressure helmet was the truly futuristic part of the headgear and was made of an extraordinary clear plastic called

polycarbonate which was known for its high impact strength. It was guaranteed proof against hypervelocity micro-meteoroid collisions and impressively in strength tests an engineer could wield a jack hammer at this transparent dome without even chipping it.

Gloves and boots

The human hand has evolved into something of unmatchable dexterity, and protecting it without hampering its abilities was going to require some remarkable engineering. There were more joints to design and build in to accommodate the fingers, thumbs and the wrists than in the rest of the suit together. And, unlike the legs or arms, there was very little

RIGHT A technician
checks lunar boots
during manufacture.
(Smithsonian Institution)

BELOW The 1965
Apollo Hamilton
Standard PLSS
backpack, without
its white thermal
protection covering.
*(Ken Thomas/Hamilton
Standard)*

room to add flexible joints around the hand. It
was said of the Apollo pressure glove that it
would need to combine the dexterity to pick up
a dime with the strength to stop a bullet.

To rise to this challenge, ILC came up with
two gloves in one: an inner single-walled rubber
bladder to fit the crewman's hand, and an
outer over-glove for added thermal and scuff
protection. At first the designers struggled to
find a suitable material to build the outer layers
from but after various permutations they settled
on a brand new material, developed for the
space suits, called Chromel-R. It was like a fine
metal chain-mail weave which flexed enough
not to impair movement and manipulation of
tools, whilst providing the durability needed for
the rigours of lunar exploration. In the
early 1960s this unique material cost $2,000
a yard, a phenomenal cost at the time and
something which the seamstresses were very
conscious of as they struggled to cut and
sew it.

In contrast the lunar boot was a lot easier to
engineer. It used the same Chromel-R material
as the gloves and was actually an overshoe
which the Apollo explorer slipped on over
the integral boot of the inner pressure suit.
These overshoes would have to protect the
astronauts from severe surface temperatures
in the sunshine and ultra-subzero conditions
in the shade. Silicon rubber soles provided
the ultimate comfort beneath the boot but the
outer upper shells of the boots also needed to
be heat-resistant. Elaborate overshoes offering
further protection were fashioned from 15
individual layers of DuPont's finest materials,
ranging from neoprene-coated nylon rip-stop to
more Teflon-coated Beta cloth.

Life-support backpacks

The nerve centre of the suits was their bulky
white Personal Life-Support System (PLSS)
backpacks built by Hamilton Standard. At first
glance they seemed rather large and unwieldy,
but each of them carried the same life-support
capabilities as an entire spacecraft, providing
temperature and pressure regulation, an oxygen
supply and electrical power.

One of the key challenges of the backpack

was to provide the maximum oxygen for the minimum weight and this was achieved with a re-breathing system which used lithium hydroxide filters to scrub the CO_2 from the exhaled air. Hamilton's re-breathe system was at least 20 per cent more efficient than a traditional aqualung. Each pack also contained an emergency oxygen supply which could extend an astronaut's life by 30 minutes if necessary.

The oxygen and water from the backpacks were carried into the suits through hoses which connected to coloured valves at the front of the suit – blue for the inlet and red for the outlet. When inside the spacecraft these connectors also allowed the astronauts to plug themselves into the Command Module or Lunar Module's life-support system. A pressure gauge was fixed to the left wrist for easy checking. Working pressure inside the suit was 3.7–3.9psi which was low enough for the suit to remain flexible whilst high enough to provide the partial pressures of oxygen needed for the astronaut to function.

The suit's temperature was continuously adjusted by the environmental control system,

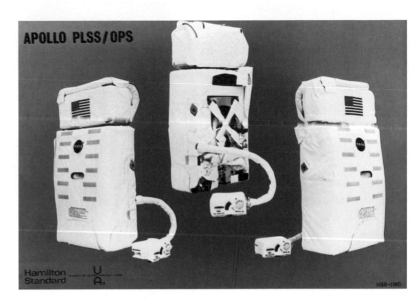

compensating for the astronaut moving suddenly from +154°C in the sunlight to –120°C in the shade, or being very active or standing still. He could control the temperature from a thermostat mounted on his chest. The water cooling proved very effective on the Moon – with astronauts reporting immediate warming or cooling in response to their controls.

ABOVE The 1965 Apollo Hamilton Standard PLSS backpack. Note the temperature controller which is mounted on the astronaut's chest in easy reach. *(Ken Thomas/ Hamilton Standard)*

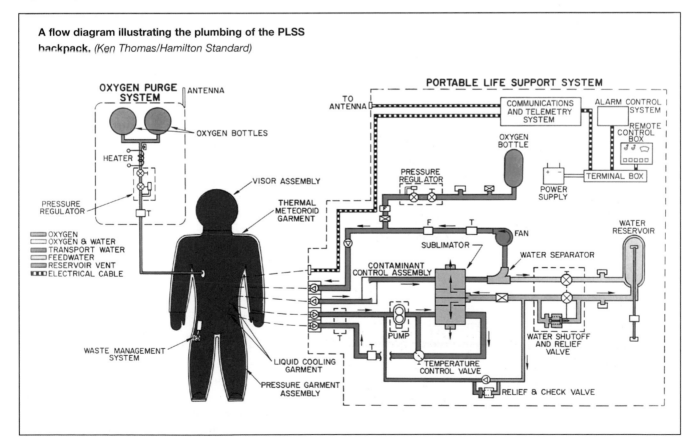

A flow diagram illustrating the plumbing of the PLSS backpack. *(Ken Thomas/Hamilton Standard)*

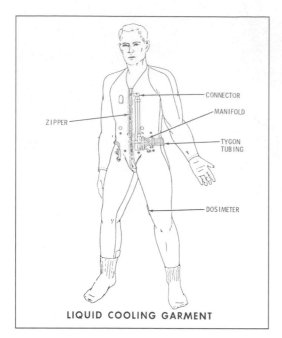

LIQUID COOLING GARMENT

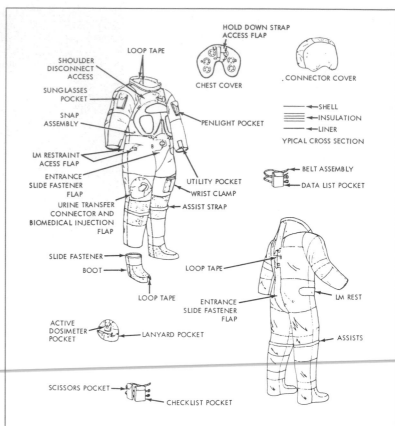

ABOVE The undergarment for the A7L suit.
(NASA)

RIGHT, TOP The Integrated Thermal
Micrometeoroid Garment. *(NASA)*

RIGHT, BOTTOM The Extravehicular Mobility
Unit, helmet and ITMG configuration on a fully
dressed astronaut. *(NASA)*

BELOW Cutaway revealing the convolutes of the
pressure suit worn beneath the ITMG. *(NASA)*

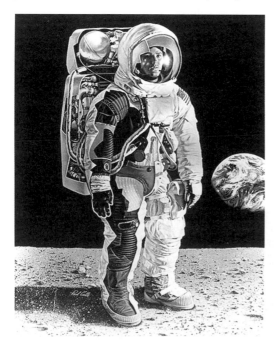

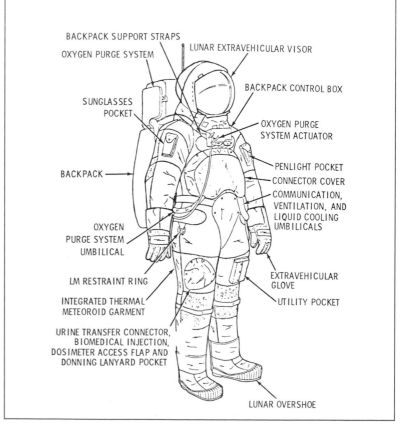

Waste management

ILC, in its capacity as suit provider, was also responsible for what was delicately referred to as 'waste management'. Urine was collected through a condom and channelled down a hose to a one-litre bag worn down one leg. The engineers nicknamed them pee pouches. For solid waste management a nappy was worn under the cooling garment whilst inside the suit, but astronauts were not encouraged to use it in case things got messy and uncomfortable.

Food and drink

During the last three missions the astronauts were out on the surface for over seven hours at a time. They needed to keep their energy levels up and stay hydrated during these strenuous hours of intense physical activity and so the suit designers incorporated drinking straws and fruit bars into the front of the helmets which the astronauts could lean their heads towards and manipulate with their lips. Coincidentally the drinking straws also provided a good way for an astronaut to relieve an itchy nose.

First test flight for the Apollo suit

Following a last-minute mission rotation, the Apollo 9 crew would get the honour of testing the first Apollo spacesuit and PLSS on a mission.

Rusty Schweikart was charged with wearing one, but he had been repeatedly sick earlier in the flight, when he had reacted badly to some decongestants he was using to dry up a cold. NASA considered scrubbing the test for fear that if he threw up again inside the suit he could asphyxiate. But Schweikart's condition improved enough on the fourth day of the mission to conduct a modified test of the suit. After depressurising the Command and Lunar Modules, Schweikart stood up in the Lunar Module hatch while Dave Scott climbed out of the Command Module hatch to take pictures of him. Scott was still plumbed into the Command Module spacecraft for his oxygen but for the first time in American spaceflight history Schweikart was now independent of

either spacecraft, breathing pure oxygen from his backpack and only attached to the LM for safety by a thin nylon cord tether. Cocooned inside the new Apollo suit and life-support system he was the first human satellite and was even assigned his own call sign, 'Red Rover', because of his rust-coloured hair.

With Apollos 8 and 9 accomplished, America was now considered to be several years ahead of the Russians in the Moon race. Barring any accidents on Apollo 10, the next space walk for the Apollo space suit would be to plant a flag on the Moon.

One small step

At 02.56 UT on 21st July 1969, exactly 6½ hours after landing, Neil Armstrong exited the Lunar Module's hatch, crawled across the porch, and dropped down the nine rungs of the ladder to the LM footpad. It had taken him

ABOVE Rusty Schweikart stands outside on the LM porch testing the first Apollo pressure suit to be worn in space. He is the first American astronaut to stand remote from his spacecraft in life-support terms. *(NASA)*

LEFT Neil Armstrong rehearses his first step on to the Moon, during a pressure-suit evaluation test prior to the Apollo 11 flight. *(NASA)*

ABOVE Neil Armstrong on the pad of 'Eagle', just seconds away from his first symbolic footstep on to the lunar surface. *(NASA)*

BELOW Buzz Aldrin stands by the American flag. Closer inspection of this image shows that Aldrin is in fact staring sideways towards the camera to see if Armstrong is still taking the picture. *(NASA)*

BELOW RIGHT Buzz Aldrin stands on the Moon – his cuff checklist raised to check on the mission timeline. *(NASA)*

and Buzz Aldrin longer than expected to don the ILC spacesuits and plumb each other into the Hamilton Standard life-support backpacks. Even squeezing through the spacecraft's hatch had proved trickier than anticipated. But now, with the whir of the life-support systems in his ears and the smell of the suit's fabrics in his nostrils, he stood on the porch, moments away from the most symbolic footstep in human history.

The environmental-control unit on his chest blocked his view of his feet as he stood in view of the black and white TV camera for the world to share this moment. Before stepping off he gave a brief description of the fine powder-like surface. And then, still hanging on to the ladder for balance, he placed his left foot into the powder-like dust declaring it as 'one small step for a man, one giant leap for mankind'.

Buzz Aldrin joined him 17 minutes later and the pair set about describing, photographing and sampling what they found. They had no trouble walking in the suits in the one-sixth gravity. Aldrin tested various methods of locomotion including a kangaroo-style two footed jump and a less strenuous loping hop from foot to foot. Stopping and starting required more concentration, with the astronauts reporting that they needed to plan their movements six or seven steps in advance. The PLSS backpack pulled their centres of gravity back a little, creating a tendency to tip backwards and requiring a slight forward lean when standing and moving. The wire pulley systems in the arms caused their rest position to be slightly raised – giving the characteristic Apollo stance.

The over-optimistic work plan for the surface took longer than anticipated, and at times the crew's metabolic rate rose higher than NASA was comfortable with as they dashed from task to task. Documented sample collecting was cut short and an extra 15 minutes was added to the time line to help them accomplish as much as possible.

After an EVA of almost 2½ hours, both astronauts returned to the Lunar Module, hauling film and rock sample boxes up with them. After they plumbed their life-support circuits back into the spacecraft's system the

Hamilton Standard PLSS backpacks were thrown back onto the surface along with their lunar overshoe boots and other non-essential kit.

Much to everyone's relief at ILC and Hamilton Standard the Apollo spacesuit and PLSS had performed flawlessly – protecting and mobilising the first human beings to explore another world.

Where are they now?

Today, alongside the Mercury and Gemini suits, the Apollo pressure suits suits lie like cadavers in a climate-controlled room at the Smithsonian's depository on the outskirts of Washington DC. Most of the inner pressure suits were made of 70 per cent rubber and 30 per cent neoprene and this mixture has not proved to be a good blend for longevity, with the rubber becoming brittle and starting to disintegrate. From Apollo 14 onwards a substance called 'age right white' was added as an antioxidant but it was later found to be carcinogenic and stopped being used. Harrison Schmitt's Apollo 17 suit has aged the best and its rubber, from an excellent batch, is still in mint condition. For over two decades it was hung on a coat hanger in a display case in New Mexico at an even temperature and low humidity. After 22 years the Smithsonian asked for it to be returned and today it lies with the others in the climate-controlled store. It is the only suit which can still hold pressure, and in that respect is considered to be more precious than Armstrong's suit.

On all the Moon missions, to save weight, it was policy to jettison the PLSS backpacks, helmet visor assemblies and over-boots from the Lunar Module hatch. Consequently only a couple of helmet visors from Apollo 11 and two pairs of boots from Apollo 17 were returned to Earth for study and preservation – making them all the more remarkable.

Studies using MRI and X-ray imaging technology are still revealing lost knowledge about how these miracles of soft engineering were constructed, helping to show the way for the new generation of lunar exploration suits now under development.

take one giant step

The first step onto the lunar surface by Neil Armstrong was truly a giant step... for mankind... for our country's technology in the eyes of the world... and for thousands of individuals in our space industry.

This giant step was made possible through years of effort by a hard-working, dedicated team—people in industrial firms such as those listed below who have assisted ILC Industries during our years as prime contractor to NASA for the Project Apollo space suits.

We congratulate astronauts Armstrong, Aldrin and Collins and the entire NASA-industry team for their outstanding accomplishments. We are proud to be associated with them and we are especially proud of our role in Project Apollo.

ILC INDUSTRIES, INC. 350 PEAR STREET, DOVER, DELAWARE 19901

ABOVE ILC's promotional advertising at the time of Apollo 11, celebrating the historic part they played in the mission. *(ILC)*

LEFT Harrison Schmitt's overshoe, returned from the Moon and still stained with the dust from the Taurus Littrow valley. *(Chris Riley)*

LEFT Neil Armstrong's visor assembly. The gold coating gave the astronauts a yellow view of the lunar landscape. *(Chris Riley)*

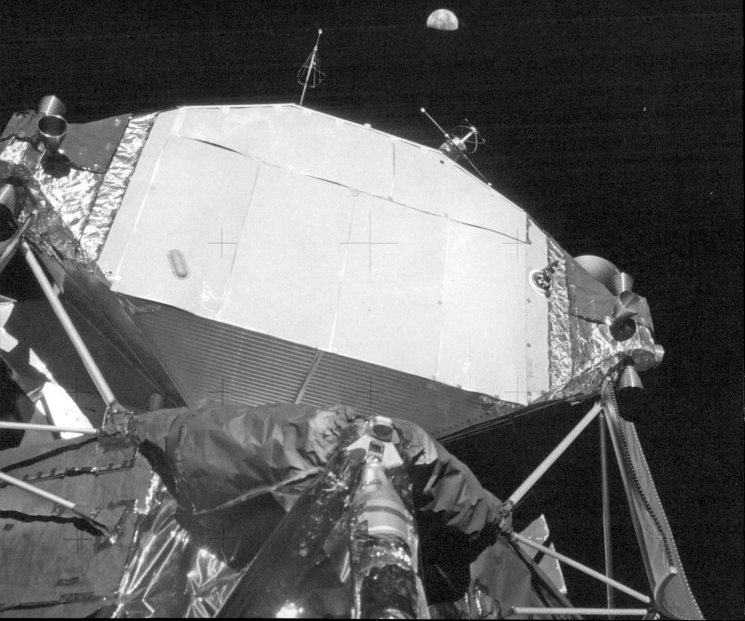

Chapter 6

Communicating from the Moon

It is Sunday 20th July 1969 and the most-watched TV event in world history is unfolding without pictures. On TV sets across the world the first Moon landing is more of a radio event – as the live audio is relayed from lunar orbit to an estimated 600 million people across the globe, accompanied by a series of crude 1960s animations which the broadcasters have designed to convey the mission's progress.

Six and a half hours of news anchor analysis, replays of the landing and informed speculation later, inter-planetary television is about to become a reality as, a quarter of a million miles from Earth, a single camera is switched on.

Cautiously Neil Armstrong is wriggling on his belly down the slight incline of the Lunar Module porch towards the top of the *Eagle*'s ladder. With his left hand he has just pulled a D-ring hanging near by. His action unfurls a panel close to the base of the ladder, upon which is fixed an upside-down black and white TV camera. From his position he cannot see the pale blue marble of his home planet which is high above his head, hanging there in the black sky. But on screens around the Earth his actions have started transmission of a live image from the camera just below him.

At first the image is upside down, with a broad white band of bright over-exposed lunar surface dominating the top and a pitch black under-exposed band of sky below it, inseparable from an equally dark spacecraft and astronaut on the left. Someone at the relay station in Australia flips a switch to reorientate the image top to bottom. An unmoving, dark, shadowy, black and white image is thrown onto TV screens across the world as a silhouetted figure drops down a ladder and into view on the right.

What unfolds next is one of the least spectacular and yet most memorable scenes to be recorded in the 20th century. Whilst picture engineers across two continents try to improve the image, Armstrong describes his limited, but unique view of the Moon's surface from near the base of the spacecraft. The picture improves a little as this first explorer from Earth prepares for the next moment. Armstrong collects his thoughts and steps gingerly towards the

LEFT The 'Eagle' lander sits silently on the Sea of Tranquillity – transmitting the astronauts' voice and telemetry data straight back to Earth, 250,000 miles above. *(NASA)*

159

camera declaring: 'That's one small step for a man, one giant leap for mankind.'

His words are carried up to an antenna on the Lunar Module above him, and then back across the great void to a world hanging on his every word. The estimated 600 million people listening and watching gasp and marvel at the moment and some of them look up in amazement at the Moon, where this historic live outside broadcast is coming from.

For all Mankind

It was an astounding triumph to be walking on the Moon, but a more invisible miracle of Apollo, which most people took for granted, was that the astronauts could talk to each other across the vacuum, hold conversations with their Command Module pilot orbiting 50 miles above their heads and chat to their Capsule Communicator on another planet over a quarter of a million miles away. To accomplish this, an ambitious network of antennae connected by 2 million miles of cables, radio circuits and communication satellites was needed to ensure continual planet-wide contact with the mission.

Beyond these operational communications, there was also the need for the world to watch the historic proceedings on the Moon. After all Apollo was billed as 'For All Mankind' and the

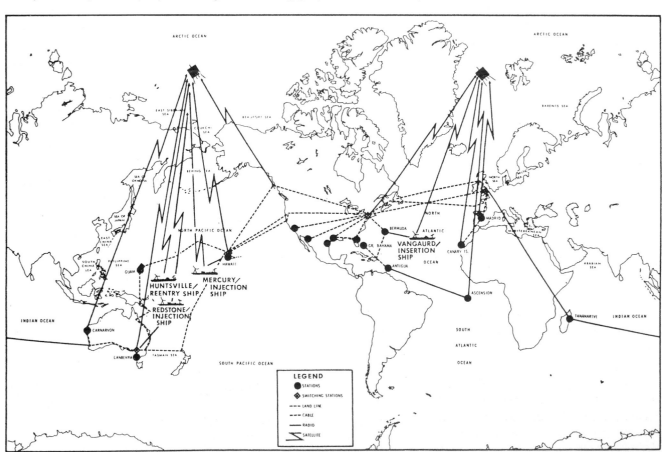

3 billion people living on Earth in the summer of 1969 were keen to share this great endeavour.

Talking across space

Inside the Command Module or the Lunar Module and unencumbered by pressurised suits the astronauts would be able to talk to each other quite easily across the capsule. But when it came to talking to each other from inside their space suits or to Mission Control back on Earth the crew had to wear their characteristic black and white 'Snoopy caps' – housing headphones and microphones. Cables connected these headsets to the main communications nerve centres, housed next to the Apollo Guidance Computer in the CM and either side of the central console in the LM.

The unit on the CM then sent their conversations and other spacecraft telemetry and crew biomedical data to Earth using a high-gain antenna (HGA) mounted on the Service Module and operating in a small frequency window (around 2.2GHz) inside the S-band of the radio spectrum. The HGA consisted of an array of four 31-inch-diameter dishes mounted on a folding arm which deployed from the SM after launch. The crew were in control of pointing these dishes towards Earth, helped by the computer to calculate the pitch and yaw angles needed to locate 'home'. Once they had established lock on a tracking station on Earth, the antenna used its own electronics to help maintain contact.

At certain times during the flight, the HGA was not able to point directly at the Earth and so four omni-directional antennae were fixed around the Command Module to ensure continuous, albeit more limited communications contact with Earth. Through these antennae, transponders onboard the spacecraft allowed a lock with the tracking stations and for ranging – providing accurate distance and velocity measurements.

The Lunar Module also carried its own high-gain S-band antenna (a 26-inch steerable, parabolic dish mounted on the roof) for direct communications with Earth both when it was in free flight and stationary on the Moon.

Back on Earth the Manned Space Flight

Network (MSFN – pronounced 'mis-fin') provided the two-way communications with the Apollo spacecraft. The MSFN had originally been designed to provide near-continuous communication with a spacecraft in low Earth orbit. It consisted of a sophisticated network of 14 ground stations and a fleet of communications ships and aircraft positioned right around the Earth. The ground stations and ships used 30-foot dishes to handle the Apollo signals whilst the ARIA aircraft (Apollo Range Instrumented Aircraft) contained a smaller 7-foot parabolic antenna housed in the aircraft's nose.

For deeper space communications beyond Earth orbit, and to help simultaneous tracking of both the Lunar Module and the Command and Service Modules, three new 85-foot dishes were added to the MSFN at the existing Deep Space Network (DSN) locations in Goldstone

Spacecraft axis and antenna locations for the CSM and the LM ascent stage. *(NASA)*

S-band inflight antenna
Crewmen optical alignment sight
VHF inflight antenna (2)
LM mounted CSM-active docking alignment target
VHF EVA antenna
Two VHF blade recovery antennas under forward heat shield
LM COAS line of sight post pitchover position
Four S-band omni antennas-flush
LM docking light
Drogue
Tracking light

CSM -Y axis
CSM -Z axis
+roll
-X
+yaw
+pitch
CSM +Z axis
CSM +Y axis

-Y
-Z
LM -Y axis
CSM axis
-Y axis
CSM -Z axis
LM -Z axis
LM +Z axis
CSM +Z axis
CSM +Y axis
LM +Y axis
+Z
+Y
60°

S-band steerable antenna
CSM mounted LM-active docking alignment target
RRT antenna
Two scimitar VHF omni antennas on SM (180 deg. apart)
Rendezvous radar antenna

Spacecraft axis and antenna locations for the CSM and the LM ascent stage. *(NASA)*

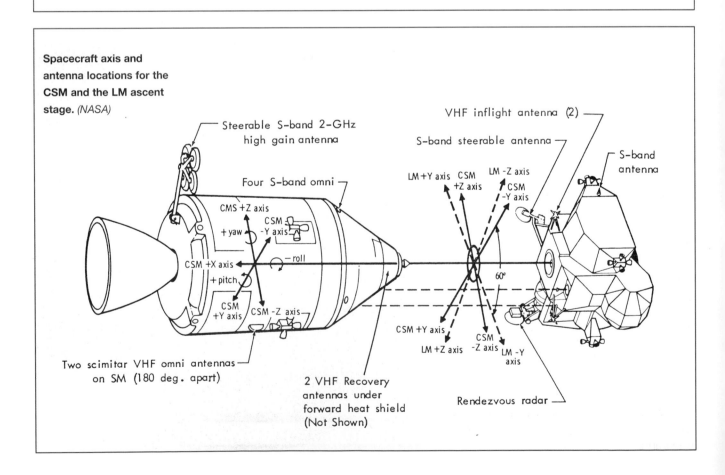

Steerable S-band 2-GHz high gain antenna

VHF inflight antenna (2)
S-band steerable antenna
S-band antenna

Four S-band omni

CMS +Z axis
+ yaw
CSM -Y axis
CSM +X axis
- roll
+ pitch
CSM +Y axis
CSM -Z axis

LM +Y axis
CSM +Z axis
LM -Z axis
CSM -Y axis
60°

CSM +Y axis
LM +Z axis
CSM -Z axis
LM -Y axis

Two scimitar VHF omni antennas on SM (180 deg. apart)

2 VHF Recovery antennas under forward heat shield (Not Shown)

Rendezvous radar

in California, Madrid in Spain and Honeysuckle Creek in Australia. These DSN station locations had been originally picked to ensure that a direct line of sight was always possible with any spacecraft as the Earth turned on its axis during a day. Signals from these ground stations were relayed to Houston through a 2-million-mile network of ground cables, sea cables, microwave links and Intelsat geostationary satellites collectively known as the NASA Communication Network (NASCOM).

NASCOM was managed by the Goddard Space Flight Center in Maryland, which received the voice, telemetry and tracking data before it was sent on to Houston. The Apollo TV signals went direct to Houston for distribution straight to the broadcasters. Two additional 210-foot-diameter dishes at Goldstone and Parkes in southeast Australia were also brought in to help receive the TV pictures, Lunar Module telemetry and voice feeds during the Apollo 11 Moon walk.

In-flight communications between the Command and the Lunar Module were conducted directly between the spacecraft through a couple of VHF (30–300MHz) aerials. By mounting aerials right around each spacecraft the astronauts could speak to each other whatever the relative orientation of the two vehicles.

Conversations from the Moon

Once the Lunar Module had landed and the crew were walking around outside each crewman was effectively now in his own spacecraft in close proximity to another one. And as with communications directly between the CM and the LM, conversations on the Moon would also be conducted over VHF radio – through small aerials mounted on the astronaut's backpacks. These transmitted voice and PLSS data to an aerial on the Lunar Module, which relayed it back to Earth through the LM's roof-mounted S-band dish.

On later flights a separate S-band antenna could be unfurled on the surface and pointed at Earth to provide a better communications link. And on the later J-class expeditions the lunar rover would also carry its own S-band antenna for voice, telemetry and TV communications with Earth.

ABOVE Buzz Aldrin stands with his PLSS backpack to us. A small antenna on the top relays his telemetry and voice data back to the LM for relay back to Earth. *(NASA)*

BELOW The portable high-gain antenna used on later missions to transmit directly back to Earth rather than via the LM. *(NASA)*

The missing 'A'

When it was first replayed back on Earth one of the most famous sentences in history appeared to be missing the crucial word 'a', changing the entire meaning of the carefully chosen words Armstrong spoke as he stepped onto the Moon's surface. Numerous press articles and reports following the crew's safe return to Earth debated the controversy in the months and years which followed, with Armstrong always insisting he had spoken the 'a' and NASA suggesting that perhaps it was somehow lost en route to Earth in the downlink or obscured by static interference.

In James Hansen's 2006 biography of Armstrong the astronaut is quoted as acknowledging that maybe he did get the sentence wrong: "It doesn't sound like there was time for the word to be there. On the other hand, I didn't intentionally make an inane statement, and … certainly the 'a' was intended, because that's the only way the statement makes any sense."

In September 2006 Australian journalist and entrepreneur Peter Shann Ford announced that he had found space for the missing 'a' in the waveform of Armstrong's transmission. Ford concluded that it had originally been spoken too quickly to be picked up and transmitted back to Earth, but this new analysis had still been able to detect the signature of the missing word. According to Ford the 'a' lasted just 35 thousandths of a second, 10 times too quickly to be heard. But the shape of the sound wave, Ford felt, was consistent with the sound made by the tongue, mouth and lips as the speech transitions from the final consonant 'r' in 'for' to the vowel 'a' and on to the opening 'm' in 'man'. Ford concluded that such a pattern would not be present had Armstrong moved straight from the 'r' in 'for' to the 'm' in 'man', as he

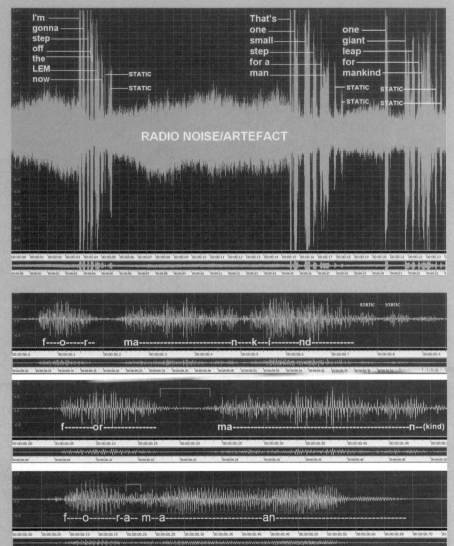

did later, with the phrase 'for mankind' which lacks the signature Shann detected earlier for the 'a'.

Subsequent more detailed analysis of the audio's waveform and spectrogram by other researchers found no such trace of an 'a' within the crackle in the actual 0.075-second gap between 'for' and 'man' and concluded that the audio moves evenly from the 'r' sound to the 'm' sound in the same way as it does for the words 'for mankind'. Whatever the interpretation of the gap between the words 'for' and 'man' the fact is that Armstrong thought the word 'a' even if he did not vocalise it and dropping the odd vowel is not uncommon for

Peter Shann Ford's September 2006 analysis of Armstrong's speech, originally published on his website and subsequently reported around the world. *(Peter Shann Ford/Control Bionics Company)*

someone who grew up and learnt to speak in north-western Ohio, as Armstrong did.

Links to a full account of Ford's work and to further discussions of the issue and spectrogram analysis of the audio can be found on the author's website at:

www.chris-riley.com/one-small-step.htm.

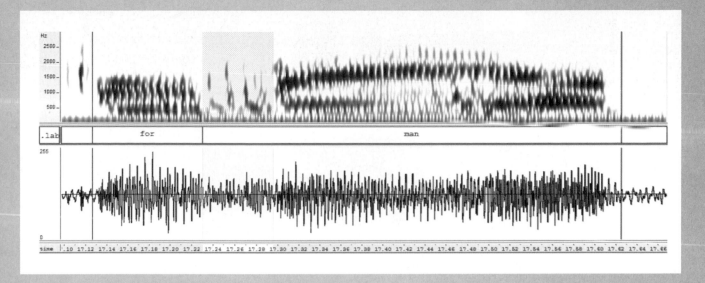

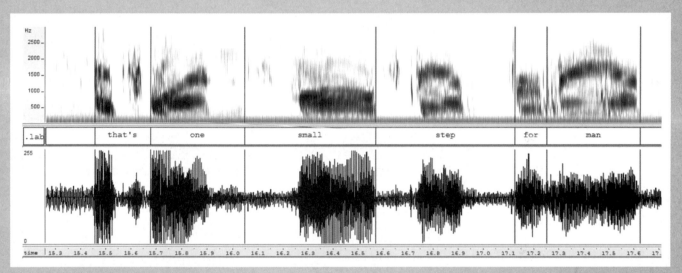

Mark Liberman's subsequent further analysis of the speech as presented on the Language Log website. *(Mark Liberman)*

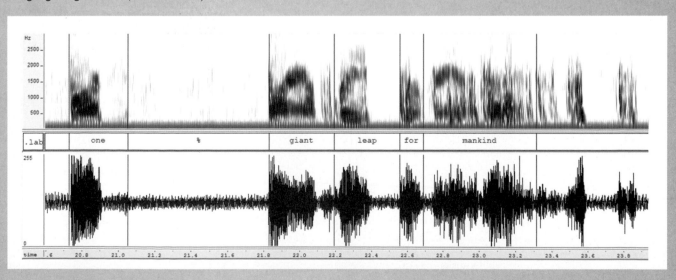

Mission Control

Through countdown and ignition to 12 seconds after launch when the rocket had cleared the tower, control of the mission was handled from NASA's Launch Control Center (LCC) at the Kennedy Space Center in Florida. After notification that the tower was cleared control switched to the Mission Control Center (MCC) in Houston. It was situated in Building 30 of NASA's Manned Spacecraft Center (later called the Johnson Space Center). The main Mission Operations Control Room (MOCR –

Roles at Mission Control and their call signs

FOURTH ROW

1. Director of Flight Operations – Overall responsibility for the mission interface to programme management.
2. MOD – Mission Operations Director was the main liaison between the control room and the upper echelons of NASA running the mission.
3. DOD Rep – Department of Defence representative. Primary interface with NASA for any Department of Defense support required during a mission, including recovery ships and DoD-controlled tracking resources.
4. PAO – Public Affairs Officer provided mission commentary to supplement and explain air-to-ground transmission and flight control operations to the news media and the public.

THIRD ROW

5. FLIGHT – Flight Director served as leader of the flight-control team.
6. INCO – Instrumentation and Communications Systems Engineer, planned and monitored in-flight communications and instrumentation systems configurations for the CSM and the LM. This role also included monitoring the telemetry links as well as voice and video feeds.

7. PROCEDURES – coordinated with launch teams and kept progress notes during the countdowns and 'go/no go' conditions.
8. AFD – Assistant Flight Director. Assisted the Flight Director.
9. FAO – Flight Activities Officer, planned and supported crew activities, checklists, procedures and schedules.
10. NETWORK – directed operational activities affecting the network of ground stations of the MSFN and the RTCC (Real Time Computer Complex) at Houston.

SECOND ROW

11. SURGEON – Flight Surgeon – monitored crew activities, coordinated the medical operations flight-control team, provided crew consultation, and advised the Flight Director on the crew's health status.
12. CAPCOM – Capsule Communicator served as the primary communicator between flight control and astronauts.
13. Vehicle Systems engineers included:
EECOM – Electrical, Environmental and Consumables Systems Engineer, monitored onboard electrical, life-support systems, cabin pressure and temperature control systems and air and water recycling systems.
GNC – Guidance Navigation and

Control Systems Engineer. Monitored all vehicle guidance, navigation and control systems, including the RCS thruster engines and the Command and Service Module's main engine.
TELMU – Telemetry, Electrical, EVA Mobility Unit Officer. Monitored the Lunar Module's electrical and environmental systems, and the spacesuits during the Moon walk EVAs. TELMU was the equivalent of EECOM for the Command Module.
CONTROL – Control Officer responsible for the Lunar Module's guidance, navigation and control systems. The equivalent of the GNC for the Command Module.
EXPERIMENTS – monitored Apollo experiments and the onboard telescopes.

FIRST ROW

14. BOOSTER – The Booster controllers monitored the launch vehicle for the first six hours of the mission. During Apollo there were three booster positions in the MOCR.
15. RETRO – Worked together with FIDO and GUIDO to monitor the spacecraft's trajectory, specialising in abort plans and retro-fire (braking manoeuvre) times. RETRO was also in charge of Trans Earth Injection (TEI) to return to Earth.

pronounced 'moh-ker'), the nerve centre for each mission, was on the third floor.

Two computers in the RTCC (Real Time Computer Complex) at MCC constantly compared the data from the spacecraft to simulations they were running to highlight unexpected variations in the flight. This processed information was also used to update the main mission status board at the front of the MOCR and the individual flight controllers' consoles. The four rows of consoles in the MOCR monitored every aspect of the mission and were broadly divided into three groups:

Mission Command and Control, Systems Operations and Flight Dynamics.

The first row, known as 'The Trench' consisted of four controllers – BOOSTER, RETRO, FIDO and GUIDO. At the second row consoles SURGEON, EECOM and CAPCOM were seated at one side and the TELMU and CONTROL people on the other side along with EXPERIMENTS. The third row housed INCO, PROCEDURES, FAO, AFD, FLIGHT and NETWORK. In the fourth row were the consoles for PAO and NASA management, including the Director of Flight Crew Operations or the 'chief

OPPOSITE A view of the Mission Operations Control Room, during the fourth television transmission from Apollo 13 while *en route* to the Moon. Eugene F. Kranz (foreground, back to camera), one of four Apollo 13 Flight Directors, views the large screen. *(NASA)*

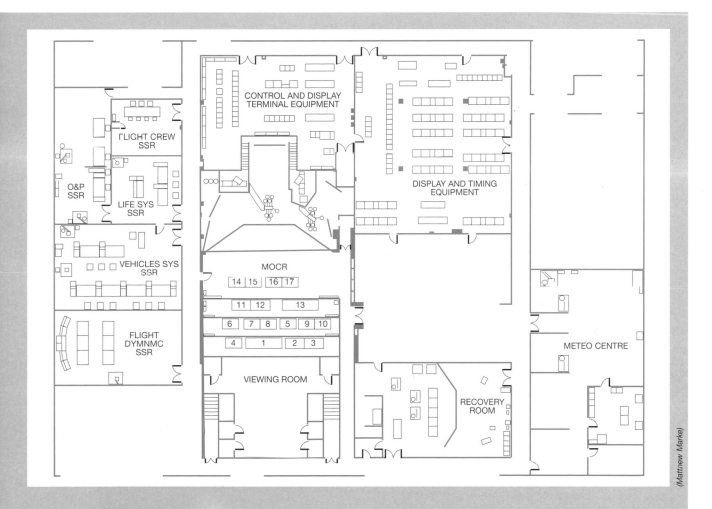

(Matthew Marke)

16. FIDO – Flight Dynamics Officer (FIDO or FDO) was responsible for the flight path of the space vehicle through the Earth's atmosphere and space. FIDO monitored vehicle performance during powered flight and assessed abort possibilities. He calculated orbital

manoeuvres and resulting trajectories for both lunar landing and Earth re-entry.

17. GUIDO – or Guidance – Guidance Officer, ensured that the onboard navigation and guidance computer software on the Command Module

was on track and monitored the spacecraft's position in space right down to the surface of the Moon.

18. Maintenance and Operations Supervisor – was responsible for the performance and status of the Mission Control Center equipment.

astronaut' a position first held during Apollo by Mercury astronaut Deke Slayton.

Backing up each man in the MOCR was a further series of seven Staff Support Rooms (SSR) which housed more people to support each system – Flight Dynamics, Vehicle Systems, Life Systems, Flight Crew, Networks, INCO, and Science Experiments. The engineers and scientists in these back rooms were themselves backed up by groups stationed around the country, often at the offices of the contractors and subcontractors who had worked on the many Apollo systems. Together this large team could provide quick responses to any situations which arose – keeping the Flight Director informed of events and, through CAPCOM, the astronauts too.

The Apollo beeps

When it comes to icons of Apollo, the audio equivalent to the Saturn V has to be the signature 'beeps' which punctuated the astronauts' conversations on each mission. They were not, as some might think, a tonal version of the human voice radio call sign 'over', but a simple way of switching the voice loop on or off. Known as 'in band signalling' the beeps, invented by a company called Quindar, avoided the need for an extra circuit to carry this on–off information. In band signalling is still in common use today

and can be heard when you dial a phone number on a modern telephone which uses the same circuit as the voice to carry a tonal signal for each dialled number 0–9 to instruct the switching system where to route the call.

On Apollo the Quindar tones were only triggered from the ground by CAPCOM pressing his 'push to talk' (PTT) button. The quarter-second 2.525kHz tone would operate an electronic circuit which switched the voice line into the subcarrier signal which was constantly streamed to the spacecraft. When he had finished speaking and released the PTT button another, slightly lower, 2.475kHz quarter-second tone would disconnect the voice line from the subcarrier. These tones were designed to be filtered out before the astronauts heard them, although in practice they sometimes leaked through for various reasons.

For periods when astronauts' speech aboard the spacecraft was not transmitted live to Earth an internal data storage tape recorder made by the Leach Corporation recorded biosensor telemetry and conversations. This data and voice record was subsequently dumped back down to Mission Control for later transcription and analysis.

TV from the Moon

With the voice, spacecraft telemetry and biomedical data pouring down Apollo's S-band communications channel there was little bandwidth left for the TV pictures. But then TV was not a top priority for NASA when the communications were being designed.

Television coverage of the Moon landings had first been raised in 1964 when the 500kHz frequency had been set aside for carrying the TV signals from the lunar surface. An RCA black and white slow-scan TV camera was initially developed for the Apollo programme, scanning at 320 lines and 10 frames a second. The Apollo 7 crew would become the first to use it. From the start Commander Wally Schirra was reluctant to try it out – preferring to concentrate on the engineering goals of the complex CSM's maiden manned flight, rather than complicate things further with more 'trivial' live TV transmissions. In the end, and under

BELOW Apollo 8's live TV camera transmission of their view of the Earth. *(NASA)*

strict orders, the crew did make seven short broadcasts from orbit.

In contrast, the Apollo 8 crew did not need much persuasion to use their TV camera from lunar orbit and the world tuned in to their 1968 Christmas broadcasts in millions. By 1969, Westinghouse had come up with a new colour Apollo TV camera and Apollo 10 Commander Tom Stafford insisted that it be test-flown on his mission. The broadcasts proved to be so good that the team received an Emmy award!

The new Westinghouse colour camera had proved it was ready for the historic first Moon walk but one insurmountable problem remained. During landing and the first EVA voice and biomedical signals would occupy all the available bandwidth. To get live colour pictures back from the surface of the Moon would need its own separate S-band antenna and by the time Armstrong and Aldrin deployed this equipment, no one would have seen their first steps!

The first historic step onto the Moon had to be a live TV event and attention turned to a new black and white camera which was able to do the job. Westinghouse had spent five years space-rating it for recording events from the harsh environment of the lunar surface. It used what was called a Secondary Electron Conduction (SEC) tube which had been developed for image intensifiers in the Vietnam War and was ideally suited to the combination of very intense shadow and bright sunlight of the Moon's surface.

All that was holding back the decision to use it was the issue of the extra weight it added and the technical challenge of converting its slow-scan 10fps pictures to the faster 30fps of interlaced pictures for the TV channels to broadcast. The weight problem was resolved when NASA management simply insisted that it was flown! The scan conversion was harder to solve, and involved an elaborate and expensive state of the art unit costing $350,000 in 1969 money. It worked using a vidicon camera pointing at a green-and-white monitor which displayed the live slow-scan image from the Moon. To turn 10fps into 30fps of interlaced pictures (that is 60 separate images) for broadcast on TV, each frame from the Moon was recorded onto a video disc and then replayed five more times, making a total of six identical images for every one from the Moon.

It worked fine when there was little movement on the screen, but when the astronauts moved too fast the image became smeared and ghostly due to an image lag effect in the vidicon and the repeating frames that the scan convertor was generating. On the slow-scan TV that was coming direct from the Westinghouse Moon camera, there was no ghosting or image lag.

Filming Apollo

It was fortunate for historians, film makers and future generations that Apollo happened when it did, when 16-mm film was still in vogue, and before the emergence of the first crude

ABOVE **Neil Armstrong floats in the tunnel connecting the LM and CM, using the Westinghouse color TV camera to document Buzz doing a LM inspection. An extra TV monitor is attached to the camera with tape to aid filming.** *(NASA)*

BELOW The flag ceremony on Apollo 11 as relayed back to Earth from the surface TV camera. *(NASA)*

169

COMMUNICATING FROM THE MOON

Why the TV picture was so bad

At the start of the Apollo 11 Moon walk, both the Goldstone dish in California and the Australian Honeysuckle Creek and the Parkes dishes were receiving the TV signal. The Australian signals travelled by Australian Postal Service microwave link to Sydney where the best signal was selected to be sent on to a satellite ground station 375 miles north. This transmitted it up to an Intelsat III geostationary satellite 22,000 miles above the Pacific, and back to a ground station in California, and finally via AT&T land line to Houston.

As the Lunar Surface Camera was switched on both the Goldstone and Honeysuckle Creek stations started to receive video. After Goldstone's reverse switch was flipped, inverting the image from its original upside-down state, it became clear that the picture coming from Goldstone to Houston was very dark with Armstrong barely a silhouette against the dark sky. From a Polaroid still picture taken at the time it is also clear that the picture Goldstone was receiving was well exposed – Armstrong's white suit is clearly defined – but somewhere within the conversion equipment which sent the picture on to Houston there was a problem which was darkening the image. Even so Houston continued to distribute the darkened image to the broadcasters and was recording it for posterity onto 2-inch video tape and 16-mm film.

Meanwhile at Honeysuckle Creek a good image was also being seen and a few seconds into the broadcast Australian TV decided to switch to the clearer Honeysuckle Creek signal rather than continuing to take the poorer one it had been getting from Goldstone. Fifty-five seconds later Houston also selected Honeysuckle's signal for distribution

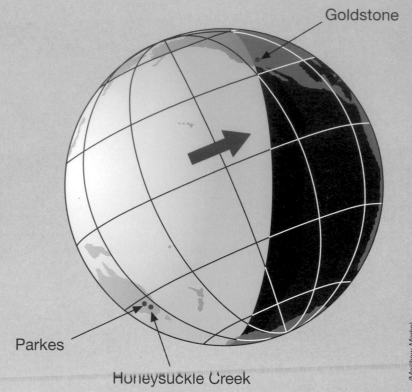

Goldstone

Parkes

Honeysuckle Creek

(Matthew Marke)

to the broadcasters, just before Armstrong took his first step. As the Earth continued to turn, nine minutes into the Moon walk, Sydney Video announced that it had an excellent picture from Parkes and Houston started to take the Parkes feed which it then stayed with until the end of the Moon walk.

As standard practice, Honeysuckle Creek, Parkes and Goldstone also recorded the signals direct from the Moon onto large 9,200-foot reels of 1-inch magnetic telemetry tape. These tapes recorded everything on the downlink from voice, biomedical and LM system data to the slow-scan TV pictures. Sadly, in the decades which have passed, these superior slow-scan TV recordings of the whole Moon walk from Parkes, Honeysuckle Creek and Goldstone have since been misplaced by NASA. Researchers were reminded of their higher quality in 2003 when Polaroid pictures of the screens in Australia were rediscovered. In 2005 unique Super 8 film footage shot by engineer Ed von Renouard at Honeysuckle also emerged, further fuelling the interest in the superior Australian recordings. The reels of tape are presumed to be stored somewhere at NASA's Goddard facility in Maryland and the search for them continues.

For more information on this story please visit the Honeysuckle Creek website: http://honeysucklecreek.net/Apollo_11/index.html.

(HoneysuckleCreek.net)

(Matthew Marke)

home video cameras, whose recordings would have been of much poorer quality. But NASA's priceless film record of mankind's first forays to another world was not intended for any 'media', PR or posterity reasons. The Maurer 16-mm cameras used onboard the missions were termed Data Acquisition Cameras (DACs) and designed for recording the performance of spaceflight hardware and experiments. From inspection of the undocked Lunar Module, filmed from the windows of the Command Module, to the dramatic views from the Lunar Module's right-hand window during landing, astronauts carefully followed instructions in the flight plans which told them when to use the movie cameras.

Thankfully these documented filming opportunities were not the only times the DACs were used. Crews were free to make more informal use of the cameras as well and often recorded scenes of life on board the spacecraft and views of the Earth rising above the lunar horizon. More than 20 hours of 16-mm film was shot on the Apollo flights, and then preserved back on Earth under liquid nitrogen for posterity. It has only been brought out of cold storage and thawed out a handful of times since it was shot and remains in mint condition.

The Saturn V launch footage on the ground was similarly recorded on 16-, 35- and even 70-mm cameras for engineering purposes; this was intended only to be of any real interest should the rocket malfunction during ignition and lift-off. For the first few unmanned Saturn 1B and Saturn V flights (Apollo 202–Apollo 6) 16-mm engineering cameras were also carried into space to record close-up views of staging. Positioned and timed to switch on moments before these key flight moments, the images they captured provided spectacular onboard views of the Saturn in space with stages falling away and others igniting and flying on further. These films were catapulted out as their final frames ran through the camera shutter and then parachuted back into the Atlantic Ocean for later retrieval. Many were lost but a handful were successfully recovered, providing some of the most iconic footage of the 20th century.

RIGHT A sequence showing the separation of the first and second stages of the Saturn V during the unmanned Apollo 6 mission in April 1968. *(Getty Images)*

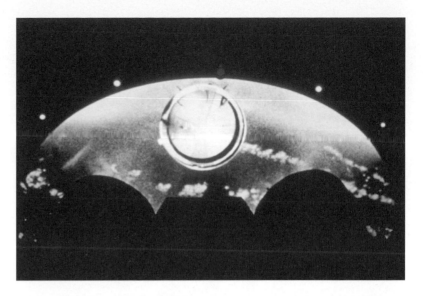

'As we leave the Moon at Taurus-Littrow, we leave as we came and, God willing, as we shall return, with peace and hope for all mankind. Godspeed the crew of Apollo 17.'

Eugene A. Cernan
Apollo 17 Commander

Chapter 7

Beyond Apollo 11 – the J-class missions

![bar graphic]

Letters from Charles Lindbergh, in 1927 the first man to fly solo across the Atlantic, were carried to the Moon on board some of the Apollo missions. The great aviator spent an evening with the Apollo 11 crew before their own historic flight, but even by 1969, when commercial flights across the Atlantic were far less common than they are now, the names of the second, third or fourth people to cross it solo were already forgotten. Had we continued to fly to the Moon after the early 1970s, Apollos 12–17 might also have been relegated to the status of 'just more solo flights across the Atlantic', with little place in the popular recollection. But when the Apollo programme was stopped in 1972 and human spaceflight got caught in Earth orbit in the decades which followed, NASA's six moon landings stood alone.

Just 24 men in all of history had flown to the Moon and only 12 of them had landed there and walked on its surface. Each of these nine incredible voyages from the Earth to the Moon deserves its own book recalling the equally extraordinary stories of engineering triumph and tribulation which enabled them to happen. Each new Apollo flight pushed the boundaries just a little bit more – flying crews to the Moon on more powerful Lunar Modules which carried more equipment and supplies than the previous flights, to more challenging landing sites.

Such breakthroughs allowed the last Apollo astronauts to call the Moon their home for three days, living and working in its mountainous highlands and even travelling across its spectacular lunar terrain in an extra-terrestrial wheeled vehicle. And thanks to live colour TV coverage, Apollo would end in the way it had started with the world marvelling at mankind's ultimate extra-terrestrial adventures.

LEFT Gene Cernan, commander of Apollo 17 stands in the Taurus Littrow Valley – the last man to walk on the Moon in December 1972. *(NASA)*

BELOW Astronaut Harrison H. Schmitt, Lunar Module Pilot, works near the Lunar Roving Vehicle (LRV) during the third Apollo 17 extravehicular activity (EVA-3) at the Taurus-Littrow site. *(NASA)*

Only four Christmases passed between the first reading of Genesis from Lunar orbit onboard Apollo 8 and the last words spoken from the Moon (quoted on page 172) on Apollo 17. But the inspiration these fleeting years bestowed upon the generation who lived through them would ripple on through the decades to come, inspiring many of the engineering innovations and technological triumphs which we all enjoy today.

The Moon shot masterplan

It was June 1966 when NASA had first thrashed out its operational plans for Apollo's human exploration of the Moon. The A-class missions would be the unmanned Command and Service Module flights; the B-class missions the test flights of the unmanned Lunar Module; the C-class missions would be manned low-Earth-orbit CSM flights; the D-class missions

the manned CSM and LM low-Earth-orbit flights; the E-class missions the manned CSM and LM high-elliptical Earth-orbit flights; and the F-class missions the manned CSM and LM flights to lunar orbit.

Not until the G-class missions would the first lunar landings be attempted. H-class flights would make further relatively basic lunar landings with two Moon walks. Finally the I and J missions would be enhanced lunar orbit (I) and lunar landings (J) flights, carrying more scientific equipment for longer expeditions which involved up to three Moon walks and a lunar roving vehicle to carry the explorers further.

Things first began to change after the setbacks of the Apollo 1 fire in January 1967 when, in order to catch up, NASA decided to accelerate its unmanned test-flight programme, allowing the first C-class mission – Apollo 7 – to take place in October 1968. Pressure from the Soviets meant that NASA promoted the next flight – Apollo 8 – to the status of an F-class mission. But with Grumman unable to deliver a fully functioning LM in time, this F-mission in December 1968, flew with just the CSM, and was re-designated as a C-prime class mission. It was followed up the following spring with a D-class mission – Apollo 9 – to test the CSM and LM in Earth orbit. Apollo 9 was such a success that the E-class missions were cancelled and Apollo 10 became an F-class test flight of the CSM and LM in lunar orbit.

This switch-around of missions also inadvertently dictated who would become the first man to walk on the Moon. Instead of the Apollo 9 backup crew, commanded by Pete Conrad, becoming the first G-class lunar landing attempt on Apollo 12, this task would now pass to the Apollo 8 backup crew, commanded by Neil Armstrong, who would now rotate into position as the prime crew for Apollo 11, with crewmates Buzz Aldrin (LMP) and Michael Collins (CMP).

The success of Apollo 11 opened up the potential for the first H-class mission the same year, with Apollo 12's extended two-Moon-walk flight taking place in November 1969. NASA's plans beyond this were for Apollos 13–17 to make further H-class flights and Apollos 18–20 to become the final J-class missions.

Following the near-disaster of Apollo 13 in the spring of 1970, NASA came under

ABOVE Apollo astronauts and Soyuz 9 crew at a backyard party: (left-to-right) Armstrong, Aldrin, Anders, Nikolayev, McDivitt, Conrad, Cunningham, Stafford, Swigert, Gordon, Schweickart, Scott, Lovell, Slayton, Sevastyanov. *(NASA)*

LEFT Neil Armstrong, CDR Apollo 11. *(NASA)*

LEFT Mike Collins, CMP Apollo 11. *(NASA)*

LEFT Buzz Aldrin, LMP Apollo 11. *(NASA)*

pressure to cut back the programme. By the autumn of that year the final three missions had been cancelled with some of their ambitions incorporated into the remaining flights. Apollo 14 would remain as an H-class mission (with two EVAs) whilst the final Apollo missions 15–17 would now become three-day J-class missions.

Apollo 12–14

Just four months after Apollo 11, Pete Conrad, Dick Gordon and Alan Bean headed off once more to the Moon on Apollo 12. The Commander's personal goal, and one which NASA also embraced, was to make the first pinpoint Moon landing at a designated site in the Ocean of Storms, near to an earlier robotic spacecraft called Surveyor III.

Conrad and Bean achieved this goal, and even made it look easy, perhaps helping to drive away public interest in their mission, which some of the public saw as a pointless re-run of Apollo 11. Kennedy had only called America to land a man on the Moon and return him safely to the Earth. With this goal now accomplished what was the point in repeating it again with

the risks and costs associated with such a flight? Apollo 12's colour TV camera was also damaged during deployment and without live pictures public interest in the programme was further dented. Curiosity was briefly rekindled when an explosion on Apollo 13 put the lives of the crew at risk in April 1970. A mixture of luck, the ingenuity of the mission controllers and stoic resilience from the crew eventually returned them safely to Earth, in what many dubbed NASA's finest hour.

The programme's return with Apollo 14 attracted enormous interest from the public again, with over a million people turning up at the Cape to watch the launch of America's first spaceman, Alan Shepard, and his rookie crewmates, Stuart Roosa and Edgar Mitchell. On board their improved spacecraft they headed for the original Apollo 13 landing site in the Fra Mauro Highlands.

After separating from the CM in lunar orbit the LM suffered two serious problems. First the computer insisted on trying to abort the landing due to a faulty switch. The computer programming team at MIT hurriedly wrote a software patch to work around the problem and read it up to Mitchell to enter manually.

RIGHT Charles Conrad Jr, Apollo 12 Commander, examines the unmanned Surveyor III spacecraft during the second extravehicular activity (EVA-2). The Lunar Module (LM) 'Intrepid' is in the right background. (NASA)

NASA's finest hour

When James Lovell, Jack Swigert and Fred Haise embarked on the third voyage from the Earth to the Moon on the 11th April 1970, the world was not paying much attention to what was beginning to look routine. But almost 56 hours into the mission, and over 200,000 miles from Earth, a routine operation to stir the cryogenic oxygen tanks resulted in one rupturing violently (explained in the CSM chapter). This shut down two fuel cells and began to leak oxygen into space. With time running out, the crew's only hope was to retreat to the Lunar Module, which carried its own supplies of oxygen. Thankfully the incident had happened at a time when the two spacecraft were still on what was known as a free return trajectory, where the Moon's gravity alone would sling shot them back towards the Earth.

Apollo 9 had even rehearsed a technique for using the LM, as a sort of lifeboat, steering the two craft using its descent engine. But whilst these broad concepts had been rehearsed the intricacies of such a rescue had never been worked out completely.

And the big question at this point was how long it would take to get the crew home. The LM was only designed to keep two men alive for 50 hours or so, but it would now need to keep three men alive for more like 100 hours. By firing the descent engine on the far side of the Moon the crew were able to accelerate their return speed back to Earth, cutting the journey time down by 12 hours. But that was still not fast enough.

Carbon dioxide levels soon started to rise, as the LM's lithium hydroxide air scrubbers began to wear out. There were unused scrubbers on the CM, but unfortunately they were packaged in square cartridges whilst the LM cartridges were cylindrical. A hurriedly assembled 'tiger team' at Mission control came up with a way of making the different shaped CSM cartridges fit into the LM using duct tape and tubing from the space suits which they had onboard to jerry-rig a connection.

Electrical power was also a problem. So to eek out the life support systems on the LM longer than they were designed for, all non-essential systems were powered down, leading to conditions on board quickly becoming very cold and life rather uncomfortable and miserable. With no power to make automated mid-course corrections the crew reverted to manually steering the two spacecraft. Quickly learning to fly all over again and using their wrist watches to time engine burns and the view of the Earth from the window to monitor their trajectory, mid-course corrections were successfully accomplished, placing them on track for re-entry at the desired spot.

As Apollo 13 neared the Earth the crew returned to the

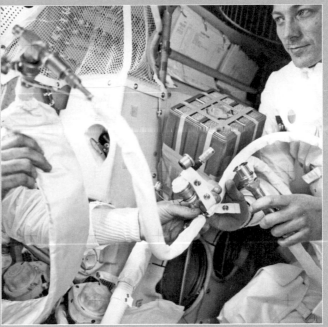

(NASA)

CSM and powered it up again for re-entry. The LM was ejected and soon afterwards the crippled service module, too, giving them their first view of the extent of the damage which the oxygen tank rupturing had caused. The usual tension of re-entry was heightened by concerns that the heat shield might have been damaged in the accident. The interminable wait during radio black out was rewarded when Apollo 13's parachutes were spotted from the deck of the recovery ship *Iwo Jima*.

When President Nixon later presented the crew with the Presidential Medal of Freedom he spoke of the way their peril had united the world: "…never before in the history of man have more people watched together, prayed together, and rejoiced together at your safe return, than on this occasion… You did not reach the moon but you reached the hearts of millions of people on Earth by what you did."

(NASA)

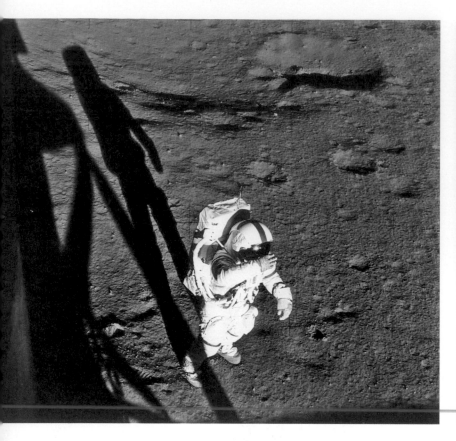

The descent continued until the LM's radar
altimeter began to cause problems when the
new software patch prevented it from locking
on to the Moon's surface. This second problem
was cured by switching the radar on and off and
Shepard went on to land the LM manually closer
to its target than any other mission before it.

On the surface Shepard and Mitchell made
two EVAs, in which they walked further from the
safety of the LM than any crew before. On one
excursion to Cone Crater, pulling a two-wheeled
experiment trolley called the MET (Mobile
Equipment Transporter), the pair became lost in
the monotonous undulating terrain and eventually
had to turn back before reaching their final
destination. On future missions, using the Lunar
Rover, better navigational aids would be added.

Apollo 15–17

O n 31st July 1971 when Apollo 15
Commander Dave Scott stepped off
the footpad of his up-rated Lunar Module
Falcon and onto the plains of Hadley in the
lunar Apennine mountains he declared 'man

must explore … And this is exploration at its
greatest.' His words hinted at the historic nature
of his expedition which had transported the
first Lunar Roving Vehicle to the Moon. Over
the next three days the pair would spend 18½
hours outside, exploring the plains at Hadley
in the south-west region of the Mare Imbrium
('Sea of Rains') – a vast impact basin 700
miles wide. Apollo 15 returned some of the
oldest rock samples retrieved from the Moon,
including a chunk of ancient anorthosite – a
sparkly feldspar-laden igneous rock which had
crystallised from the original molten Moon about
4 billion years ago.

The following spring Apollo 16 made the
penultimate flight to the Moon. During descent
to the lunar surface a back-up guidance
system problem in the CSM engine almost led
to a cancellation of the landing. After Houston
reassessed the dangers it posed, John Young
and Charlie Duke were given the green light to
continue with their descent. The pair spent over
20 hours outside, during three excursions, and
collected over 200 pounds of samples. What was
thought to be a region of volcanic rocks turned
out to be covered in a fragmented rock called

Lunar Rover

Concepts and designs for a giant, pressurised three tonne Lunar Roving vehicle had begun in the early 1960s. But when NASA picked the lightweight Lunar Orbit Rendezvous technique for Apollo these over ambitious wheeled vehicles looked unlikely to ever fly to the Moon. The idea for a slimmed down Lunar Roving Vehicle (LRV) was resurrected in May 1969, when Boeing and General Motors were awarded the contract to build it. Their ingenious folding design could be fitted into a blunt triangular shaped space just 5ft tall, 5ft wide and 5ft deep inside the descent stage of the LM. On the surface springs would deploy the front chassis before the astronauts lowered it down onto the surface and unfurled the rear wheels. It was driven using a T-bar control from either seat and was powered by four independent ¼ horse power electric motors sealed into each wheel hub. A crude inertial guidance system and a backup Sun compass were used to navigate on journeys which could carry the astronauts up to 6 miles from the safety of the Lunar Module. Three LRVs were flown to the Moon onboard Apollos 15, 16 and 17. Together they carried the their astronauts across 56 miles of rugged lunar terrain, helping to return well over half a tonne of rock samples which revolutionised our understanding of the Moon's geology and the Earth's history. Harold Urey's original scientific argument for urging NASA into further exploration of the Moon had been vindicated.

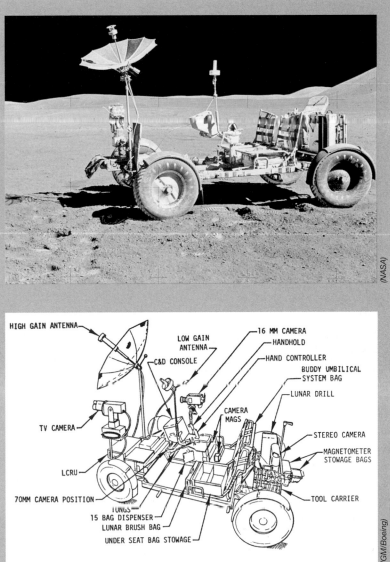

(NASA)

(NASA/GM/Boeing)

LRV STOWED PAYLOAD INSTALLATION

FAR LEFT Astronaut David R. Scott, Commander, salutes while standing beside the US flag during the first Apollo 15 lunar surface EVA. *(NASA)*

LEFT The white anorthositic rock, dubbed the 'Genesis Rock' photographed during the second Apollo 15 EVA. *(NASA)*

breccia, formed by impacts. Their discoveries overturned previous theories about the evolution of the Moon's ancient highland crust.

The final Moon mission, Apollo 17, in December 1972, carried Eugene Cernan and geologist Harrison Schmitt, (swapped in from the cancelled Apollo 18 mission) into the dramatic Taurus-Littrow valley. This final landing site had been chosen from orbit as there seemed to be plenty of boulders which had tumbled down slope from the surrounding ancient mountain peaks. Everyone was hopeful

that this region would also prove to be truly volcanic, after the surprise of the impact origin of the Apollo 16 landing site.

Riding on the final Lunar Roving Vehicle, Cernan and Schmitt roamed 21 miles through the valley during their three days, discovering a volcanic orange soil and delivering the most comprehensive Apollo Lunar Surface Experiment Package (ALSEP) ever left on the Moon. The crew returned the biggest cache of lunar samples of any Apollo mission – over 243 pounds – more than the first three Moon missions put together.

Apollo 18–20 (the cancelled missions)

From late 1968 to early 1970 NASA's Moon shot plans had called for 13 manned Apollo flights – Apollos 8–20. Plans for these last three ambitious J-class flights even involved a landing on the far side of the Moon, using a supporting network of lunar telecommunications satellites to keep contact between the crew and Earth. Apollo astronaut-geologist Harrison Schmitt was a strong advocate of such bold expeditions, and also pushed hard for a landing site inside one of the big impact craters like Copernicus. When Apollo 20 was axed on 4th January 1970, the

LEFT Jack mounting the Rover – taken by Gene Cernan at Station 9. *(NASA)*

Copernicus landing site was transferred to Apollo 18. But the wake-up call to the dangers of Moon flights provided by Apollo 13 a few months later led to further cancellations and ultimately the loss of a chance to visit Copernicus.

Pressure to keep Harrison Schmitt, the only scientist astronaut with a chance of a Moon landing, on a flight meant that he was ultimately moved up to the surviving Apollo 17 mission, replacing Joe Engle. Neither Engle nor any of the other Apollo astronauts from these cancelled missions would ever walk on the Moon and many of them would have to wait a long time even to fly in space on board the Space Shuttle.

The next Apollo

We started this book with a quote from Gene Cernan, the last man to leave his footprints on the Moon. 'The president had plucked a decade out of the 21st century and inserted it into the 1960s and 70s.' Cernan's heady statement implied that a visit to the Moon might have been more likely in the 21st century, but the further we get from Apollo the less likely it seems that a human visit to the Moon will ever happen again.

Presidential proclamations about returning to the Moon and going on to Mars have been made in the past couple of decades. NASA has even started to chant the mantra 'Moon, Mars and beyond …' But the reality of human exploration beyond Earth orbit is no more guaranteed today than was the prospect of landing a man on the Moon when it was first discussed at NASA in the late 1950s. And perhaps it is less likely. To send humans to the Moon you need a reason and a strong purpose; and without these drivers, the sort

ABOVE Artist's rendering of NASA's new constellation programme, showing a lunar lander undocking from a crew exploration vehicle (CEV) while in Moon orbit. *(NASA)*

LEFT Computer rendering of two proposed Mars habitation modules and a Mars Rover vehicle for future human spaceflights to the red planet. *(NASA)*

of dedication, commitment and resolve to accomplish this endeavour will be lacking.

Landing humans on the Moon is extremely expensive – perhaps even more costly today relatively, than it was in the 1960s. And, with the economic downturn of the early 21st century and the prospect of expensive climate change issues and sustainable energy challenges to solve here on Earth, a human return to the Moon is currently not a top priority for the nations who raced there before. Perhaps another nation like China or India might one day return humans to the Moon, maybe kicking off a new space race with the United States. But without such national pride at stake, returning to the Moon might not happen any time soon.

Beyond the Moon a human flight to Mars is even more unlikely. It is at least an order of magnitude harder to accomplish than a manned flight to the Moon, perhaps two orders. And, judging by the recent performances of wheeled robotic explorers on the surface and the flotilla of 'spy satellite'-grade orbital missions around the Red Planet, perhaps the need to physically land humans there for exploration will diminish before we choose to go.

This is not to say that we should not strive to return to the Moon and go on to Mars as part of what it means to be human. Whilst these are difficult and expensive endeavours, they offer great excitement and adventure for our species and what is life for if not adventure? Whether adventure alone is enough reason to plant another footprint on the Moon though is for the next generation to decide.

Misconceptions and conspiracy theories

One of the fastest ways to get a heated argument going with a group of strangers is to bring up the subject of the Moon landings. Within a few sentences someone will always raise the lunar conspiracy theory. Perhaps this is a reflection of people's understanding of how close to impossible it was to land a human on the Moon back in the 1960s. But it is more likely to be because of a lack of knowledge of the science and engineering facts about Apollo.

The notes below are only included in response to the countless times I have been asked these questions over the years by people who often want to believe in Apollo but lack the knowledge of physics and the environmental conditions on the lunar surface, which reassures the rest of us that Apollo was real. They are also aimed at those of us who are informed enough not to doubt the reality of Apollo, but who are sometimes lost for words when we do meet another less enlightened human being who truly believes that the Moon landings were faked!

Radiation

The first astronauts to pass through Earth's Van Allen radiation belts, where charged solar particles are channelled by the Earth's magnetic field, were the crew of Apollo 8. There was concern at the time about the sort of radiation dose they would be exposed to but after careful consideration it was felt that they would be travelling so fast (over 25,000mph) that they should be safe. By monitoring their radiation exposure using the dosimeters which each crewman wore, the science teams back in Earth could confirm that they had received no more than the equivalent radiation dose of a chest X-ray.

BELOW The Apollo flags were stretched out along wires running through the top to display them properly in the vacuum. *(NASA)*

Flags

The American flags hang out from their flag poles on the Moon because there are wires pushed through the top seam of the flags to hold them out proudly. The nylon fabric was sometimes wrinkled as it was pulled out along these wires, giving the illusion that the flags were flapping in a breeze, but without them the flags would have simply hung down limply. Today the flags are likely to have been bleached white by the decades of strong sunlight, but nylon would not have melted in the sunlight, as some people suggest.

Dust

Clouds of dust did not linger around the lunar landers after the engines were switched off as there was no air in which dust could be suspended. In the vacuum of space the disturbed dust, blown aside by the descent engine, dropped straight to the surface again. This effect even surprised the astronauts themselves. Years later Armstrong recalled that "I was absolutely dumbfounded when I shut the rocket engine off and the particles that were going out radially from the bottom of the engine fell all the way out over the horizon, and when I shut the engine off, they just raced out over the horizon and instantaneously disappeared, you know, just like it had been shut off for a week. That was remarkable. I'd never seen that. I'd never seen anything like that. And logic says, yes, that's the way it ought to be there, but I hadn't thought about it and I was surprised." (Quoted from: http://history.nasa.gov/alsj/a11/a11.html)

Shadows

Also, because of the lack of any atmosphere, light bounces and scatters from the lunar surface in a different way to what we are used to seeing and experiencing on the Earth, giving shadows a different quality and appearance.

Stars

There are no stars in the images because, despite the black sky (due again to the lack of atmosphere) it is day time. It is clearly day time because the Sun is shining, and as on Earth you cannot see stars during the day because the Sun is too bright. No Apollo mission ever landed on the Moon during a lunar night because the astronauts would not have been able to see enough to land safely or explore.

Why did we stop going to the Moon?

We stopped going, not because we never really went in the first place as some hoax proponents would have you believe, but because the public lost interest and with the space race won and nine manned flights to the Moon accomplished, financial and public support for Apollo dried up.

Finally, if you ever find yourself in the presence of a die-hard conspiracy theorist and want to put a swift end to their nonsense, just remember Apollo 11 Command Module Pilot Mike Collins's witty put-downs at the end of our documentary feature film *In the Shadow of the Moon*. "I don't know two Americans who have a fantastic secret without one of them blurting it out to the press. Can you imagine thousands of people able to keep the secret?"

For a more complete rebuttal of all the Apollo conspiracy points, please visit the links on the author's web page: www.chris-riley.com/one-small-step.htm

ABOVE Dust is scattered by the LM's ascent engines, but drops to the ground immediately the force is removed, as there is no air to hold it in suspension. *(NASA)*

The legacy of Apollo

For many, Apollo was no more than a piece of cold war bravado. For others it was an inspiring act of human willpower, creative ingenuity and determination – a celebration of all our best qualities as a species.

Four hundred thousand engineers and scientists had toiled day and night for the best part of a decade so that twelve men could walk on the Moon for a total of just eighty hours. It seems at first glance like a lot of effort for such a fleeting human encounter with the Moon. But in the decades which have passed since Apollo came to an end it is clear that the legacy of those nine flights to another world has proved to be of far greater significant than anyone imagined.

The act of sending representatives of our species to explore somewhere beyond the Earth on our behalf united the world, briefly, in admiration for what we humans were capable of. It was an effect which lingered into the 1970s – with the world united once more by Apollo 13 through prayer and pledges of assistance for the safe return of the beleaguered crew.

Such ephemeral sentiments were soon forgotten as Apollo disappeared from the news; but the generation who had grown up watching seemingly impossible things being accomplished by driven and determined Apollo engineers, would not forget what they had witnessed. Many were inspired to reach for greatness themselves in the decades which followed and the technological revolution which they have helped to bring about in the decades since the Moon landings continues to touch all our lives.

The influence which the Apollo programme had on the silicon chip industry has already been noted in Chapter 3, but thousands of other spin off products and industries emerged from the Apollo programme. They range from medical technologies like heart monitors and premature baby incubators, to the strong, lightweight materials used in the construction of sports stadiums, shopping centres and airport terminals. Over 30,000 documented products are in common use today thanks to Apollo.

The 838lb of lunar rocks returned by the six landing missions continue to supply cosmochemistry investigators around the world with samples to study. With no guarantee of a new supply of lunar rocks the Apollo samples are used sparingly and ingeniously to ensure that future generations of researchers won't run out of Moon rock for centuries to come. Analysis of the samples to date has suggested a common origin of the Earth and the Moon and has started the job of piecing together the complex geological history of our nearest neighbour and the secrets of the Earth's own lost geological youth.

From the first black and white picture of the Earth rising above the Lunar horizon, snapped by one of the Apollo 8 crew in December 1968 to the familiar view of our marbled blue and white planet captured by Harrison Schmitt on Apollo 17 just four Christmases later; our perspective on the Earth was also changed forever. The view of our home planet for the first time as a fragile and vulnerable place and the environmental awareness which these images stirred within us still influences our behaviour today.

As Apollo 8 astronaut Bill Anders pointed out "we came all this way to explore the Moon and the most important thing which we discovered was the Earth."

This is perhaps Apollo's most precious and enduring legacy.

Epilogue

*'To see the earth as it truly is, small and blue and
beautiful in that eternal silence where it floats, is
to see ourselves as riders on the earth together,
brothers on that bright loveliness in the eternal cold,
brothers who know now they are truly brothers.'*

Archibald Macleish
*US poet and writer,
December 25th 1968*

Appendices

Apollo acronyms and abbreviations

ACA	Attitude Control Assembly	MCC	Mission Control Center
AGC	Apollo Guidance Computer	MC&W	Master Caution and Warning
AGS	Abort Guidance Systems (LM)	MDC	Main Display Console
AK	Apogee Kick	MESA	Modularised Equipment Stowage Assembly
APS	Ascent Propulsion System (LM)	MOCR	Mission Operations Control Room
	Auxiliary Propulsion System (S-IVB stage)	MSFN	Manned Space Flight Network
ARIA	Apollo Range Instrumented Aircraft	MSI	Moon Sphere of Influence
ASLEP	Apollo Lunar Surface Experiment Package	MTVC	Manual Thrust Vector Control
BMAG	Body Mounted Attitude Gyro	NAA	North American Aviation
CAPCOM	Capsule Communicator	NACA	National Advisory Committee for Aeronautics
CDH	Constant Delta Height	NASA	National Aeronautics and Space Administration
CDR	Commander	NASCOM	
CM	Command Module		NASA Communications Network
CMC	Command Module Computer	NCC	Combined Corrective Maneuver
CMP	Command Module Pilot	OAMS	Orbit Attitude and Maneuvering System
COI	Contingency Orbit Insertion	OPS	Optical Alignment System
CRS	Concentric Rendezvous Sequence	PDI	Powered Descent Initiation
CSM	Command and Service Module	PIPA	Pulse Integrating Pendulous Accelerometer
CSI	Concentric Sequence Initiate	PLSS	Portable Life Support System
DAC	Data Acquisition Camera	PNGS	Primary Navigation and Guidance System
DAP	Digital AutoPilot	PRO	PROceed
DEDA	Data Entry and Display Assembly (LM AGS)	PTC	Passive Thermal Control
DFI	Development Flight Instrumentation	PTT	Push To Talk
DOI	Descent Orbit Insertion	PUGS	Propellant Utilization and Gaging System
DPS	Descent Propulsion System	RAE	Royal Aircraft Establishment
DSKY	Display and Keyboard	RAM	Random Access Memory
ECS	Environmental Control System	RCS	Reaction Control System
ELS	Earth Landing System	REFSMMAT	
EOR	Earth Orbit Rendezvous		REFerence to Stable Member MAtrix
EPO	Earth Parking Orbit	RHC	Rotation Hand Controller
EVA	Extra-Vehicular Activity	RTC	Real-Time Command
FDAI	Flight Director/Attitude Indicator	ROM	Read Only Memory
FITH	Fire In The Hole (LM ascent abort staging)	S-IC	Saturn first stage
FTP	Full Throttle Position	S-II	Saturn second stage
GN&C	Guidance, Navigation and Control	S-IVB	Saturn third (final) stage
GNCS	Guidance, Navigation and Control Systems	SCS	Stabilisation and Control System
HGA	High-Gain Antenna	SEC	Secondary Electron Conduction
IGY	International Geophysical Year	SHE	Supercritical HElium
ILC	International Latex Corporation	SIM	Scientific Instrument Module
IMU	Inertial Measurement Unit	SLA	Spacecraft LM Adaptor
IRIG	Inertial Rate Integrating Gyro	SPS	Service Propulsion System
ITMG	Integrated Thermal Micro-meteoroid Garment	STL	Space Technology Laboratories
LCC	Launch Control Centre	SWIP	Super Weight Improvement Programme
LEVA	Lunar Extra-vehicular Visor Assembly	TEI	TransEarth Injection
LH_2	Liquid Hydrogen	THC	Thrust Hand Controller
LM	Lunar Module	TIG	Time at Ignition
LMP	Lunar Module Pilot	TLI	TransLunar Injection
LOI	Lunar Orbit Insertion	TLSA	Torso and Limb Suit Assembly
LOR	Lunar Orbit Rendezvous	TPF	Terminal Phase Finalization
LOX	Liquid OXygen	TPI	Terminal Phase Initiate
LPD	Landing Point Designator	TTCA	Thrust/Translation Controller Assembly
LPO	Lunar Parking Orbit	TVC	Thrust Vector Control
LRV	Lunar Roving Vehicle	VAB	Vehicle Assembly Building

Table 1 – Missions

Mission name/ call sign Launch date	Prime Crew	Backup Crew	Spacecraft Names/ Numbers	Mission summary
No name (AS-201) 26-02-1966	Unmanned	Unmanned	CSM-009	First flight of the Saturn IB and a block 1 Command & Service Module
Apollo 2 (AS-203) 05-07-1966	Unmanned	Unmanned	No CSM or LM	A six hour, four orbit flight to investigate the effects of weightlessness on the fuel in the S-IVB tank, using 83 sensors and two TV cameras. The flight also tested a new Instrumentation Unit
Apollo 3 (AS-202) 25-08-1966	Unmanned	Unmanned	CSM-011	Sub-orbital test flight of the Saturn IB and Command and Service Modules to test the heat shield during a simulated re-entry from the Moon.
Apollo 1 (no call sign) 21-02-1967	Command Pilot: Virgil 'Gus' Grissom Senior Pilot: Ed White Pilot: Roger Chaffee	Command Pilot: James McDivitt/ Walter Schirra Senior Pilot: David Scott/Donn Eisele Pilot: Rusty Schweickart/Walter Cunningham	CM-012 SM-012	First flight of the new Apollo Command Module (Block I) in Earth orbit, (14 days) to test launch operations and ground tracking and control facilities A fire on the pad during a test killed the crew on 27th January 1967
Apollo 4 (AS-501) 09-11-1967	Unmanned	Unmanned	CSM-017 LM: LTA-10R (a dummy LM)	First flight of a fully stacked Saturn V, and the first flights of the S-IC and S-II stages. The flight carried a Block I CM into orbit for testing of a new heat shield and hatch. A model of the LM was also carried as ballast
Apollo 5 (AS-204) 22-01-1968	Unmanned	Unmanned	LM-1	First unmanned flight of the Apollo Lunar Module in Earth orbit, to test the descent and ascent engines and the pyrotechnic system to separate the stages
Apollo 6 (SA-502) 04-04-1968	Unmanned	Unmanned	CM-020 SM-014	The second and last unmanned flight of a Saturn V launch vehicle. The objectives were to test new launch support infrastructure, and a new Command Module re-entry system. J2 engine failure prevented this last test
Apollo 7 'Phoenix' (unofficial crew call sign never used) 11-10-1968	Commander: Walter Schirra CMP: Donn Eisele LMP: Walter Cunningham	Commander: Thomas Stafford CMP: John Young LMP: Eugene Cernan	CM-101 SM-101	The first manned Apollo mission and first three man American spaceflight. An eleven day Earth orbit 'shakedown' mission for the CSM and the SPS; launched on a Saturn 1B from Launch Complex 34 (all other Apollo flights launched from Complex 39)
Apollo 8 SA-503 21-12-1968	Commander: Frank Borman CMP: Jim Lovell (replaced Mike Collins) LMP: William Anders	Commander: Neil Armstrong CMP: Buzz Aldrin (replaced Jim Lovell) LMP: Fred Haise. (Replaced Buzz Aldrin)	CSM: (103) LM: LTA-B (test article flown as ballast)	Originally planned as a low Earth orbit LM/CM test flight the mission was changed in mid-1968 to become the first Apollo flight to the Moon. After launch the crew took three days to reach the Moon, entering lunar orbit on Christmas Eve and making 10 further orbits over the next 20 hours. One of the crew's major tasks was to scout out potential landing sites for future missions; especially Apollo 11

Mission name/ call sign Launch date	Prime Crew	Backup Crew	Spacecraft Names/ Numbers	Mission summary
Apollo 9 SA-504 03-03-1969	Commander: James McDivitt CMP: David Scott LMP: Russell Schweickart	Commander: Pete Conrad CMP: Dick Gordon LMP: Alan Bean (replaced Clifton Williams)	CM: Gumdrop (CM-104) SM: (SM-104) LM: Spider LM-3	Originally conceived as a test flight in Lunar Orbit, Apollo 9 and 8 swapped objectives in 1968, making Apollo 9 the first manned spaceflight of the CSM with the LM in Earth orbit. Navigation systems and docking manoeuvres were tested along with the LM's descent and ascent engines. It was also a chance to test the first Apollo pressure suit and life support back pack in space
Apollo 10 SA-505 18-05-1969	Commander: Thomas Stafford CMP: John Young LMP: Eugene Cernan	Commander: Gordon Cooper CMP: Don Eisele LMP: Edgar Mitchell	CM: Charlie Brown (CM-106) SM: SM-106) LM: Snoopy LM-4	First flight of the Lunar Module in Lunar orbit. LM4 was not equipped to land but descended to within 8.4 nautical miles of the Lunar surface, before returning to the CSM above. Surveys of the Sea of Tranquillity were carried out and colour TV was broadcast from space for the first time – winning a prestigious Emmy award for the crew
Apollo 11 SA-506 16-07-1969	Commander: Neil Armstrong CMP: Michael Collins LMP: Buzz Aldrin	Commander: James Lovell CMP: William Anders /Ken Mattingly LMP: Fred Haise	CM: Columbia (CM-107) SM: (SM-107) LM: Eagle (LM-5)	The first manned mission to land on the Moon. On the 20th July 1969 Armstrong and Aldrin became the first humans to land and walk on the Moon, whilst Collins remained in orbit above inside the CM. During their 2½ hours out on the surface an Apollo Scientific Experiment Package (EASEP) was deployed and over 20kg of lunar regolith and rock core samples were collected to return to Earth. A US flag was planted during a ceremony involving President Nixon speaking to the astronauts from the Oval Room at the White House
Apollo 12 SA-507 14-11-1969	Commander: Pete Conrad CMP: Dick Gordon LMP: Alan Bean	Commander: David Scott CMP: Alfred Worden LMP: James Irwin	CM: Yankee Clipper (CM-108 SM: (SM-108) LM: Intrepid (LM-6)	The second manned lunar landing and the first pinpoint landing on the Moon in the Ocean of Storms – close to Snowman crater – the landing site of an earlier robotic lunar lander called Surveyor III. Over two excursions outside, lasting almost eight hours in total Conrad and Bean collected rock samples and set up Lunar surface experiments, whilst Gordon, orbiting above took multi-spectral photographs of the Moon
Apollo 13 SA-508 11-04-1970	Commander: Jim Lovell CMP: Ken Mattingly (Replaced by John 'Jack' Swigert) LMP: Fred Haise	Commander: John Young CMP: John Swigert LMP: Charles Duke	CM: Odyssey (CM-109) SM (SM-109) LM: Aquarius (LM-7)	Planned as the first manned mission to the Lunar highlands of Frau Mauro. A rupture of the number 2 oxygen tank in the SM and subsequent loss of electrical power 200,000 miles from Earth caused the landing to be abandoned. Using the LM as a 'lifeboat' – to keep the crew alive and to steer them around the Moon and back to Earth the three astronauts made it home alive – transferring, in the final hour before re-entry, back to the CM
Apollo 14 SA-509	Commander: Alan Shepard CMP: Stuart Roosa LMP: Edgar Mitchell	Commander: Gene Cernan CMP: Ronald Evans LMP: Joe Engle	CM: Kitty Hawk (CM-110) SM: (SM-110 LM: Antares (LM-8)	A re-flight to the Apollo 13 Frau Mauro landing site. On their second EVA Shepard and Mitchell walked over a mile from the landing site pulling instruments behind them in a special two-wheeled trolley called the MET. The pair collected over 100 pounds of Lunar rock samples, conducted a number of surface experiments and were the first to use a colour TV camera on the Moon. From above Roosa conducted the first extensive manned orbital lunar science mission

Mission name/ call sign Launch date	Prime Crew	Backup Crew	Spacecraft Names/ Numbers	Mission summary
Apollo 15 SA-510 26-07-1971	Commander: David Scott CMP: Alfred Worden LMP: James Irwin	Commander: Richard Gordon CMP: Vance Brand LMP: Harrison Schmitt	CM: Endeavour (CM-112) SM: (SM-112) LM: Falcon (LM-10)	The first J-class mission to fly to the Moon – Apollo 15's focus was more on science than previous missions, Scott and Worden spent 3 days exploring the area around the Hadley rille in Lunar Apenninus mountains. They were the first crew to carry a lunar rover to the Moon and drove it 17.25 miles during their 18½ hours of exploration. It helped them to collect 170 pounds of rock samples. From orbit Worden used the Scientific Instrument Module on the SM to study the Moon's environment and map the surface in great detail – leading to the selection of the Apollo 17 landing site in the Tarus Littrow valley
Apollo 16 SA-511 16-04-1972	Commander: John Young CMP: Ken Mattingly LMP: Charlie Duke	Commander: Fred Haise CMP: Stuart Roosa LMP: Edgar Mitchell	CM: Casper (CM-113) SM: (SM-113) LM: Orion (LM-11)	The second J-class mission to the mountains of the Moon, Apollo 16 landed in the Descartes Highlands. John Young and Charlie Duke used the second Lunar Rover, spending three days exploring the region, whilst Mattingly conducted a lunar remote sensing science programme from above
Apollo 17 SA-512 07-12-1972	Commander: Gene Cernan CMP: Ron Evans LMP: Harrison Schmitt (replacing Joe Engle)	Commander: John Young CMP: Stuart Roosa LMP: Charlie Duke	CM: America (CM-114) SM: (SM-114) LM: Challenger (LM-12)	The sixth and final manned lunar landing mission, Apollo 17 touched down in the Taurus Littrow Valley on the 11th December. Cernan and Schmitt drove the third and final lunar rover over 22 miles during their three days exploring the site. They spent the longest time of any Apollo mission outside on the lunar surface, returning 243 pounds of rock samples
Apollo 18 SA-513 Cancelled	Commander: Richard Gordon CMP: Vance Brand LMP: Harrison Schmitt (moved to Apollo 17)		N/A	Cancelled mission – partial crew switch to Apollo 17. Would have visited either the Schroter's Valley or Gassendi craters or Copernicus crater
Apollo 19 SA-514 Cancelled	Commander: Fred Haise CMP: William Pogue LMP: Gerald Carr		N/A	Cancelled in September 1970 Planned to visit the Hyginus rille or Copernicus or Hadley rille (assigned to Apollo 15 after cancellation)
Apollo 20 SA-515 Cancelled	Commander: Pete Conrad CMP: Paul Weitz LMP: Jack Lousma		N/A	Cancelled in September 1970 Might have visited Hyginus rille or Marius Hills or Tycho

Field guide to the Apollo hardware

The Saturns

It is commonly noted that of the 365 feet of fully stacked rocket, all that returned to Earth was the conical apex at the top of the leviathan – the Command Module. But the truth is that all the first and second stages of the Saturn V rockets, along with the rocket's pinnacle launch escape towers all fell into the Atlantic Ocean. Including those stages from the Apollo-Soyuz launch vehicle thirteen S-IC and S-II stages lie today on the Atlantic Ocean floor off the coast of Florida (see table 2 below). The final S-IVB stages along with their Lunar Module Adaptor housings and Instrumentation Units are all still in solar orbit, or crashed onto the Moon.

The first and second stages of the Saturn V built for SA-513 (Apollo 18) were used to launch Skylab, it's third stage built from a converted S-IVB #212. Two complete Saturn V's were never used after the Apollo programme, SA-514 and SA-515, as well as the third stage of the SA-513.

These rockets along with some test stages which never flew have been preserved for future generations to marvel at. An encounter with them today in one of the three visitor centres around United States where they lie is as close as most of us are ever likely to come to comprehending the scale of Apollo.

The stack lying on its side in the large air conditioned warehouse on the outskirts of the Johnson Space Center is made up of the first stage of SA-514 (Apollo 19), the second stage from SA-515 (Apollo 20) and the third stage from SA-513 (Apollo 18). A second Saturn V mounted high enough to walk beneath, inside the Kennedy Space Center visitor center in Florida, is made up of an S-IC-T (a test stage) and the second and third stages from SA-514 (Apollo 19). The final Saturn V on display is at the Davidson Center for Space Exploration at the US Space and Rocket Center in Huntsville (Alabama). It is constructed entirely from test stages which were never built to be flown; S-IC-D, S-II-F/D and S-IVB-D.

In addition to these fully Stacked Saturn Vs, the S-IC stage from SA-515 (Apollo 20) is on display at the Michoud Assembly Facility in New Orleans, Louisiana. The S-IVB stage from SA-515 (Apollo 20) was converted for use as a backup for Skylab and is now on display at the National Air and Space Museum in Washington DC.

Table 2 – The fates of the Saturn V stages from the 15 planned Apollo flights.

Mission	S-IC	S-II	S-IVB	IU
SA-501: Apollo 4	Impact on Atlantic Ocean	Impact on Atlantic Ocean	Lasted 0.34 days re-entering on the 09-11-1967	Same fate as S-IVB
SA-502: Apollo 6	Impact on Atlantic Ocean	Impact on Atlantic Ocean	Lasted 22 days re-entering on the 26-04-1968	Same fate as S-IVB
SA-503: Apollo 8	impact on Atlantic Ocean 353.462nmi downrange, 30.24N 74.109W	Impact on Atlantic Ocean 2245.91nmi downrange, 31.83N 37.277W	Left on a ballistic trajectory to fly by the Moon and enter heliocentric orbit with a period of 340.8 days	left on a ballistic trajectory to fly by the Moon and enter heliocentric orbit with S-IVB-503N
SA-504: Apollo 9	Impact on Atlantic Ocean 346.635nmi downrange, 30.183N 74.238W	Impact on Atlantic Ocean 2413.2nmi downrange, 31.46N 34.04W	Propelled into heliocentric orbit	Burned up in Earth's atmosphere with S-IVB-504

Mission	S-IC	S-II	S-IVB	IU
SA-505: Apollo 10	Impact on Atlantic Ocean 348.8nmi downrange, 30.188N 74.207W	Impact on Atlantic Ocean 2389.29 nmi downrange, 31.522N 34.512W	Left on a ballistic trajectory to fly by the Moon and enter a heliocentric orbit	Left on a ballistic trajectory to fly by the Moon and enter heliocentric orbit with S-IVB-505
SA-506: Apollo 11	Impact on Atlantic Ocean 357.1nmi downrange, 30.212N 74.038W	Impact on Atlantic Ocean 2,371.80nmi downrange, 31.535N 34.844W	Injected into heliocentric orbit	Injected into heliocentric orbit with S-IVB-506
SA-507: Apollo 12	Impact on Atlantic Ocean 365.2nmi downrange, 30.273N 73.895W	Impact on Atlantic Ocean 2404.40nmi downrange, 31.465N 34.214W	Lacking the energy to escape the Earth–Moon system the S-IVB ended up in a semi-stable orbit around the Earth & Moon – was eventually ejected into a heliocentric orbit in 1971. The stage returned to Earth orbit briefly in 2002	Same fate as the S-IVB-507
SA-508: Apollo 13	Impact on Atlantic Ocean 355.3nmi downrange, 30.177N 74.065W	Impact on Atlantic Ocean 2452.60nmi downrange, 30.177N 74.065W	Impact the Moon on April 15, 1970 at 01:09:41.0UT 2.75S 27.86W. 1.60 miles/sec 76 degree	Impact on moon with S-IVB-508
SA-509: Apollo 14	Impact on Atlantic Ocean 351.7nmi downrange, 29.835N 74.042W	Impact on Atlantic Ocean 2462.10nmi downrange, 29.049N 33.567W	Impact the Moon on February 4, 1971 at 07:40:55.4UT 8.09S 26.02W. 1.58 miles/sec 69 degree	Impact on moon with S-IVB-509
SA-510: Apollo 15	Impact on Atlantic Ocean 368.8nmi downrange, 29.42N 73.653W	Impact on Atlantic Ocean 2261.30nmi downrange, 26.975N 37.924W	Impact the Moon on July 29, 1971 at 20:58:42.9UT 1.51S 11.81W. 1.60 miles/sec 62 degree	Impact on moon with S-IVB-510
SA-511: Apollo 16	Impact on Atlantic Ocean 351.6nmi downrange, 30.207N 74.147W	Impact on Atlantic Ocean 2312nmi downrange, 31.726N 35.99W	Impact the Moon on April 19, 1972 at 21:02:04UT 1.3N 23.8W. 1.55-1.61 miles/sec 79 degree	Impact on moon with S-IVB-511
SA-512: Apollo 17	Impact on Atlantic Ocean 356.6nmi downrange, 28.219N 73.878W	Impact on Atlantic Ocean 2292.8nmi downrange, 20.056N 39.7604W	Impact the Moon on December 10, 1972 at 20:32:42.3UT 4.21S 12.31W. 1.58 miles/sec 55 degree	Impact on moon with S-IVB-512
SA-513: Apollo 18 partially used to launch Skylab 1	Impact on Atlantic Ocean	Remained in orbit for 606 days re-entering on the 11-01-1975	Displayed at the Johnson Space Center	Remained on top of the Skylab Orbital work shop – and re-entered the atmosphere with Skylab in 1979.
SA-514: Apollo 19 not flown	On display at the Johnson Space Center, Houston	On display at the Kennedy Space Center, Florida	Displayed at the Kennedy Space Center, Florida	Unknown
SA515: Apollo 20 not flown	On Display at the NASA Michoud Assembly Facility, LA	On display at the Johnson Space Center, Houston	Converted into a backup space station workshop for Skylab 1 and now on display at the National Air and Space Museum in Washington DC	Unknown

The spacecraft

From Apollo 12 onwards the Lunar Modules were deliberately crashed into impact the Moon to provide artificial moonquake sources for seismic experiments. Their impact sites are noted below. LM-2 and LM-9 were never assigned to an Apollo mission and are currently on display at the Air and Space Museum (LM-2) in Washington DC and the Kennedy Space Centre (LM-9) near Orlando, Florida.

The Command Modules were the only pieces of space hardware to return to Earth from the vicinity of the Moon and along with some of the Apollo pressure suits and other mission kit and equipment, they rest today in Museums and science centres around the world, noted in the table below. The Service Modules all burnt up in the Earth's atmosphere soon after their corresponding CMs safely re-entered.

Mission	Location of Command & Service Modules	Location of Lunar Module
Apollo 1	CM-012 – Inside a private storage facility, NASA Langley, Virginia. SM-012	No LM
Apollo 2	No CSM	No LM
Apollo 3	CM-011 – on display on the Hornet in Alameda, California. SM-011 burnt up in Earth's atmosphere.	No LM
Apollo 4 SA-501	CM-017 – on display at NASA's John C. Stennis Space Center, Bay St. Louis, Mississippi. SM-017 burnt up in Earth's atmosphere.	LTA: Lunar Module Test Article – LTA-10R – burnt up on re-entry.
Apollo 5	No CSM	LM-1 upper stage – burnt up on re-entry.
Apollo 6 SA-502?	CM-020Fernbank Science Center, Atlanta, Georgia. SM-020 burnt up in Earth's atmosphere.	LTA-2R
Apollo 7	CM-101 Frontiers of Flight Museum, Dallas, Texas. SM-101 burnt up in Earth's atmosphere.	No LM
Apollo 8 SA-503	CM-103 Chicago Museum of Science and Industry, Chicago, Illinois. SM-103 burnt up in Earth's atmosphere.	LTA-B – test article – flown as ballast – and burnt up in the Earth's atmosphere.
Apollo 9 SA-504	CM-104 San Diego Aerospace Museum, San Diego, California. SM-104 burnt up in Earth's atmosphere.	LM-3 Descent Stage burnt up in the Earth's atmosphere – 22nd March 1969. Ascent Stage: burnt up in the Earth's atmosphere on 23rd October 1981.
Apollo 10 SA-505	CM-106 Science Museum, London, England. SM-106 burnt up in Earth's atmosphere.	LM-4 In heliocentric orbit. The only surviving LM ascent stage to fly in space.
Apollo 11 SA-506	CM-107 The National Air and Space Museum, Washington, DC. SM-107 burnt up in Earth's atmosphere.	LM-5 Ascent stage jettisoned into Lunar Orbit on the 21st July 1969 at 23:41 UT (7:41 PM EDT) impact site unknown. Descent stage: on Moon, Sea of Tranquillity (0.67409N, 23.47298E).
Apollo 12 SA-507	CM-108 Virginia Air and Space Center, Hampton, Virginia. SM-108 burnt up in Earth's atmosphere.	LM-6 Ascent stage impacted the Moon on the 20th November 1969 at 22:17:17.7 UT (5:17 PM EST) 3.94 S, 21.20 W at 1.00 miles/sec 3.7 degree. Descent stage: on Moon, Ocean of Storms (3.01381S, 23.41930W).
Apollo 13 SA-508	CM-109 Kansas Cosmosphere and Space Center, Hutchinson, Kansas – formerly at Musee de l'Air, Paris, France. SM-109 burnt up in Earth's atmosphere.	LM-7 - Burned up in Earth's atmosphere 17th April 1970.

Mission	Location of Command & Service Modules	Location of Lunar Module
Apollo 14 SA-509	CM-110 Astronaut Hall of Fame, Titusville, Florida. SM-109 burnt up in Earth's atmosphere.	LM-8 – Ascent stage impacted the Moon on 7th February 1971 at 00:45:25.7 UT 3.42 S, 19.67 W at 1.04 miles/sec 3.6 degrees. Descent stage: on Moon, Fra Mauro (3.64544S,17.47139W).
Apollo 15 SA-510	CM-112 USAF Museum, Wright-Patterson Air Force Base, Dayton, Ohio. SM-112 burnt up in Earth's atmosphere.	LM-10 – Ascent stage impacted the Moon on 3rd August 1971 at 03.03.37.0 UT 26.36 N, 0.25 E at 1.05 miles/sec 3.2 degrees. Descent stage: on Moon, Hadley-Apennine (26.13224N, 3.63400E).
Apollo 16 SA-511	CM-113 U.S. Space and Rocket Center, Huntsville, Alabama SM-113 burnt up in Earth's atmosphere.	LM-11 – Jettisoned on the 24th April 1972. A loss of attitude control made targeted impact impossible. Impact site unknown. Descent stage: on Moon, Descartes (8.97341S,15.49859E).
Apollo 17 SA-512	CM-114 NASA Johnson Space Center, Houston, Texas. SM-114 burnt up in Earth's atmosphere.	LM-12 – Ascent stage impacted the Moon on 15th December 1972 at 06:50:20.8 UT 19.96 N, 30.50 E at 1.04 miles/sec 4.9 degrees. Descent stage: on Moon, Taurus-Littrow (20.18809N, 30.77475E).
Apollo 18 SA-513	CSM-115A – on display at the Johnson Space Center as part of the Saturn V stack.	LM-13 – Not flown. Both stages at the Cradle of Aviation Museum, Mitchell Field, Long Island. It was used to film the HBO Mini-series *From the Earth to the Moon* and features in the Discovery Series Moon Machines.
Apollo 19 SA-514	CM-116 – flown as Skylab 1 – on display at the National Museum of Naval Aviation, Pensacola, Florida.	LM-14 – Not flown. On display at the Franklin Institute in Philadelphia.
Apollo 20 SA-515	CM-117 – flown as Skylab 2 – on display at the Glann Research Center, NASA Cleveland, Ohio.	LM-15 – Scrapped.

(TopFoto)

October 1957 – Sputnik 1 orbits the Earth – first artificial satellite.

November 1957 – Soviet dog Laika becomes the first living animal to orbit the Earth.

February 1958 – First US satellite Explorer 1 reaches Earth orbit.

October 1958 – NASA formed.

December 1958 – Mercury Seven astronauts announced.

4 January 1959 – Soviet Luna 1 mission flies within 3,000 miles of the Moon.

Mid-1959 – US Airforce plans announced for project 'Lunex' Moon base.

Mid-1959 – US Army plans announced for project 'Horizon' Moon base.

4 December 1959 – Sam (Rhesus macaque) first primate Mercury Flight on Little Joe 2 to 53 miles.

21 January 1960 – Miss Sam (Rhesus macaque) second primate Mercury flight on Little Joe 1B to 9.3 miles.

July 1960 – NASA's advanced manned spaceflight programme Apollo announced.

Dec 1960 – Vostok (Sputnik 6) – dog flight – burns up.

20 January 1961 – *Kennedy becomes President.*

31 Jan 1961 – Ham (chimpanzee) Mercury sub-orbital flight on a Mercury-Redstone 2.

9 March 1961 – Vostok (Sputnik 9) animal flight success.

24 March 1961 – Unmanned Mercury test flight.

April 1961 – Gagarin orbital flight.

5 May 1961 – Shepard first sub-orbital Mercury flight on A Redstone rocket.

25 May 1961 – *Kennedy speech to congress about Moon.*

21 July 1961 – Gus Grisson Mercury sub orbital flight (spacecraft sinks on splashdown).

6 August 1961 – Herman Titov Vostok 2 orbital Flight – first to spend over a day in space completing 17 orbits.

13 September 1961 – Unmanned Mercury orbital flight.

29 November 1961 – Enos (chimpanzee) Mercury flight on a Mercury-Atlas 5 – 2 orbits.

20 February 1962 – John Glenn's first manned Mercury orbital flight on an Atlas ICBM booster.

May 1962 – Lunar Orbit Rendezvous (LOR) selected as NASA's method for Apollo.

24 May 1962 – Carpenter Mercury Flight – lands 350 miles off target.

11 August 1962 – Nikolayev Vostok 3 flight (rendezvous with Vostok 4).

12 August 1962 – Popovich Vostok 4 flight (rendezvous with Vostok 3).

12 Sept 1962 – *Kennedy Rice Speech: "We choose to go to the Moon…"*

3 October 1962 – Schirra Mercury Flight Sigma 7.

15 May 1963 – Cooper Flight 22 orbit mission of Faith 7.

14 June 1963 – Vostok 5 flight – Bykovsky (record breaking 5-day solo flight).

16 June 1963 – Vostok 6 flight – Valentina Tereshkova (first woman in space).

Autumn 1963 – *Kennedy and Kruschev agree to a joint venture in space.*

22 November 1963 – Kennedy assassinated.

8 April 1964 – Gemini 1 – first test flight (unmanned) of the new two-man US spacecraft.

12 October 1964 – Voskhod 1 – first multi-person spaceflight.

19 Jan 1965 – Gemini 2 – Sub-orbital (unmanned) flight to test the heat shield.

19 March 1965 – Voskhod 2 – first spacewalk performed by Alexi Leonov.

23 March 1965 – Gemini 3 – first manned Gemini flight makes three orbits.

3 June 1965 – Gemini 4 – first EVA by an American astronaut – for 22 minutes.

21 August 1965 – Gemini 5 – first week long flight – first use of fuel cells for electrical power and evaluation of guidance and navigation systems.

4 December 1965 – Gemini 7 – first two-week mission and rendeavous with Gemini 6A.

15 December 1965 – Gemini 6A First space rendezvous – station keeping for over five hours.

January 1966 – *Korolev dies.*

22 February 1966 – Cosmos 10 – 22-day test flight with two dogs. Landed safely.

16 March 1966 – Gemini 8 – first docking with another space vehicle – thruster malfunction terminated the mission early.

3 June 1966 – Gemini 9A – rendezvous practice – docking impossible due to technical fault. Two hour EVA.

5 July 1966 – Apollo 2 test flight to test the S-IVB tank.

18 July 1966 – Gemini 10 – rendezvous and docking practice. 49 minute EVA.

26 August 1966 – Apollo 3 test flight of the CSM-011.

12 September 1966 – Gemini 11 – rendezvous and docking practice – 33 minute EVA and two hour stand up EVA.

11 November 1966 – Gemini 12 – manual rendezvous and docking. New EVA record of 5 hours 30 minutes.

28 November 1966 – Cosmos 133 launch (beginning of the Russian Soyuz programme).

27 January 1967 – Apollo 1 fire kills the crew.

7 February 1967 – Cosmos 140 – third (unmanned) launch attempt for the new Soyuz programme.

23 April 1967 – Soyuz 1 flight – kills Colonel Vladimir Komarov – when his spacecraft crashed on its return to Earth.

27 October 1967 – Cosmos 186 (unmanned) launched (Soyuz programme).

30 October 1967 – Cosmos 188 (unmanned) launched (Soyuz programme).

9 November 1967 – Apollo 4 – first all-up test of the Saturn V.

22 January1968 – Apollo 5 – first LM flight (unmanned).

4 April 1968 – Apollo 6 – second all-up test of the Saturn V.

14 April 1968 – Cosmos 212 (unmanned) launched (Soyuz programme) docked with Cosmos 213.

15 April 1968 – Cosmos 213 (unmanned) launched (Soyuz programme) docked with Cosmos 212.

28 August 1968 – Cosmos 238 – final unmanned launch before Soyuz 3 to test manoeuvring systems re-entry, descent and landing.

15 September 1968 – Zond 5 launched to make the first circumlunar flight – returning safely to the Earth. The spacecraft carried turtles and other animals.

11 October 1968 – Apollo 7 – first manned Apollo flight – to test the CSM in Earth orbit.

25 October 1968 – Soyuz 2 launched (unmanned) as a target for Soyuz 3.

26 October 1968 – Soyuz 3 launched – first manned flight since Soyuz 1 – designed to dock with Soyuz 2. Rendezvous occurred – but docking not possible.

10 Nov 1968 – Zond 6 makes a second circumlunar flight carrying livestock.

21 December 1968 – Apollo 8 – first manned Apollo flight to the Moon – completing 10 lunar orbits and a test of the CSM and SPS and navigation systems.

20 January 1969 – Zond 1969A (unmanned) attempted lunar flyby – launch aborted.

21 February 1969 – Zond L1S-1 (unmanned) attempted lunar orbiter launched on N1 rocket.

3 March 1969 – Apollo 9 – first manned LM flight in Earth orbit – first test of the Apollo pressure suit in space.

18 May 1969 – Apollo 10 – first manned LM flight in lunar orbit.

3 July 1969 – Zond L1S-2 (unmanned) attempted lunar orbiter and N1 rocket test.

16 July 1969 – Apollo 11 – first manned lunar landing.

(NASA)

Acknowledgements

Phil Dolling first came up with the idea for this book in the summer of 2008 and I am most grateful to him for suggesting to Haynes that I wrote it. Phil brought his life-long love of Apollo and his considerable experience in story telling to bear on this book as it took shape, and made the time in his busy diary to work through the early manuscripts with me.

From the beginning of the project it was clear that there was never going to be enough room to write a nut-and-bolt guide to all the highly complex machines needed for an Apollo Moon shot. There are over five-and-a-half million parts in a Saturn V alone! So, instead, we decided early on to use this book to tell some of the remarkable engineering stories that led to the vehicles that carried men to the Moon. From the giant fire-breathing Saturn V rocket to the individual stitching on the finger tip of an Apollo pressure-suit glove, each chapter in the book covers a separate part of the 'daisy chain' of technology required to take us to the Moon and back. I would like to thank the team at Haynes who shared this vision for the book and made time in their tight schedules to accommodate my research and writing needs. Particular thanks go to Steve Rendle, Jonathan Falconer and Mark Hughes.

Even with years of research, no one person can know all of the details of the diverse stories retold in this book, and I am extremely grateful to a number of devoted Apollo history scholars who have helped me to make the following chapters as accurate as possible.

Chief amongst them is the Apollo historian David Woods, creator and editor of the *Apollo Flight Journal* and someone who has unstintingly supported and encouraged my often faltering attempts to get to grips with the considerable technical details of Apollo. His own book *How Apollo flew to the Moon* should be on the essential-reading list for any Apollo aficionado who is keen to learn more detail than the pages of this book would allow.

David's friend, Frank O'Brien, has been equally supportive and encouraging of my efforts – and has provided invaluable advice and corrections to ensure the chapter on the Apollo Guidance, Navigation and Control system is as good as it could be. Frank's own book *The Apollo Guidance Computer: Architecture and Operation* is the last word on this remarkable part of Apollo's history.

In addition to Frank's guidance, I feel privileged to have had input on this chapter from some of the men at the Draper Lab who actually designed, built and programmed the Apollo Guidance systems themselves. Jerry Gilmore, Fred Martin, Norm Sears, Hal Laning, Dave Hoag, Eldon Hall, Alex Kosmala and Malcolm Johnston all took the time to help me tell their story. Eldon Hall's own account of the story *Journey to the Moon: The History of the Apollo Guidance Computer* is another essential read for those interested in the emergence of digital computing and Apollo. Other staff at the lab who have generously supported my research over the years include Drew Crete,

Kathleen Granchelli and Jacky Bonarrigo.

One other Apollo spacecraft engineer helped in the writing of the book. Jerry Goodman, who worked at NASA's Manned Spacecraft Center in Houston during the Apollo years, proof read the chapters on the CSM and the Apollo Space Suits – both of which he was professionally involved with. The dedicated space suit historian from Hamilton Standard, Ken Thomas, and his counterpart at ILC, Bill Ayrey, also kindly contributed their time to ensure that the pressure suit's story is correct. Ken's own book *US Spacesuits* is a must for readers who want to delve into this topic further.

Colin MacKellar from the Honeysuckle Creek Earth Station took the time to help me with the chapter on communications and, along with the former Deputy Director of Honeysuckle Creek from Apollo 7 to 13, Mike Dinn, has ensured that this chapter has done justice to a subject which, in all honesty, deserves a book of its own.

Saturn historian Alan Lawrie kindly helped me to correct the introduction and the chapter on the Saturns, and helped me to compile the appendix. He also generously offered his time to help me source many of the pictures in the preceeding pages. His own book *Saturn* is a treasure trove of meticulously researched and well-written stories, and I highly recommend it to any fan of the most iconic engineering symbol of Apollo.

Apollo aficionado Scott Schneeweis also devoted his time and expertise to help me trace some of the figures reproduced here, as did the brilliant Heather Walsh.

NASA has always been very supportive of the various spaceflight projects which I've been lucky enough to have worked on over the years, and this book has been no exception. The priceless resources which the agency donates, through their web sites, to the public domain, and the tireless support provided by their staff at the various NASA centres around the United States are remarkable gifts to the world which we should all pause to reflect on from time to time. In particular on this project I would like to say a special thank you to Mike Gentry at the Johnson Space Centre picture archives and to Gwen Pitman and Stephen Garber at NASA Head Quarters in Washington.

Without the generous help of all these people this book ould never have been completed. I must take the final blame for any errors which have, despite their best efforts, still reached its pages.

Finally I would like to thank my patient and supportive wife Jacqui Farnham and our little daughter Eve, who have both put up with the long hours which I have spent trying to turn years of assembled research notes and stories into this final manuscript. Without their understanding and love I would have given up a long time ago.

CDBR Spring 2009